MW01490385

The Stephenson County Historical Society: [advanced copies] of the latest book by Joyce Salter Johnson. Their books are titled **The Freedman Settlement of Good Hope, Mississippi -The Beginning By Joyce Salter Johnson** and are uncorrected proof copies also known as the reader edition. They are "Bound Advance Review" copies that may contain editorial marks, may be missing photographs, illustrations, charts, and even text that will, however, eventually appear in the final finished edition. **The Stephenson County Historical Society: The Wurtzel Publication Fund- Freeport, Illinois**

This book is the finished edition and is titled

The Freedmen Settlement of Good Hope, Mississippi -The Beginning
By Joyce Salter Johnson

2017

The Freedmen Settlement of

Good Hope, Mississippi

The

Beginning

By

Joyce Salter Johnson

Cover photograph:

Copyright by David Rae Morris

Used with permission

Published by Stephenson County Historical Society, Freeport IL
Wurtzel Fund

ISBN: 978-1548715557
ISBN 10: 1548715557

"It would be here, on this land that I would begin to trace the footsteps of my ancestors"

Dedication

To my mother and father, Archie and Edna Hayden Johnson, to my aunt, Opal Johnson Ford whose sprit continues to live on the land, to my uncle, Filmore Clarence ("Unkie") Johnson who cared enough to keep the land in the family, to Reverend O.J Edison for guarding the legacy and keeping a family member in the pulpit of Good Hope Missionary Baptist Church. Many of these families are listed below:

Most of all, I dedicate this book to the early families who cleared the land, built the church building and the little school house in the Good Hope Freedmen Settlement in Newton County, Mississippi during the early years: The Anderson Family, The Bates Family, The Beason Family, The Bogan Family, The Bolton Family, The Brown Family, The Chapman Family, The Cole Family, The Cook Family, The Croft Family, The Curry Family, The Davis Family, The Dawkins Family, The Doby Family, The Dyes Family, The Edison Family, The Evans Family, The Ford Family, The Fielder Family, The Gaddis Family, The Garner Family, The Gibbs Family, The Gipson Family, The Gooden Family, The Graham Family, The Griffin Family, The Gully Family, The Hall Family, The Hamilton Family, The Hardy Family, The Hayden Family, The Horn Family, The Johnson Family, The Jones Family, The Kirby/Curby Family, The Kidd Family, The Lee Family, The Levy Family, The McCarty Family, The McMillian Family, The McCune Family, The Mitchell Family, The Norman Family, The Overstreet Family, The Petry/Petree Family, The Potts Family, The Pruitt Family, The Riley Family, The Russell Family, The Salter/Saulter Family, The Stephen Family, The Suttles Family, The Tanksley Family, The Tankson Family, The Tatum Family, The Thompson Family, The Tillman Family, The Toles Family, The Tullos Family, The Walker Family, The Wall Family, The Wash Family, The Watts Family, The Williams Family, The Wright Family, The Youngblood Family.

Foreword

By Dorothy Hayden-Watkins, Ph.D.

It is my great honor to congratulate and express gratitude to Joyce Salter Johnson on the publication of her latest book and her first book signing for this book in the state of our birth, "Ole Miss." I applaud the author's years of dedication and tremendous passion, energy, and enthusiasm in researching, documenting and sharing "our history, heritage, ad culture." The book establishes for the first time authentic, inclusive, documented history of the Good Hope Hickory, Mississippi Community.

As a resident of the Good Hope Hickory Community, I can attest to the spirit and of the community and its families as they are introduced in this publication. Specifically, as daughter of the late Reverend Daniel and Mrs. Salome Chapman Hayden, and great granddaughter of Frank and Dora Salter, and the author's first cousin, I commend everyone who takes pride in and honors their individual family heritage and history and that of the communities of their ancestors. We acknowledge and celebrate our commonality and the people who remind us of who we are and the priceless experiences we hold true. The author painstakingly sought out and presented us with the story of our extra-ordinary journey and beginnings as a community of record and importance. It is upon this historical platform that the generations represented in this book have achieved and contributed greatly to the American story; and, we continue to do so.

The Good Hope Hickory community with its strong, determined people of vision and pride have made an indelible impact on the Magnolia State and the nation through educational attainment, success in the professions, and unwavering faith in God! Like many such communities, the church was pivotal in the growth and development of the families and the community through the generations to this day.

This publication, The Freedmen Settlement of Good Hope, Hickory, Mississippi reiterates our commitment, obligation, and opportunity to preserve and continue the proud legacy which we have been fortunate to inherit and now perpetuate! Thank you, Joyce, on behalf of your immediate family and all the many Good Hope families and their progeny for this great gift.

It is now our opportunity to "continue" to remind Mississippi and the Nation of the barriers of the "deep south" which our diverse southern community, working together, overcame; and, the determination of Good Hope Hickory families and their descendants to embrace our history and authenticate it by telling our story. We will continue to successfully meet the myriad socio-economic and political challenges, wherever we find them in the culture, without bitterness but rather with love and goodwill toward all.

There is no better time than now to embrace the opportunity to confront the residual barriers faced by our community in the 21st Century; and, to capitalize on present -day opportunities that have been hard fought-for, justly won, and yet to be fully realized!

To this end, on behalf of all the families of Good Hope Hickory, Mississippi we the author, the families, the supporting entities and readers with boundless gratitude and unceasing commitment. We commit individually and collectively, to cherish and preserve the memories and events that we have been so beautifully reminded of in this book. We resolve to perpetuate the author's gift to us with the same integrity and love of family, community and country that her work epitomizes!

Dorothy Hayden-Watkins is Founder and Owner of Hayden-Watkins & Associates, LLC
Aurora, CO 80016
Associate Professor University of Phoenix (UOPX)
Lone Tree, CO 80124
Retired Executive, National Aeronautics and Space Administration (NASA)
Washington, DC 20546

The Author's Note

There are several Good Hope communities in the state of Mississippi such as: Good Hope, Holmes County; Good Hope, Leake County; Good Hope, Marion County; Good Hope, Neshoba County; Good Hope, Perry County; Good Hope in Scott County, plus the Good Hope Baptist Church Community on Fellowship Road in Newton County and the Good Hope Colored Community on Good Hope Road also in Newton County. The book will deal primarily with the people and events of the two Good Hope communities in Newton County before and following Emancipation Proclamation through the 1950s.

I was inspired to begin the research because the story of the two Good Hope communities in Newton County is a part of my family's history. I am originally from Newton County and lived in the Good Hope Freedmen Settlement Community the first ten years of my life. I am fascinated by history and the family lore that goes along with it. Also writing down these stories helped me to get to know the Good Hope Settlers for myself and to realize that it was all of these things that helped to shape my life.

My desire to write this book is not merely to honor my ancestors: the Johnsons, Levys, Petrees, Kirbys, Suttles and the Toles, the Salters, Haydens and the Garners, but hopefully to give a clear and precise account of where they came from and why we understand the need for unity and traditions in the family and community. I believe we inherited this legacy from the founding ancestors and other members of Good Hope Freedmen Settlement Community.

A small part of the book will pertain to what I remember about my great grandfather, Filmore Johnson, and what was told to me by my elders as a young girl. With the help of the oral historians and the family elders, I will also make an effort to identify the slaveholding families: Levy, Petree, Suttles and Johnson. Some information in this book regarding the Hardy Salter family was obtained from my book, In search of Hardy Salter, published November 2011. Information pertaining to the Great Migration was gathered from my book, The Early Black Settlers In Stephenson County, Illinois 1830 – 1930, published in 2009 by the Stephenson County Historical Society of Freeport, Illinois.

As for myself, I agree with the author Willie Morris, a native of Yazoo City, Mississippi, who said "the older I am the more [the South] means to me, the closer the ties."

My favorite quote by Willie Morris is:

"If there is anything that makes southerners distinctive from the main body of Americans, it is a certain burden of memory and a burden of history.... I think sensitive southerners have this in their bones, this profound awareness of the past."

Preface

The Freedmen who settled communities after Emancipation Proclamation were largely ignored in the "telling" of America's history. They were either omitted from historical documentation or portrayed in imagery that lacked depth or accuracy. Many early historians did not see the relevance in the experiences of emancipated men and women. This book is a modest attempt to bring light to these events and pay the early settlers of Good Hope Freedmen Settlement in Newton County, Mississippi their due. The book will attempt to explain the historical links and ties of the first two Good Hope Communities and the role the original Good Hope Baptist Church on Fellowship Road played in the development of Good Hope Freedmen Settlement. The Good Hope community on Fellowship Road was known during that period as the "White Good Hope Church Community" and will be referred to in this book as the original Good Hope Community on Fellowship Road, unless necessary to the telling of the story when "White Good Hope Church" may be used. Freedmen Settlement, Colored Community and Good Hope Community, will be used interchangeably throughout the book.

To offer scope and content to the book, biographical and genealogical sketches of the early settlers and their descendants are presented, which will include: correspondence, obituaries, funeral notices, tax receipts, land deeds, United States Census information, journal entries, church records, Indian Daws Roll, wills and other documentation pertaining to the emancipated Freedmen and those who held them enslaved. The genealogical research done on my great grandfather, Filmore Johnson/Petree, his ancestors and his many descendants from 1860 until present will make up a large portion of the information in this book.

The lives of the families of Good Hope Freedmen Settlement will reveal novel information pertaining to the history of the settlement from its beginning to the present. Plus it will review historical information that pertains to the areas surrounding the settlement towns such as: Union, Chunky, Conehatta, as well as Hickory, Newton, Leake, Scott, Jasper, Lauderdale and other surrounding counties in Mississippi. Another so called "Slave Town" known as Davis Bend, Mississippi (see appendix), will be referenced in this book because of its close ties to the ancestors of the author's paternal grandmother, Elizabeth Levy Johnson and her father, Simon Levy.

The facts documented in the book concerning Fillmore and the Johnson/Petree families and their descendants were discovered through researching and gathering information over many years from the few remaining descendants of these pioneer founding families. Some of the material in the book regarding Filmore Johnson/Petree is from family elder's recollections, as well as memories and stories from community elders.

The census offered the most detailed and accessible records and provided the foundation upon which much of the book's research rests. Yet, the census had its limitations; the data was used with caution and subjected to verification wherever possible. The period immediately following the emancipation of enslaved men and women remained treacherous for newly freed men and their families. Fearing return to slavery and retribution, some residents did their best to avoid documentation which limited the reliability of census reports.

Race and ethnicity in the United States Census, as defined by the Census Bureau, are self-identification data items in which individuals chose the group or groups with which they most closely identified.

From 1850–1870 the census designated people of African descent as Black and Mulatto. In the censuses from 1880–1930 responders could self-identify as Colored in addition to Black or Mulatto. Freedmen is one of the terms given to the emancipated enslaved and their descendants after slavery was abolished in the United States following the American Civil War and will be used throughout this book.

The word Negro was used to refer to a person of African ancestry prior to the shift in the lexicon of American classification of race and ethnicity in the late 1960s. In the book I opted to refer to enslaved African as the Enslaved and Native American as Indians in a historical context. The terms Indian, Black, White, Colored and Negro, in the period when those terms were in use, will be capitalized. I will use the term for African American as people of African descent or African ancestry. The term "nigger" is used in this book where necessary for historical accuracy, otherwise n——— is used to represent that word.

The Native American connection:

Attempts will be made to address the Native American connections with the families in the community. Family members of Native American descent can often be found in the regular Federal population censuses, however, there will be no indication in most cases that they are of blood descent and will be listed in the United State Censes as Mulatto or Negro. Any Indian person not living on well-known reservation areas were more likely to be recorded as Mulatto than either Indian or White. (*The following are the instructions given to enumerators [census takers] regarding mixed Indian and Negro. Indians-A person of mixed White and Indian blood should be returned as Indian, except where the percentage of Indian blood is very small, or where he is regarded as a white person by those in the community where he lives. Negroes-A person of mixed White and Negro blood should be returned as a Negro, no matter how small the percentage of Negro blood. Both Black and Mulatto persons are to be returned as Negroes, without distinction. A person of mixed Indian and Negro blood should be returned as Negro, unless the Indian blood predominates.*)

The following are the instructions given to enumerators [census takers] regarding mixed Indian and Negro.
Indians-A person of mixed White and Indian blood should be returned as Indian, except where the percentage of Indian blood is very small, or where he is regarded as a white person by those in the community where he lives.

Negroes-A person of mixed White and Negro blood should be returned as a Negro, no matter how small the percentage of Negro blood. Both Black and Mulatto persons are to be returned as Negroes, without distinction. A person of mixed Indian and Negro blood should be returned as Negro, unless the Indian blood predominates.

Those of Indian ethic identify were first reported in the United States Federal Census for 1860 for Indian Lands west of the Mississippi only. There were no officially sanctioned reports for the census years 1870 or 1880, the first available census being 1900; only. however, in the cases of Neshoba and Newton Counties, the enumerators made exception to the rule and reported Indians. Therefore, there are such entries in the 1880 Federal Census of Newton County, Mississippi, as "Jack Amis (Amos), age 40, Indian, and his wife Sallie living north of Hickory.

I will also attempt to address the Native American connection with the community families: the Garners, Amis/Amos and other community members and see where that takes us. Family ancestors of Native American descent can often be found in the regular Federal population censuses, but there will be no indication in most cases that they are of Indian descent and will be listed as Mulatto or Negro.

Acknowledgments

I am indebted to David Rae Morris for the use of his work: the photograph on the cover of this book and photos in the book. I am indebted to Dr. Harold Graham and the Historical and Genealogical Society of Newton and to my friend, Basia Pulz, who provided many hours of untiring support and helpful insight.

With profound respect I try here to honor the Good Hope Fellowship Church Community Members: Miss Aline Williams, the Church secretary who spoke to me many times on the phone in her last years, the information I received from her gave me the key to begin my research; to Dan Williams, who guided me to the well-kept cemetery, marked "Colored Cemetery", where some of the ancestors are buried during and after the time of enslavement; to the late Pastor John West, the late Deacon Bill Williams and to the Good Hope Church members on Fellowship Road who invited us in and made us feel part of their congregation.

To Cousin Cliff Edison, who added flavor to the stories with his rare gift of hospitality; to Pastor George Smith and the late Mrs. Bernice Mitchell, for their knowledge of the recorded history of Good Hope Missionary Baptist Church; to my cousin Carroll Johnson, who drove me around the community to help jar my memories. To Basia Pulz, who did much more than edit and to Joseph Roy (of RoyTek), who was there advising me technically all the way. To the settlers whose stories I endeavored to tell and for the trust and encouragement that I found among their descendants, which made this project possible and multiplied the personal rewards that I derived in the process.

To my daughters: Jacquelyn, Jewelynn, Jocelynn, my grandchildren and great grands, for allowing me the time away. Lastly, I want to thank Charles Williams of Save the Family Institute, for the many personal hours put into the research and traveling over the country when necessary. I am ever so grateful.

Major Publications and Contributors

<u>The Great Migration to the Mississippi Territory 1798-1819 by</u> Charles Lowery

<u>History of Newton County 1834 -1894</u>, by A. J. Brown, The Clarion-Leger Press, Jackson, Mississippi, 1894, Reprint by Melvin Tingle.

The Suttles and Petry Family Research by Carolyn Whittier

Levy Family Research: by Edward Sanders,

The Jewish Historical Society of South Carolina

Kershaw County, South Carolina Historical Society

With additional notes from: Melvin Tingle, Greg Boggan and Dr. Harold Graham

Darrell Fielder, Family Researcher

Britta Pruitt, Family Researcher

Contents

Introduction

Filmore Johnson Remembered

I remember very little of my great grandfather. He died in 1945, four months after my sixth birthday. What I know most about him is what I was told by my elders, and that was a lot. I was told he died at the home of a daughter, Mary Johnson and her husband, Isaac Salter. (*Isaac Salter was a member of the Salter family living in the community and a brother to my maternal grandmother Susie Anna Salter Hayden.*)

The first memories of my great grandparents, Filmore and Elizabeth Levy Johnson [Bettie], were when I was about five years old and they were living apart. I never questioned it. Years later I learned that grandpa Filmore had become what the elders called "cantankerous." Because of his senility it was very hard for Grandma Bettie to live with and care for him. They lived apart until his death.

While gathering information for the book I interviewed my aunt, Opal Johnson Ford, the granddaughter of Filmore and Bettie, who was eighty years old at the time. She told me this story: "My mama, your grandma, Lilia [Toles] Johnson, died when I was about thirteen years old and "poppa", your grandpa, Daniel Johnson married again after her death to a woman named Mahala. We called her Mama Hallie. Just when she came to live with us, I went to live with Grandma Bettie and Grandpa Filmore. Poppa had sent me there to help Grandma Bettie with Grandpa Filmore and with chores around the house. During the time that I lived with them we lived in a little house past the church and the cemetery near Mus Godden's house." She continued, "Before long they were separated; he went to live with Uncle Ike and Aunt Mary.

I went back home and Grandma Bettie went to live with their other daughter, Aunt Nupsy [Lela Johnson Edison],for a while. Later she lived with us until Grandpa Filmore died. After that she went to live with Aunt Mary and Uncle Ike. Although when they lived apart Grandma Bettie would walk every day the short distance down the road to Aunt Mary's house to visit with grandpa."

In his later years, on most Sundays, my dad would take us to Aunt Mary's house to visit Grandpa Filmore. I remember him lying in what looked like to me a very large feather bed in the front room of the house. The front room, or the parlor as it was sometimes called, had been changed around to suit grandpa's needs. One by one, we who were old enough would walk up to the head of the big feather bed and say, "How do you feel grandpa?"

He would sometimes nod and reply, "fine," or just nod. Our sister Doris, who we called "Beet", is a year or so older than I and who remembered things more vividly than others, said Grandpa Filmore said to her, "I feel with my damn hands, how do you think I feel?" I didn't hear him say that, however I have no doubts that he said it.

CHAPTER ONE

The Mississippi Territory 1798-1819

The rich lands east of the Mississippi were originally inhabited by Indian tribes who had made it their home for many centuries. When the Europeans first came to America the Choctaw people were already one of the largest and most advanced Indian tribes east of the Mississippi River. They were noted for their high quality farming, trading and their high level of success. They were the chief exporters of agricultural products among the Indian tribes of the Southeast. Nevertheless in 1798 Congress organized the land as the Mississippi Territory and opened it for settlement.

By 1817, when Mississippi was made a state, residents of older states, such as Virginia, the Carolinas and Georgia moved to the new state of Mississippi believing they were taking up residence in a land of unsurpassed opportunities. Economic opportunities were declining for most planters living in the states of Virginia, North Carolina and South Carolina as the available supply of fertile land was decreasing. This made the rich virgin land of the Mississippi all the more attractive. Some who came were land speculators, others were merchants and general tradesmen hoping to make investments and many came to buy land for permanent settlement. What lay at the heart of this wealth was land purchased at minimal prices and the use of unpaid labor to produce cotton and other crops. The economic prospects expected by the settlers were true, although certainly not for the many enslaved men, women and children or for the Indian tribes who had lost their home lands to what became the state of Mississippi.

The Removal of the Choctaw Nation

Before 1830, the United States government had reason to cultivate friendship with the Choctaw Indians. The tribe was considered a barrier between the United States and the Spanish as well as the French. Once Spain and France had been defeated and were no longer a threat to America, the Choctaw Nation was no longer needed as protection.

However, their land was in high demand by scores of settlers. By 1830, the census was increasing and much of the good lands were being taken. Settlers in need of more land immediately made plans to acquire more fertile Choctaw land.

The Treaty of Dancing Rabbit Creek was ratified by the U.S. Senate on February 25, 1831. Once the treaty was signed close to eleven million acres of Choctaw Land were lost to the tribe and more settlers moved into the area.

The Choctaws were removed to the lands west of the Mississippi [Oklahoma] which created room for more settlers. Not all tribal members were removed. Some stayed on and refused to be moved. Following the enactment of the Trail of Tears, President Andrew Jackson issued a degree declaring that the Indians were allowed to homestead forty acres on the conditions that they no longer could speak their own language, practice their religion or call themselves a tribe. These resisters hid in the forests and swamps east of the Mississippi. Others became sharecroppers. Some were held enslaved, especially those of mixed African blood. They were considered aliens in their own land, without the recognition as United State citizens.

In 1945, after many years of hardship, the Mississippi Band of Choctaw Indians was federally recognized by the United States government. The Choctaw people continued to struggle economically due to bigotry, cultural isolation, and lack of jobs. The Choctaw, who for 150 years had been neither "white nor black," were left, where they had always been, in poverty. With reorganization and establishment of tribal government, however, over the next decades they took control of schools, health care facilities, legal and judicial systems, and social service programs.

The Choctaws witnessed the social forces that brought Freedom Summer and it's after effects to their ancient homeland. The Civil Rights Movement produced significant social change for the Choctaw in Mississippi, as their civil rights were enhanced. Prior to the Civil Rights Act of 1964, most jobs were given to whites, then to people of African descent. Donna Ladd, a Choctaw, now in her 40s, wrote, "as a little girl, she thought that a 'white only' sign in a local store meant she could only order white or vanilla ice cream." It was a small story, but one that shows how a third people group can easily get left out of the attempts for understanding.

On June 21, 1964 James Chaney, Andrew Goodman and Michael Schwerner (renowned civil rights workers) disappeared; their remains were later found in a newly constructed dam. A crucial turning point in the FBI investigation came when the charred remains of the murdered civil rights workers' station wagon was found on a Mississippi Choctaw reservation. Two Choctaw women, who were in the back seat of a deputy's patrol car, said they witnessed the meeting of two conspirators who expressed their desire to "beat-up" the boys.

The end of legalized racial segregation permitted the Choctaws to participate in public institutions and facilities that had been reserved exclusively for white patrons. Phillip Martin, who had served in the U. S. Army in Europe during World War II, returned to visit his former Neshoba County, Mississippi home. After seeing the poverty of his people, he decided to stay to help. Martin served as chairperson in various Choctaw committees up until 1977. Martin was elected as Chief of the Mississippi Band of Choctaw Indians. He served a total of 30 years, being re-elected until 2007. Martin died in Jackson, Mississippi on February 4, 2010. He was eulogized as a visionary leader, who had lifted his people out of poverty with businesses and casinos built on tribal land.

CHAPTER TWO

Neshoba County, Mississippi (1833) to Newton County, Mississippi (1836)

Originally Newton was part of Neshoba County and was included in the Indian lands taken with the Treaty of Dancing Rabbit. Soon the pioneers living in the southern half of the large county of Neshoba wanted a county of their own. Thus on February 26, 1836, the Mississippi Legislature admitted Newton as a separate county. (*Newton County is 64 square miles and uses the Township Range System. A section is a basic unit of the system, a square tract of line one mile by one mile containing 640 acres. A Township is 36 sections ranged in a 6x6 array, measuring 6x6 miles. Lake is a town in both Newton and Scott counties, Mississippi. Most of Lake lies in Scott County while the smaller portion of the city lies in Newton County.)*

Settlers of Newton County 1840

1840 and 1850 Census Slaveholders

The United States Census taken in 1840 was Newton County's first federal census. Of the residents in Newton County; thirty-five were slave holders that held approximately 560 men, women and children enslaved. The census shows the population of Newton County's early settlers at only 341 not including their enslaved workers or the Choctaw Indians living in the county. Throughout this period many settlers came from Georgia and Alabama and other counties in Mississippi with hundreds of enslaved workers. The population in the county from 1840 to 1850 nearly tripled. The many reasons behind the decisions to leave their homes, and sometimes their families, were countless. Many chose to move in search of a better life.

The people they held enslaved however were brought along as free labor. Like the livestock, they had no choice, they were there to work. They were taken away from their families, often never to see them again. Most worked on small farms and toiled alongside their slaveholders. Some were plantation workers and worked from sun up to sun down and ate and slept in "slave houses". In 1840 planters such as A.E. Benjamin and Hiram Walker, James Thomas, James Hollingsworth, A.

Other planters who owned large plantations held a greater number of enslaved workers. For example: Edward Chapman held twenty workers enslaved; Deed Safford held forty four workers; Milton and James Baylock each held fifty enslaved men, women and children; Henry Evan held twenty five; Catharine Watson held twenty-eight; Charles Williamson reported seventeen and Duncan Thompson reported eighteen enslaved. Ten years later the Slave Schedule of 1850 shows the slaveholders of Newton County with more than 1,000 enslaved people.

Abel Edwards Chapman and Edward Edwards Chapman were heads of the large Chapman family. Abel Edwards Chapman was a railroad surveyor and Edward E. Chapman worked mostly as a land surveyor. Both were farmers and slaveholders. Edward E. Chapman was the owner of six slave houses and held twenty-nine people enslaved. Abel Chapman held twenty-one enslaved workers. The brothers lived in adjoining communities near the small town of Hickory, Mississippi. *(Information regarding the Chapman of Newton County taken from The Chapman papers at the Mississippi Department of Archives & History) By Bradley Chapman Pierce, Margaret Olivia Chapman)*

Willis Roy Norman, the central figure in the Norman families of Newton County, was a native of Wilkes County, Georgia who arrived in Newton, County about 1842, in company with his brother, Jesse Norman. They were soon joined by William Norman, a third brother, also a slave holder. The Normans became one of rural Hickory's largest slaveholders and sharecroppers. Other plantation owners who held enslaved workers were: Samuel, Starling and William Boyd Johnson, James Biggs, Alfred and John Brown, T. R. Overstreet, William Graham and Isaac Hollingsworth.

CHAPTER THREE

The Origin of the Original Good Hope Church

One of the early churches formed in the county was near to what would be the town of Hickory. Information from the Regular Baptist Church of Christ records shows on September 29, 1855 the constitution of the original Regular Baptist Church of Christ, "the White Church" [as it was later known], was organized by several community members and signed into charter. The charter was signed by the following community members: Jacob S. Ishe, Richard Sinclair, David Richee, Lydia Richee Temp Sinclair, Mary Skinner, Eliza Tatum, Martha Ishe and Phoebe Sission. Elder N.L. Clark was appointed Moderator Protem and John William as Protem. David Richee was appointed Church Clerk. Good Hope Regular Baptist Church of Christ held its first service in the Tatum schoolhouse on Tatum Road. For a short period Church services were held on the Saturday before the third Sunday of each month in Tatum School building.

Some years after 1855, a church building was erected. [The date as of this printing is not known.] The building was in the vicinity of what is called the "Short Cut Road" or as known by some community members as the "Straight Road." (*Near the Enterprise Road*) A short time after the church was organized a small piece of land was donated by the membership to be used as a Colored or "Slave" cemetery. The area surrounding the Good Hope Regular Baptist Church of Christ became known as the Good Hope Community. The church was and still is located on Fellowship Road near the town of Hickory. The leading church and community members then were: the Johnsons, Gibsons, Suttles, Walkers, Walls, Tatum, Ishee, Thompsons and the Sinclairs. Some were slaveholders who settled in the area. Some had large plantations and held a large number of people enslaved. Others worked small farms and held only a few enslaved workers. *(The acreage that was set aside for the Colored cemetery is still being used for that purpose. All told it appears likely that there are well over fifty graves in the cemetery.)*

CHAPTER FOUR

The Town of Hickory, Mississippi

1860 Slaveholders

In 1860, the town of Hickory was settled and named in honor of Andrew Jackson, "Old Hickory". Living in the area were three classes of people: the Choctaw Indians [the original land owners], the plantation owners and the land workers, the latter being known as "slaves." The 1860 Slave Schedule shows more planters who moved into the county near Hickory. The settlers owned several thousand acres of land and many enslaved workers. Plantation owners like B. Saffold produced large crops there and held as many as fifty eight enslaved workers. William Norman held forty three enslaved laborers and had eighteen slave houses on the plantation. His brother, Jesse Norman, held fourteen people enslaved and owned two slave houses. William Thompson held thirty two men, women and children enslaved and he produced large amounts of cotton. Ben and William Walker together held twenty six enslaved laborers. Joseph Hughes and Duncan Thompson held twenty five each. Art Harrington was listed holding twenty four men, women and children enslaved. John McRea was listed in the Slave Census holding sixteen workers enslaved on a large cotton and sugar cane plantation. Henry D. Jones had three slave houses and held nineteen people enslaved.

Most settlers, however, in the area owned small farms and held less than ten enslaved people. John Blakely and Jane Brown each held nine persons enslaved. Isaac Hollingsworth held eight. Burgess Garner had seven. Absalom Loper and Thomas Mc Mullin held six each. All were producers of cotton. Some planters such as John Dyes, Emely Dyes and James Levy held less than five workers. Samuel Brown and Thomas Wall held as few as two workers. Walter Johnson and James Overstreet each held only one on their small farms. Almost every man, woman and child who were held enslaved on plantations and farms in rural Hickory before the War would become the ancestors of the former and present day families of the Good Hope Freedmen Settlement of Newton County, Mississippi after the War. *(Information found in 1860 Slave Schedule on Newton County)*

CHAPTER FIVE

What Caused The Civil War

Most historians would agree that a number of issues ignited the Civil War: states' rights, the role of the federal government, the preservation of the Union and the economy; which all were inextricably bound to the institution of slavery. By the beginning of the 19th century slavery in the United States was firmly instituted with a series of statutes and penal codes enacted in a number of states to regulate the activity of enslaved people and all matters concerning the enslaved. *(Judy Woodruff, PBS News Hour What Caused the Civil War)*

Beginning with the Louisiana Purchase, the question of slavery ushered in a period of national debate between pro-slavery and anti-slavery states. In 1820, Congress was in debate over how to divide the new territories into slavery states and free states. After Missouri's admission to the Union in 1821, no other states were admitted until 1836 when Arkansas became a slavery state. Debates over slavery states and free states remained reasonably calm for almost thirty years. However, by the late 1840s several events happened that upset the balance: America added new territories after the Mexican war; Texas had claimed that its territory extended all the way to Santa Fe; and in January 1850, a bill passed known as the Compromise of 1850. According to the compromise Texas would relinquish the land in dispute but be given ten million dollars to pay off its debt to Mexico.

The territories of New Mexico, Nevada, Arizona and Utah would be organized without mention of slavery. In the District of Columbia slavery would still be permitted. Finally, California would be admitted as a free state. To pacify slavery state politicians, who would have objected to the imbalance created by adding another free state, the Fugitive Slave Act was passed. The Compromise of 1850 kept the nation united but the solution was only temporary. The compromise lasted until the passage of the Kansas-Nebraska Act in 1854, when Illinois Senator Stephen Douglas proposed legislation allowing the issue of slavery to be decided in the new territories.

In 1857, Dred Scott, an enslaved man, was taken by the man who held him enslaved into Illinois and Wisconsin Territory in which slavery was prohibited. He sued for his freedom.

The Supreme Court decided he was not a United States citizen and did not have the right to sue. The court also found the Missouri Compromise unconstitutional, ruling that the federal government did not have the authority to prohibit slavery in the territories.

The Freeport Doctrine

The doctrine known as the Freeport Doctrine was articulated by Stephen A. Douglas at the second Lincoln-Douglas Senatorial Debates on August 27, 1858 in Freeport, Illinois. The question put to Stephen A. Douglas by Abraham Lincoln on that day in Freeport, Illinois was, "Can the people of a Territory in any lawful way, against the wishes of any citizen of the United States, exclude slavery from their limits prior to the formation of a State constitution?" Douglas answered, "In my opinion the people of a Territory can, by lawful means, include or exclude slavery from their limits prior to the formation of a State constitution."

Douglas continued, "It matters not what way the Supreme Court may hereafter decide as to the abstract question whether slavery may or may not go into a Territory under the Constitution, if, on the contrary, they are for it, their legislation will favor its extension no matter what the decision of the Supreme Court may be."

The Freeport Doctrine separated many southern Democrats who did not want to see slavery extended into the territories. Douglas had previously stated the principle of the doctrine but its deliberate public statement at Freeport added to alienating those in the southern United States who were demanding more defense for slavery, and who later insisted on the rejection of the Freeport Doctrine [the passage of a congressional Slave Code for the territories]. The answers led to the split of the Democratic Party in 1860 and Douglas' loss in the 1860 presidential election to Abraham Lincoln. Freeport newspaper stated on November 6, 1860, "Abraham Lincoln, who had declared "Government cannot endure permanently half slave, half free...," is elected president."

The following year the Southern Confederate States was established. Representatives of the new "Confederate" states convened in Montgomery, Alabama on February 4, 1861 and inaugurated Jefferson Davis as president on February 18. When Abraham Lincoln took the oath of office on March 4, 1861 seven slavery states had seceded and four others were soon to follow. Weeks after President Lincoln took the oath more southern states began seceding.

On April 12, 1861, the Civil War began when the South fired on the federal garrison at Fort Sumter in South Carolina.

The War had gone on for more than a year and many lives were lost. The South was using enslaved men to aid the war effort. Enslaved men and women had been forced to build fortifications, work as blacksmiths, nurses, and laundresses and to work in factories and armories. In 1862 President Lincoln was considering emancipating enslaved men under Confederate control as a military strategy to win the war. He warned the Confederacy if it did not surrender at once he would free the people enslaved in the South. In August 1861 Congress passed a confiscation act that conferred "contraband" status on all slaves who had been used in direct support of the Confederate war effort. In March 1862 Congress enacted a new article of war forbidding army officers to return fugitives to the slaveholders. Emancipation had weakened the enemy and before the war was a year old the slaves themselves had taken the initiative that forced northern authorities to move toward making it a war for freedom.

When Lincoln did permit the Freedmen to enlist, the men rushed to sign up. Contrabands and Negro Troops served in Colored units commanded by White officers. Though they faced segregation and discrimination, they fought with valor, and their contributions helped turn the course of many battles. By the end of the war, roughly 180,000 troops were men of color, some earning the highest military honors. Several Freedmen from the Good Hope Freedmen Settlement enlisted and fought in the War. Men such as Henry Dyes I, Prince Dyes and Daniel Johnson I and more, fought and died unnoticed but not in vain.

Migration After The Civil War

After the War several descendants of the first generation land owners and slaveholders in Newton County relocated to other counties and states that had an available supply of fertile land for sale in hope of starting new lives.

Several planters who had withstood wartime destruction and postwar uncertainties faced spiraling debt. Some of the wealthiest planters in the regions forfeited their land to pay off their debts. Many of the large plantations were broken up into small farms. Some farms, however, were still owned by a few well to do absentee landlords who had relocated to other states. The Wyatt family moved to Texas. Charles Cornett and his family relocated to Scott County in Mississippi. Some of the Johnson families migrated to Kentucky, Tennessee, Arkansas and Texas, leaving behind their former enslaved labor force, several friends and neighbors, much of whom were too poverty-stricken to make the move.

CHAPTER SIX

Emancipation Proclamation

Emancipation as a War aim was never universally popular in the North. In a letter that would be read aloud to a Union mass meeting in Springfield, Illinois, on September 3, 1863, Lincoln explained that "if White Americans did not want to fight for Black Americans then they should fight to save the Union." Only force could quell the rebellion, and emancipation had weakened the enemy and provided soldiers for the North. But having made a pledge of freedom to black soldiers and their families, Lincoln was determined to keep the promise once the Union was saved. The executive order abolished slavery in all Confederate states on January 1, 1863. As a result, black soldiers were able to fight for the Union and slavery became a central issue in the Civil War.

Few events in American's history matched the drama of the Emancipation Proclamation. Centuries later it continues to stir the deepest emotions. The 16th president of the United States, President Abraham Lincoln, regarded slavery as a moral evil and supported the notion of gradual emancipation. Nonetheless, on January 1, 1863, Abraham Lincoln signed the Emancipation Proclamation. The proclamation declared, "That all persons held as slaves" within the rebellious states "are, and hence forward shall be free," after many years of hardships four million people who had lived years enslaved had gained their freedom. In the United States emancipation accompanied the defeat of the world's most economical and powerful slaveholding class.

Soon after the War, things changed throughout the South for both former slaveholders and the newly freed residents. Former slaveholders were now in need of workers and the newly freed men and women needed work and a place to live. One Freedman said, "The master called us up to the big house and told us we were as free as he was and we could stay on and work on the farm. He said, 'I need help and you need work.' " All over the South most of the country's enslaved population had been born on plantations and some considered it a part of their family. The plantation had always been their home, and for many, the work they did there was the work they knew best. The now freed workers were offered a piece of land, seeds, fertilizer and at the end of the year they would share the profits with the land owners. The planter told them he would continue to look after them when they were old and sick; just as he had done before the War.

In spite of these promises nearly all who heard the good news of freedom began shouting and rejoicing and running from plantation life. Yet some stayed behind. Planters and Freedmen of Newton County who stayed behind settled in the Good Hope Fellowship sections of Township 5 Range 12 south of Hickory, Mississippi.

Freedmen Bureau

In March of 1865, one month before President Abraham Lincoln was assassinated the Bureau of Refugees, Freedmen and Abandoned Land [Freedmen Bureau] was established. The Freedmen Bureau was established to provide for the distribution of "unoccupied land" to the Freedmen and to aid in negotiating labor contracts between the Freedmen and their employers. Plus it provided legal advice, facilitated resettlement and help Freedmen families to register in the 1866 State Census. The bureau also assisted in obtaining food and helped establish hospitals, schools, churches and cemeteries. With the support of the Freedmen Bureau, the newly freed people were able to make their familial relationships official. Scores of couples formalized their "slave marriages." Even so, the greatest importance for the newly freed men and women were finding lost loved ones and obtaining land and independence. *(Congress allowed the Freedmen Bureau to sell only 5 to 10 acre tracts of land to each head of families)*

1866 Mississippi States Census

In1866, a state census was held in most southern states and emancipated head of households were mandated by law to register in the census. Prior to the 1866, Mississippi and other southern state census, the enslaved were listed in census records not with a name, but enumerated separately under the slave owner's name by age and gender only. After 1866, Freedmen were required to have a surname for themselves and their family members. Former enslaved men and women were able to choose any surname they desired. The common view and records show that most Freedmen who were held enslaved in rural Hickory chose the surname of their former slaveholders.

In some cases they did choose the surname of a previous slaveholder. And in other cases they did not choose a surname of any slaveholder. Some wanted to distance themselves from slavery altogether. In a few cases, they seem to have had concealed surnames while enslaved which emerged after freedom.

Some slaveholders asked the people they had held enslaved not to take their surname at all. From all indications and research information a large percentage of the Freedmen chose the surnames of their last slaveholders.

Surnames such as: Garner, Lee, Evans, Barnett, Dyes, Walker, Chapman, Thompson, Norman, Brown, Suttles, Salter, Gibson, Johnson, Petree/Petry, Dawkins, Gaddis, Kidd and other surnames appeared in the1866 Mississippi State Census in Newton County as the surnames chosen by the Freedmen in the county.

The Reconstruction Era 1867-1876

The Reconstruction Era is considered one of the most turbulent times in American history and is even considered a second Civil War by many. The Reconstruction Era for Freedman and former slaveholding citizens was particularly intense. From 1867-1876 the South was under Radical Reconstruction with Union soldiers to protect the civil rights of Freedmen citizens. During this period more than two hundred Freedmen were elected to local, state and federal offices as members of the Republican Party. However, political equality would soon be challenged by the Democratic Party and by terrorist groups such as the Ku Klux Klan.

Andrew Johnson was sworn into the presidency after John Wilkes Booth assassinated Abraham Lincoln. Upon Lincoln's death, leading the task of reconstructing the South became the responsibility of Vice President Andrew Johnson as he became the 17th president of the United States. The devastated South had to be rebuilt economically, socially and politically. Citizens and politicians at the state and national levels became divided over how to rebuild the South. On May 29, 1865 when President Johnson issued his reconstruction plans for the South he deflated the hopes of the Freedmen and Civil Rights activists when he vetoed the Freedmen Bureau Bill and Civil Rights Bill of 1866 and opposed the 14th and the 15th amendments to the constitution. The president's plans forced Congress to pass the bills over his vetoes. (*The 13th, 14th, and 15th Amendments, known collectively as the Civil War Amendments, were designed to ensure equality for recently emancipated people. The 13th Amendment banned slavery and all involuntary servitude, except in the case of punishment for a crime.*) In 1868 President Andrew Johnson was impeached in the House of Representatives. He was acquitted in the Senate by one vote. As a result, he was able to stay in office. President Johnson was pressed to repeal certain reconstruction issues in exchange for those Senate votes needed to keep him in office. He ordered the return of land to pardon Confederates, null and voided those wartime orders that granted Freedmen forty acres and a mule, and removed many of the Freedman troops from the South.

Feeling empowered by the President's action the Confederates instituted a series of discriminatory "Black Codes."

Violence and election fraud kept most Freedmen and Republicans from voting. Democratic candidates committed to "White Rule" were swept into office. Yet some White southerners were supportive of the original reconstruction plans. The supporters themselves were in great personal danger. In 1872, Adelbert Ames, the twenty seventh and thirtieth governor of Mississippi, tried organizing a state militia to protect the voting process. Ames pleaded for federal troops to help keep order, but President Ulysses S. Grant refused. Governor Ames tried organizing a state militia to protect the voting process. But the tide had already turned against Republican rule in Mississippi, and Governor Ames was forced to resign. He lamented that the Freedmen "are to be returned to a condition of serfdom — an era of second slavery."

Newton Knight was another strong supporter of the Republican Party. Governor Ames had appointed him as a deputy U.S. Marshal for the Southern District to help maintain the fragile democracy. Also, in 1875, he was appointed as Colonel of the First Regiment Infantry of Jasper County, Mississippi. After Reconstruction ended, Knight retired from politics, as White Democrats took over county and state offices.

Newton Knight was born in Jones County, Mississippi, a Unionist who did not believe in the War for poor White farmers nor in slavery and was considered a deserter. On October 13, 1863, Knight and a band of deserters and enslaved men from Jones, Covington, Jasper, Newton and adjacent counties organized to protect the area from Confederate authorities. Jones County had mostly yeoman farmers and cattle herders, who were not slaveholders. They had little use for a war over a "state's right" to maintain the institution of slavery. By the spring of 1864, the "Knight Company" had taken effective control from the Confederate government in the county, and in July 1864 Newt Knight and the Knight Company, with other derserters, declared Jones County's independence from the Confederacy. After the war Newt Knight lived in Jasper County, where he was active in the Republican Party. In 1872, he was appointed as a deputy U.S. Marshal for the Southern District. After Reconstruction ended, Knight retired from politics, as White Democrats took over county and state offices. Newton Knight and his second wife, Rachel, and their children lived the rest of their lives after the Reconstruction era in SoSo, Jasper County. (Newton Knight 's wife, Rachel,was a former enslaved woman who had aided in the resistance) (see the Free State of Jones)

CHAPTER SEVEN

The Great Changes

Excerpts from the book by AJ Brown: The History of Newton County "*The whites and Negroes agree remarkably well. It is rarely the case that there is a difficulty between them. There is no disposition on the part of the Negroes for social equality. He knows his place, and he conducts himself well, and the white people respect him. The white people largely educate the Negroes, assist them to build all their churches, and when they are unfortunate and have their houses burned, or other such ill-luck, their white neighbors assist them and treat them kindly. The Negro is not cheated out of his wages in Newton County. He is given a fair price for his work and is expected to give reasonable labor. If he had a farm of his own, his white neighbors will 'treat him kindly if he behave himself and use only his own things. In this way the white and Colored people get on well and there is very little trouble with the Colored man appropriating anything to his own use that does not belong to him.*"

AJ Brown writes "*Many parts of the State have been troubled with a class known as "white caps," and this county [Newton County] has not been altogether an exception. But at present there appears to be but little or none of it left in the county. Some very good people may, in an evil moment, have been drawn into participating with this lawless order and some others might have wished it success, but it is not so now. People all over the country find that such lawless proceedings are wrong and will not be tolerated by law or accepted by good citizens.*" "*The result is the order of "white caps" appears to be in the things of the past, with a hope that it will not be revived again. No arrests were ever made and but little trouble was experienced in the county in reference to it. The general behavior of the people of the county will compare well with the best in the State. No man need have any fears of going anywhere in this county on any business he may have, and the officers can execute any warrant they may have at any time without fear of being molested.*"

The End of Reconstruction

The end of Reconstruction and the demise of the Freedmen's Bureau and the advent of the Black Codes brought about enormous changes for the Freedmen families. The Federal Government had restored white supremacist control to the South and adopted a relaxed policy in regard to the newly freed men and women. This policy resulted in disenfranchisement. The Freedmen were reduced again to a status of quasi-slavery. From the onset, the Reconstructionist Government aroused bitter opposition among the majority of southerners.

The essential reason for the growing oppositions to the reconstruction plan was, most southern "whites" could not accept the idea of the newly freed men voting and holding office. Also for them it called for a redefining of their relationship between the former slaveholding families and former enslaved families.

Relationships and Unrest

In an effort to drive out Republicans from office and restore white supremacy, widespread postwar violence erupted throughout the South. The effects reached Newton County and the terror it created made its way to the small Colored Settlement in rural Hickory, Mississippi. Darrel Fielder, family history writer and former resident, wrote: "Information on the 'Dyess Rebellion of rural Hickory can be found in the book "History of Newton County" by: A J Brown, pages 162-169. It also references an article in the Meridian Mercury dated February 8, 1868. "To me, this is a very important event," Fielder said, "since African American men took the initiative to fight back against being accused of stealing as a pretext of driving them from their land that was granted to them during reconstruction. *(Dyess in this article is spelled Dyess; in other documents it is spelled Dyes.)*

*An article published in the Meridian Mercury on February, 1868 declares (**From the perspective of the reporter in 1868**); "In 1868 the Freedman Bureau was well established in the state and the Military Government was toughly engrafted upon it. This new state of things begat idleness among the Negroes, they also became more insolent to white peoples and were harder to govern and thus began trouble that ended in very tragic events in the county of Newton.*

The article continues; "When a Negro felt himself aggrieved or insulted, he reported it to [Military] Headquarters and if it were thought proper the white man was brought upon trial. Negroes would not work, and in many instances resorted to taking things. The most lamentable occurrence took place in (South- Eastern) part of the county in which two men were killed and another wounded. The particulars are as follow. "The two Denis brothers, living about 6 or 8 miles South-East of Hickory a farmer missed some hogs and went in search of them among the Negroes living nearby, who they suspected of being the thieves and made a close search and found a portion of the pork buried in the yard of one of the Negroes. After an unsuccessful attempt to settle the matter by compromise, one of the Denis brothers went to Hickory and sued a warrant to have the guilty parties arrested."

"The precise scene of the shocking deed is about midway, between Hickory Station and Garlandsville. [The area that is Good Hope Colored Community] Daniel A. Denis and Edward Denis originally from the state of Georgia but more recently from the state of Alabama, and came to this State about 10 years ago and settled on a plantation and have since been working together. Industrious and honorable men they both served in the war. Their ages were 54 and 51."

The *Meridian Mercury* story continues "There is a family of Negroes living near the Denis plantation formerly belonging to the Dyess plantation family. They lived nearby when they were slaves. They are four brothers perhaps five believed to have been concerned in the murderous assault. Their names are Prince, Orange, John, Sonny and Joe all are Dyess Negroes. They were squatters here nearby.

The Mrs. Denis had missed a hog they suspected the Dyess Negroes having stolen from them. Ed. Denis; with Mr. Tucker went to Prince Dyess' home to search. They found Prince's wife cooking fresh hog meat asked where she got it she said she got it from Uncle Henry Dyess. They went to Uncle Henry about it who said they did not get it from him. This was Friday: Prince was not at home. Went after dark and he was not at home yet. Went in the morning and still not home. Told the woman she would have to go to Hickory [for questions]. She then showed them the meat buried in a box. They started to leave with her; and met with her husband and Orange [Dyess] his brother; both had doubled barrel shot guns. A conversation ensued Prince confessed that he killed the hog and said the woman should not be held. Then Denis told Prince that he must go [to Hickory] and he would make it as light as possible provided he would leave the County, he said he would but he was hungry and would go after he had something to eat. Denis with Tucker waited until evening and Prince did not come as promised. So they sued for a warrant. The warrant was given to Mr. Gibson special deputy to execute. A posse of the Denis brothers, Ben Griffin, Jonas Nelson, and Jack K. Horn and Sim Perry after dark went to Prince's [Dyess] house. They did not find him at home failing in their object and not suspecting a conspiracy, lighted a torch, call upon some dogs, and turned it into a possum hunt. They caught one possum returned home.

They were in 100 yards of home, crossing a branch, Ed Denis bearing the torch next to Daniel Denis in advance, others following, when a volley was fired into the party at close range. Daniel Denis, it is supposed fell dead. Gibson and Griffin and Nelson were more or less severely wounded by the fire. The Negroes rushed from their ambush. Old John Dyess the father of the five sons encountered Ed Denis who seemed to have stood his ground were killed. Edward was heard to exclaim "Prince don't kill me; the voice of Little John Dyess was heard saying kill him. Daniel Denis laid dead shot twice. Ed was apparently run through with a sword. The Black Prince [Dyess a Civil War Veteran] wore a sword by virtue of his service in the War with Old John the old daddy of these young devils.[John Dyess and his sons were Civil War Veterans] The next morning about 20 men from Garlandville appeared upon the scene. The Negroes too seemed to have improved the time to recruit their forces. Flushed with victory and confident of their numbers they sent a message to the party to come and arrest them.

The Party of whites from Garlandville went up to old John's house and several were wounded, the first was returned and two Negroes were shot. It is Negroes news that one was killed but doubtful. Old John was wounded and sent to Hickory where we lose track of him and will not attempt to find him again; Tobe Gentry in the Sat. night's massacre has been arrested and put in county jail. Besides old John, Joe and his son, Uncle Henry Dyess' brothers both in Saturday's fight, were caught. "

Daniel Johnson I was in the Sunday fight and had been arrested and committed to Jasper County jail. "A certain restless Negro [Possibly Daniel Johnson] who is well known in Newton County has on several occasions shown a disposition to incite his people to violence, was out early on Wednesday morning It was said here "on Wednesday morning Negroes engaged in war on Newton had sent here for reinforcements" The law was not troubled with any trials of those assassins. The vengeances of the white people were speedy'. But they did not enjoy the rest as soon as the facts doubtless, greatly exaggerated, against the whites and mitigated. The Law was not on the part of the Negroes. The Blacks arrested on Murder and lynching were tried before military court some that had but little to do with the punishment of Negroes were tried and set free." (The article is from the perspective of the reporter who wrote the article in 1868) (An article published in the Meridian Mercury on February 1868) (See more on Daniel Johnson I in the Frank Petry/Petree I Story)

Violence Erupted Near Hickory

In 1890, violence erupted near the small town of Hickory, Mississippi. In the Newton Record on December 15, 1908 the headlines read: "Slayer of A. J. Wall Has Not Been Apprehended." The article continues: "Dee Dawkins a friend of Jones meets death at the hands of a mob. For several days following the tragedy there was considerable excitement in the community where A. J. Wall was murdered last week at the hand of the Negro Shep Jones. Things have quieted down somewhat now but so far as known, the Negro is still at large. Some think that he was captured and killed but this cannot be confirmed."

Darrell Fielder wrote: "Regarding the incident involving Shep Jones, William Fielder and D. Dawkins, bear in mind, this was written from the perspective of the majority population. Cousin Ruby Jean, Shep's granddaughter, tells it differently. Shep Jones married Scotia Fielder. Shep and Scotia had a daughter, Mae Ida. Mae Ida is the mother of Ruby Jean." The article must be balanced against her personal oral story. Shep escaped (with the help of William Fielder and D. Dawkins) but was never heard from again. Shep was able to escape "overseas" according to Ruby Jean." (*Mrs. Ann Burke at the Newton County Genealogical and Historical society was very instrumental in locating this article and transcribing it*)

On July 31, 1890 in near-by Jasper County, Mississippi, Marsh Cook, organizer of Jasper County [Negro Republican Party] was shot and killed. "He had been warned of his danger. Cook was making a canvass of the county under the management of the chairman of the Republican Executive Committee of Jasper County. The chairman was a notorious Negro politician and Cook's speeches were arousing bad feelings between the Blacks and the Whites. "When asked to quit the canvass on the grounds that his speeches would create race trouble, he refused to do so and said he would continue no matter what the cost might be." Marsh Cook was on his way to his next appointment when he was killed. (*Hamilton Times, Marion County, Alabama, July 31, 1890 Transcribed by Veneta McKinney*)(*The Negro Republican Party is one name of the African American branch of the Republican Party formed in the southern United States by the Union League in 1867 during the Reconstruction Era. After 1890 the faction was usually called the Black -and -Tan faction.*)

CHAPTER EIGHT

The Good Hope Freedmen Settlement

The Founders

The Good Hope Freedmen Settlement is legendary for having been founded by former enslaved men and women who were held enslaved on plantations in the original Good Hope Community area. Many were members of the original Good Hope Regular Baptist Church known by the Freedmen during that period as the "Masters' Church" and later as the "White Good Hope Church." No defined period or precise records were uncovered that suggests the advent of the settlement or specific records as to its founders. Some believe that soon after Emancipation Proclamation during the time of Reconstruction several Freedmen who had fought in the Civil War had received land grants in the area. John Dyes and his sons had served in the Civil War with the Union and may have received their land by virtue of their service in the War. Oral history and land records lean also toward the Johnson brothers. Daniel I, William, Preston I, Frank Petry II and young Filmore Johnson, who were held enslaved on the Gibson/Johnson plantations in the Good Hope Fellowship area during the time of enslavement and who may have been gifted the land by their former slaveholders.

Daniel Johnson I and the Dyess family may have been living in the Settlement as early as 1867 or 1868. Research shows on February 8, 1868 Daniel I was reported in the Meridian Mercury newspaper "arrested and committed to Jasper County Jail". Daniel Johnson I was said to have been helping the Dyess family hold on to land granted to them. Other Freedmen who settled the area were large extended families such as: the Gibsons, Browns, Longmires, Ishees, Barbers and other names, which were not legible in historical records. This list contains only some of the many early farmers who broke the land, planted fields, raised families and eked out an existence in the Good Hope Freedmen Settlement, near Hickory, Mississippi in Newton County.

Land ownership and independence were very important for the Freedmen but trying to buy only a small piece of very poor land was a long and difficult struggle. Yet in spite of the terrible conditions of those first years, the early settlers persevered and acquired a few acres of land, most of it was by renting and a small amount was by purchasing. Some elders said "We ain't going nowhere; we plan to stay." The settlement was to be their home. It was families, friends and community. They resolved it would take more than hard times, hard work, the threat of violence and violence to induce them to abandon their land and their quest for more land. This was said by the descendant's many times, "They had faith in themselves, their ability to work hard and they had faith in God."

The Advent of

Good Hope Freedmen Settlement

During these chaotic times the Freedmen were faced with major encounters and had many decisions to make. The new laws, unrest, disorders and the turmoil throughout this period may have caused the Freedmen to end their ties and their church affiliation with their previous slaveholders. Subsequently, several Freedmen had begun to seek land to farm and to construct a new existence in a settlement of their own, in an area just south of Hickory, a short distance from the original Good Hope Church Community on Fellowship Road.

Some said that there was a time period before the War and before Reconstruction the former slaveholders and the people they held as slaves "were somehow bound together." They said, "Each of us in own way was struggling to make it." AJ Brown wrote in his book, *The History of Newton County*, "The Whites and Negroes agree remarkably well. It is rarely the case that there is a difficulty between them."

However, during and after the times of Reconstruction things changed. Mississippi and other southern states passed legislations creating "Black Codes." These laws generally restricted nearly all rights of the Freedmen. Jim Crow Laws, as they were called, brought about great changes in relationships between the Freedmen and former slaveholders. The new laws created various social barriers that had affected many areas of their life. The greatest source of controversy was the new social order. The former slaveholders had difficulty accepting the new freedom of former enslaved workers. The Freedmen had to adjust to a new way of life. They were not enslaved but not yet free.

Also, the Freedmen were no longer allowed to worship with the church congregations which their ancestors, both enslaved and free, had been a part of for many years.

The "forty acres and a mule" that was promised them, never materialized. The Jim Crow Laws had provided a system where many had to work as sharecroppers with a limited and often total lack of opportunity to achieve land ownership and operate independently. For several years sharecropping and working for others appeared to be the main method by which they could gain access to land. Step by step they were being pushed back into slavery. Instead of allowing themselves to be pushed back into slavery a number of determined men like the Johnson brothers, the Dyes family, the Gibsons, Browns and others agreed that going back to the plantation was not part of their plans. Before long others followed but less than five families held deed to their land. On the whole they were land squatters settling on unclaimed land deserted by fleeing plantation owners after the War or on unproductive land not in use by their former slaveholders. "Freedom Settlements", as they were sometimes called, were to a large degree an anomaly in a postwar South where white power rapidly resumed social, economic and political control and the agricultural system of sharecropping came to dominate. The ability of Good Hope Freedmen Settlement to withstand under these conditions may have been in some extent shielded by former slaveholding benefactors in the area.

The Freedmen Settlement that was developing was less than two miles from the original Good Hope Fellowship Community and the plantations where the Freedmen had toiled in the fields for many years and for most a lifetime. The settlement was to be called the "Good Hope Freedmen Settlement."

By 1920, it was referred to as the Good Hope Colored Community. (*As of this printing (2017) it is known as Good Hope, Mississippi, in Newton County*)

The Household Kinship System

The 1866 Mississippi State Census report shows many Freedmen living in large family groupings. Some families in the houses were related, others were not related. This system known as "Household Kinship" and was practiced during this period as a source of housing, mutual assistance and cultural continuity. The system escalated due to the enactment of the Mississippi Black Codes and the rising fear created by the Black Codes Vagrancy Laws. Under the new "Black Codes" [Jim Crow Laws] every man, woman and child were mandated by law to have a formal abode "a place to live."

The "Household Kinship" system served its purpose for shelter while, on the other hand, it created problems in documenting an accurate genealogical family history. *(The Vagrancy Law states "Newly freed men, women and children, if unemployed and homeless shall be arrested for vagrancy.")*

The 1870 Federal Census was the first census to include former enslaved men and women by first and last names. Before that enslaved men and women were not listed in the United States Census by name at all. By 1870, the census shows former enslaved men and women of Newton County in District 5 Range 12 continued to live in multi-family groupings. More confusion was added in documentation when the Freedmen were living in multi-family groupings and when sisters of one family married brothers of another family, plus scores of relatives with the same first and last names, all made it difficult when attempting documenting an accurate genealogical family history. For example: Daniel Johnson, the brother of Filmore Johnson and Daniel Johnson, the son of Filmore Johnson and Daniel Johnson, the great grandson of Filmore Johnson and Daniel Johnson, the great great grandson of Filmore all lived in the same area or in the same household. In spite of the many obstacles created by the Household Kindship System and other familial dynamics, with the help of the census and the "Roman Numeral Suffixes Rules", the settlers were classified. *(See more information on the pioneers in the Biographical Sketches of Good Hope Colored Settlement)*

To help identify family members with the same given name the "Roman Numeral Suffixes Rules" will be used. *(Such as Roman Numeral I II or III) for example: Daniel Johnson I the brother of Filmore Johnson and Daniel Johnson II the son of Filmore and Daniel Johnson III the grandson of Daniel Johnson IV and Daniel Johnson V the grandson of Daniel Johnson III. The first Daniel gets the first Roman number suffix I and the son the second II nephew get the third number III and so on...* **(Josiah Schmidt–professional Genealogist)**

CHAPTER NINE

Exploring the Connection of

Two Good Hope Baptist Churches

The legends surrounding the links between the two churches, the Good Hope Regular Baptist Church of Christ and the Good Hope Missionary Baptist Church, have been passed down for many generations and the stories they tell are undeniable. The oral accounts from the elders regarding the connections of the two communities were not always clear and needed more verification.

Exploration into the churches histories revealed a great deal. On the southwest portion of the Good Hope Regular Baptist Church of Christ property a marker was found posted "Colored Cemetery." Additional investigation revealed names of many enslaved ancestors who were buried there as early as 1861. Crumbling headstones list such names as: Edgar Brown, Hunter Brown, Lucius Brown, Richmond and Susan Gibson, George (GW) Gibson and Elvira Gibson. Cemetery and death records also confirmed: Eliza Petry Cook, the daughter of Frank Petree/Petry I, Clay Petree, the son of Frank Petree/Petry II and Angelina Petree/Petry plus Mary Kirby/Curby, the mother of Filmore Johnson all were buried there in later years. Other stones were too faded and weather worn to read.

Dan Williams, a current member of the original Good Hope Baptist Church, said, "In years past I have seen many more Black folks' graves up here in the Colored cemetery, no tombstones; most were marked with pretty pieces of glass. Some who were buried there were members of the Church during slavery days and a few years after slavery. Other Colored folks were buried there." Williams said, "They lived and worked on plantations and farms in the area."

While scores of early records have been lost, or are incomplete, reliable evidence proves "the Masters' Church" had enslaved members in its congregation. The church records of 1861 show the congregation had twenty Colored persons in its membership, recorded as "our Colored Brethren." The twenty enslaved members listed in the registry revealed such surnames as Longmire, Dyess, Johnson, Brown, Gibson, Ishee, Barber, Petree and other names that were not legible.

The records clarify in 1893 that the entire Colored membership requested dismissal from the church body to establish a house of worship of their own.

The Advent of the Good Hope Colored Church

Good Hope Missionary Baptist Church

Throughout the time of enslavement on most plantations a religious life had developed in the slave quarters. Certain masters had encouraged religion among their enslaved workers, sometimes for benevolent reasons but on the whole because they believed it would make their property more docile. Regardless of the viewpoint of the slave master, religion was very important in the lives of the enslaved men and women. While they were living enslaved on plantations in the Good Hope Fellowship area many became members of the slaveholder's church.

Good Hope Missionary Baptist Church

AJ Brown wrote from his book <u>The History of Newton County</u>**:** "Up to the close of the War Between to the States the Colored population had church membership with their owners, each according to his choice. Once they were made free however, they thought it best to go to themselves, thus forming their own Colored churches, first in the stronger communities and then in the weaker communities so that almost all the Colored people in the county now have a church privileges within their reach. "These churches," Brown continues, "are self-sustaining and do not call on the whites for help, unless to aid in building houses of worship."

The demise of the Freedman Bureau, the new Black Codes and the advent of the Jim Crow Laws had created many challenges for the newly freed families. These ordeals had produced the many reasons why the Colored church members had requested dismissal from the former "masters' church" rolls. Once dismissal from membership was granted the residents of the settlement were free to assemble, worship and to hold services as they desired. Within a few years plans to erect a settlement church were being discussed. The task of reorganizing as a religious community was another element of their larger need. As a result, all efforts were put forth by the Freedmen Community to build a church.

There are many stories surrounding the advent of the Good Hope Colored Missionary Baptist Church. Many were recounted and much research was done and new research continues to be presented. In 1994 results concerning the advent of Good Hope Colored Missionary Baptist Church were prepared by current pastor Reverend George Smith and the late Brother Costeller Dawkins, then the church clerk. They concluded: "the Good Hope Colored Missionary Baptist Church was established in 1855 by local White slave owners.

As a result many slaves attended the church with their owners. However, in the early 1900's the Freedmen established the church as their own." The research done by Reverend Smith shows the current Good Hope Colored Baptist Church on Good Hope Road was organized in 1908 and held its first service that same year."

In 2004, eighty six year old Broomsy Salter, a grandson of Filmore Johnson, said, "After they left the White folks church, before our church was built, they had attended services for a few years at Mt. Pleasant Baptist Church near Pachuta. Some attended other Colored churches in the area. Before they had land enough to build the church, they met in homes." "Other times," he said, "they just held church in the pine groves."

Regardless of the many different stories surrounding the advent of Good Hope Missionary Baptist Church it still stands on the nine acres of land that were purchased in 1909 just a few miles west of the original Good Hope Baptist Church Community on Fellowship Road where the ancestors were once members.(*(In 1909 records indicate that nine acres of land were purchased for the members of Good Hope Colored Settlement to build a church, a school and cemetery. There are some discrepancies regarding the advent of the church and its cemetery. New research uncovered information showing Good Hope Colored Church Cemetery is older than it was first documented. A master plat of the property with the church, cemetery and the school and playground and other landmarks located were documented by Ricky Harrison and student from East Central Community College Decatur, Mississippi and it is on display in the sanctuary at Good Hope MB Church on Good Hope Road Hickory, Mississippi. Some community elders and church historians hold a different view as to the year Good Hope Colored Settlement Church was built and the when first service were held.)*

Past Pastors

Reverend J.M. Brooks 1908 -1910

Reverend J.R. Graham 1911 -1922

Reverend S.A. Tullos 1922 -1923

Reverend H.M. Moore 1923 - 1939

Reverend C.M. Chapman1939 -1950

Reverend Fred Chapman 1950 -1977

Reverend Rubin Tatum 1977 -1978

Reverend George Smith 1983 - Present

Mothers of the Church 1921

Sister Bettie Johnson

Sister Maggie Brown

Deacons

Filmore B. Johnson

Frank Williams

Thomas. J. Petree

G. W. Gipson

Luther Gipson

Price C. Cole

I. S. Salter

Joe Brown

General Johnson

Ardell Edison

L. D. Griffin

Oscar Mitchell

Don Dawkins

H. P, Williams

Albert Johnson

Rev. Daniel Hayden

The 1909 researched information shows the people of the community were able to purchase ten acres of land to build a church and several acres for a burial ground, plus a much needed school for the children of the settlement. Plans went forward and in the early 1900s the church was organized in the community as Good Hope Colored Missionary Baptist Church. Later the name was altered to Good Hope Missionary Baptist Church. [This name will be used when referring to the church after 1930 and will refer to it as Good Hope Colored Baptist Church when it is necessary to relate to that era in history.] The 119 year old cemetery in Good Hope Colored Settlement lies on about three acres of land. It is situated in the corner South West of North West section 25 Beat 5 Range 12 in Newton County located near the town of Hickory.

The office of the Record of Deeds in Newton County shows in 1909 thirty dollars was received by J.K. Kirkland from Good Hope Colored Baptist Church members to buy land situated in the county of Newton and the state of Mississippi described as ten acres of land in Township 5 Range 12 in Newton County.

Good Hope Colored Baptist Church Cemetery

Oral historians' report the cemetery may have been used as a burial ground as early as 1880 and the families of the deceased are thought to have brought their loved ones from as far away as Hickory for burial. The earliest marked burial stone is dated 1898 and lies on the highest ridge in the cemetery.

A cedar sprig was planted to commemorate this loved one and now has grown to gigantic proportions. The name on the head stone is not legible and the stone itself is in need of repair. Over the years evidence of numerous burial places was located throughout the cemetery.

Research found at least 500 burials in the cemetery, many of which are unmarked. Only a few burials are listed here. For more burials see the Researched document complied **by Dr. Harold Graham Newton County Mississippi: A Cemetery Census 1782 – 1992** The Anderson Family, The Bates Family, The Beason Family, The Boggan/Boggan Family, The Bolton Family, The Brown Family, The Chapman Family. The Cole Family, The Cook Family, The Croft Family, The Curry Family, The Davis Family, The Dawkins Family, The Doby Family, The Dyes Family, The Edison Family, The Evans Family, The Ford Family, The Fielder Family. The Gaddis Family, The Garner Family, The Gibbs Family, The Gibson Family. The Gipson Family, The Gooden Family, The Graham Family, The Griffin Family. The Gully Family, The Hall Family, The Hamilton Family, The Hardy Family, The Hayden Family, The Horn Family, The Johnson Family, The Jones Family. The Kirby/ Curby/Kirby Family, The Kidd Family, The Lee Family, The Levy Family, The Mc Carty Family, The Mc Millian Family. The Mc Cune Family, The Mitchell Family, The Norman Family, The Odson Family, The Overstreet Family, The Love Family, The Petry/ Petree Family, The Potts Family, The Pruitt Family. The Riley Family, The Russell Family, The Salter/ Saulter Family, The Tullos Family, The Stephen Family, The Suttles Family, The Tanksley Family, The Tankson Family, The Tatum Family, The Thompson Family, The Tillman Family, The Toles Family, The Wall Family, The Wash Family, The Watts Family, The Walker Family, The William Family, The Wright Family, The Youngblood Family

Some Early Settlers burials found in the Colored Good Hope Church Cemetery Census 1913 – 1940

Parents: John Curry and Viola Evans
Dyes, Frances Rebecca: Died 1914 age 5 days
Parents: Henry Dyes and Louise Salter.
Dyes, S. T.: Died 1914 age 0-3-2.
Parents: Dan Dyes and Mary Clay
Evans, Cherry: Died 1915 age 53
Parents: Sylvia Walker
Ford, Green: Died 1913
Parents Dave Ford and Carline Davis
Gibbs, Squire: Died 1915 at age 62,
Parents not given
Informant: Ham Gibbs
Gibson, Cora: Died at age 1924
Parents: George Gibson and Jennie Jones
Gibson, Elvia: Died 1919 at age 19
Place of burial not given
Parents: Joe Brown and Maggie Petrey
Gibson, Minerva: Died 1941 at age 53
Wife of George Gibson
Father: Frank Petri.
Informant: Birdie Carroll, Picayune, Mississippi.
Hall, Sarah Died 1921at age 104
Widow of Peter Hall
Informant: Roy Curry
Hamilton, John: Died 1941 at age 72
Wife Rilla Hamilton
Mother: Rebecca
Johnson, Walter Died 1941 at age 17
Occupation: soldier
Parents: Dan'l Johnson and Lillie Toles
Informant: Dan'l Johnson
Cause of death: pneumonia
Johnson, Baby: born and died December 12, 1920,
Parents: Walter Johnson and Ida Berry
Johnson, Eliza: Died June 7, 1919 at age 34.
Grave marker not located
Buried in Old Good Hope Cemetery
Parents: Filmore Johnson and Bettie Suttles
Informant: Fannie Lee
Johnson, Fannie Died December 12, 1919 age about 75
("Old ex-slave")
Widow of Daniel Johnson I
Parents not given
Cause of death: "Burned to death accidentally—dead when found."
Johnson, Harriett: Died1917
Place of burial not given
Cason Pruitt: Died November 31, 1919 at age 24
Place of burial not given.
Parents: Phil Pruitt and Alice Salter.
Cause of death: tuberculosis.
Quince, Kitson Died June 23, 1915 at age 41

Place of burial not stated.
Parents: Cason Saulter and Cherry Johnson
Infomant: Isaac Salter.
Salter, Cherry Anderson:
Midwife
Wife of Cason Salter
Burial marker not located
Parents: John Anderson and Betsey Johnson
Informant: Cason Salter
Cause of death: heart lesion.
Tanksley, Infant Died October 1, 1929 at age 5 hours
Tansley, Inez Grey Died November 23, 1925, at age 6 years
Parents: Isiah Tansley and Viola Brown.
Informant: Jesse Brown
Tankson, A. B: Died October 13, 1924 at age 0-3-10
Parents: Early Tankson and Ona Bell Gibson.
Informant: George Gibson.
Kidd, Jessie Died April 18, 1914 at age 4 months
Parents: Henry Kidd and Bessie Kidd
Informant: Henry Kidd.
McCune, John: Died February 13, 1920 at age 6
Parents: Wade McCune and Mary Jefferson
Petre, Angie: Died April 7, 1921 at age 74
Parents: Nelson Walker and Angel Walker
Informant: Frank Petrey
Pruett, Ruth: Died March 23, 1925 at age 21
Parents: Phil Pruett and Alice Salter.
Pruitt, Alice: Died July 14, 1926 at age about 60
Parents: Cason Salter and Cherry Anderson
Informant: Frank Salter
Quince, Kitson: Died June 23, 1915 at age 41
Parents: Cason Saulter and Cherry Johnson
Place of burial not stated
Filmore Johnson
Infomant: Isaac Saulter
Hannah and Julius Garner
Maggie Missouri Petree Brown died in 1923
Joe Brown husband of Maggie
Price and Eliza Cole

More burials were found listed on a wall hanging in the Good Hope Church sanctuary Titled "Rest In Peace"

Amie Lee Gaddis
Dan Youngblood
Sylvia Overstreet
Lillie Beason
Rebecca Rigby
Frank Williams
Teagre Cole
C. Dee
Magra Corn
Julius Corn
Mary Bender
Mildred Jones
Etta M. Griffin
William Cole
Eliza Cole
Charlotte Freedmen
Betty Ford Johnson
Reed Tillman

Maude Tanksley
Tomas Tanksley
Clyde Pugh
Leslie Pugh
Ben Amber Pugh
Sylvia Dawkins
Ed Edison
*Anna Hayden
Milton Hayden
Robert Johnson
Viola Curry
John Curry
Lamar Curry
DH Johnson
Maude Pruitt
Willie Salter
Rufus Ford
Ike Salter

*Anna Salter Hayden the Maternal Grandmother of the author is buried in Freeport, Illinois City Cemetery

In times gone by the care of the cemetery was a community effort with the primary responsibility belonging to the families and friends of the deceased. During church service twice a year, the pastor would announce a date for the community clean up that took place every Saturday before Memorial Day and the first Saturday in August in anticipation of the church's annual revival meeting. The men, women and children would clean and the elder women would prepare food and drinks. These two events were major community activities and served to renew community ties and bonds.

In recent years clean-up and restoration is done by the descendants of those laid to rest in the small cemetery. On the first Saturday in August many family members throughout the United States journey home to the almost deserted settlement to do as their ancestors have done for the past hundred years: to care for the cemetery and to ensure it will continue to be a beacon and a visual history for the generations to follow.

Good Hope Colored Community School

The 1884 Mississippi law sent down by the Federal Government passed; which mandated that all children between the age of five and eighteen must be educated. In the slave states and all throughout the South a law was passed during the time of slavery making it a crime to teach enslaved people to read and write.

Therefore most people coming out of enslavement could not read or write. The first generation of freed people in the Good Hope Community embraced education as a freedom right. Many saw education as the way to full citizenship, economic success and community standing.

Still there was no access to school for Colored children. Broomsy Salter said, "Long before the rule was sent down 'Fessa' Tullos had already started to teach us boys to read and write. Before the schoolhouse was built," Broomsy said, "we had class in the church house. Sometimes Reverend Stephen Tullos went into the homes of settlement members in the evening to teach boys who had farm chores during the day. "School," he said, "was first held in the church building. The government said we would have to have a proper school building and they would be responsible for the teacher's pay. But the community had to pay for the building of the school. So, about 1921, a new school building was constructed by Lemon Chapman and members of his family. Papa [Isaac Salter], as the church trustee, authorized the cutting of timber on church property to pay for building the school, then, as school trustee, he took the responsibility for the school's finances."

In 1921, a two room school house was built across the road from the church. The school contained two rooms and students were grouped according to achievement levels. At the center of the building was a pot-bellied stove and the older boys were required to cut and split wood for the winter months. Separate outhouses on opposite ends of the property were situated for use by the boys and the girls. The Good Hope Colored School System gave the community children an excellent first through eighth grade education. Students were taught reading, writing and arithmetic in the lower grades and science, geography, history and literature in the upper grades. None the less, in 1953 the school was closed and students were required to attend the Hickory Colored School thereafter in Hickory, Mississippi. *(Ricky Harrison and crew spent about three hours at the Good Hope school site and cemetery and were able to locate the school, the porch in front, and a hitching rail out front that we had not looked for earlier. A drawing of the property including the school, church, cemetery, and other landmarks were created by Ricky Harrison. On his drawing he included photographs and a short narrative history of the church, school, and community.)*

See names of settlement children enrolled in the school between 1885 and 1940

School Enrollment 1931
Ardell Edison Age 12
P C Edison Age 10
Chester Edison Age 6
Clifton Edison Age 7
Maude Lee Edison Age 8
Edna Hayden Age 17
Paul Hayden Age 14
Daniel Hayden Age 15
David Hayden Age 18
Sherman Overstreet Age 8
Annie Overstreet Age   9
Doretha Overstreet Age 7
Lee Gertha Salter Age 13
Alexander Tullos Age   12
MaryTullos Age 7
Oscar Pruitt   Age 8
Lonzo Pruitt Age 7

School Enrollment 1933
Lillie PruittAge 12
Maude Gibson Age 6
Jessie Dobie Age 9
AC Dobie Age 8

Lavererne Dobie Age 7
Elowesse Riley Age 17
Nancy Riley Age 11
Ray Gibson Age 8
Frank Dyess Age 14
Sophia Dyess Age 17
George Gibson Age 6
Ray Dyess Age 8

School Enrollment 1935
Jeanette Wright Age 6
Hattie Gaddis Age 17
Samella Brown Age 18
Cleo Johnson Age 13
Tom E. Johnson Age 13
Rebecca Johnson Age14
Ethel Beason Age 16
Le Roy Beason Age 18
Walter Brown Age 9
Maggie Brown Age 7
Bertha Brown Age 16
Gaddis Tullos Age 6
Rosie L. Johnson Age 7
Clifton Curry Age 16

Bill Curry Age 20
George Gibson Age 7
L M Beason Age 14
Orleane Beason Age 11

School Enrollment 1939
Charles Dawkins Age 6
Nancy Brown Age
Oj Edison Age 7
Erlene Edison Age 9
Johnnie Edison Age 11
Saul Johnson
Otho Johnson Age 17
TL Johnson
Emma Johnson
Willie Mae Pruitt Age 8
Thomas Pruitt Age 6
Betty Jean Johnson Age 7
Marshall Johnson Age 10
Daisy Johnson
Johnnie R. Johnson Age 11
Mary R. Johnson Age

CHAPTER TEN

Good Hope Settlers Between 1900 And 1910

Much of the land the Good Hope Settlement farmers were able to purchase in 1900 and 1910 was adjacent to or near farmland owned by "White" landowners. Sterling Johnson and his wife, Sarah Johnson, were former slaveholders who owned farmland they used for tenant farming. Another former slaveholder and landowner, Jessie Gibson and his wife, Mary Jane Gibson, lived on the next plantation. More plantation owners were living near the Good Hope Colored Settlement including Sam Gibson and his wife, Francis Gibson and their two daughters, Bettie and Mineron Gibson.

In 1910, many second generation community members like Daniel Johnson II and his wife, Lilia Toles Johnson and their sons, France, Robert, Charles and a daughter, Blanch, were living on farmland owned by Sam Gibson; Claud Dawkins and his wife, Sylvia, rented the farm near the Gibson place. Other second generation community members: Daniel Arnold and his wife, Irene, and their daughter, Lucy May, also lived near the Dawkins farm; forty year old Ellen Chapman lived alone on a small farm near Minerva Petry Brown Carter; Minerva was the daughter of early settler Frank Petry II who had lost two husbands and was running her farm with the help of her children: two daughters; Henrietta and Annabel Carter and a son, Willie Brown. The family's farm in 1910 was operated by a son, Thomas Petry and his wife, Lillie, and their six sons: Willie, Eldon, Dios, Arthur, Bennie, Lawyer and one daughter, Willie Mae Petry.

The land that adjourned the Petry farm was a small farm rented by Nacky Washington. Living with Nacky Washington was her infant great niece, Daisy Washington, and three year old great nephew, James Washington. Boarding with the family was twenty one year old Thomas Dyes. By 1920 more second generation Good Hope families had earned enough money to buy small plots of land. Some were able to acquire land by working for other farmers picking cotton and working in lumber camps.

And some had received small plots of land through land grants. In spite of the many difficulties, records show the Freedmen were able to band together and survive the early years of freedom in the Good Hope Colored Settlement.

There were only a few isolated opportunities for the Colored settlers to buy land. Many Freedmen in the Good Hope Settlement who owned their farm had gained their land through working relationships with the landowners. The landowners expected to profit by offering tenant farmers an opportunity to buy certain tracts of land in exchange for what they believed would increase farming efficiency. However, some may have for benevolent reasons. Unfortunately, the land that was for sale to the Freedmen was somewhat of a wilderness often not much use for farming. The area was unbroken and unreachable by road. These obstacles did not deter the Freedmen from their goals of owning farmland. They worked very hard preparing what appeared to be unproductive land into useful farm land. Before long things were progressing a roadway were cleared and land was broken and fields were made ready for planting.

CHAPTER ELEVEN

Biographical Sketches of Good Hope Families

Between 1880 and 1940

*Several Freedmen families documented in this chapter may or may not have been a resident of the Good Hope Colored Settlement yet played an integral part in its development. Since most people of African ancestry were enslaved in the decades prior to 1863, the information shown here is taken from the individual census years of 1870, 1880, 1900, 1910, 1920, 1930 and 1940. Census data may show family information different from decade to decade. An example: in 1880 the family dynamics may have changed from what was listed in 1870. Other children might have been born or a family member may have died in the ten years between the censuses. Plus over the years in each census the given names of individuals spelling varied. Therefore all information documented here regarding families is taken from the census record reported in that year. It does not always reflect other year's information. Also as much as possible there will be information regarding the families who held Freedmen families enslaved. If no information was uncovered as of this printing it will not be documented. The research done here regarding the slaveholders will be information found in historical documentation, family histories and oral history from the descendants. Therefore in all cases this information has been carefully researched. When I am not sure of my findings it will be stated with expressions such as; maybe, perhaps, possibly or some records show. And as much as possible I will source that information. **Joyce Salter Johnson**

Beginning with their names, what else would these individuals want us to remember about them? What would they want us to reveal about their lives, both enslaved and free? The information here regarding the early settlers and their children were woven together from the memories of their descendants and has been passed down from generation to generation. Many facts were gathered through research based on a variety of documents and historical evidence. While an overall picture of their lives can be constructed, a number of details will still remain a mystery. The Newton County Court House at Decatur was destroyed by fire along with the greater portion of important records. Fortunately most of the records in the Chancery Clerk's office were saved practically intact. In the Circuit Clerk's office everything was burned.

Many surname spellings were altered for various reasons. Of the many reasons some are more apparent than others. The spelling skills of the record keepers were often weak and spelling errors were common. Plus record keepers and almost certainly planter families chose to distinguish names between "White and Black" individuals by changing the spelling in surnames such as Kirby/Kerby/Curby, Johnson/Johnston, Gipson/Gibson, Petry/ Petree /Petrie/, Cook/Cooke, Salter/Saulter, Amis/Amos and scores of others. It was this aspect of the system of slavery which created many questions for families. Some blood relatives emerged from slavery with different surnames than that of their parents, brothers and sisters and other family members. Consequently in most cases the family member was lost forever. From this terrible time in America's history, these families emerged and the information is sketchy at best. However, every effort was put forth to insure all information regarding the settlers was valid. The Freedmen Bureau's marriage records were perhaps some of the most important records available for the study of Freedmen family marital relations before and after the time of slavery. (*In most southern states, between 1867 and 1887, "Enslaved Marriages" were recognized and the children of such marriages were legitimate*)

The Amis/Amos Family

Slaveholding Amis Family

The ancestor of the oldest Mississippi branch of the slaveholding Amis family was John Woodson Amis. John Woodson Amis was born in North Carolina in 1795, and died in Scott County, Mississippi in 1849. Hayward, one of the former enslaved men held by John Woodson Amis, said "I was born in North Carolina and lived there until I was about fifteen years old. My "old Marster " name was William Amis. He was the father of John Woodson Amis. My Marster wife was a Woodson and that they lived near Pittsboro, Chatham County, North Carolina." He continued, "When "old Marster" [William Amis] died his son, John Woodson Amis, was living in Wilkinson County, Mississippi where he married Martha Wadkins of Copiah County, Mississippi."

John Woodson Amis went back to North Carolina to get his share of his father's estate. John received from his father's estate four enslaved people: Hayward, an enslaved man, a woman and two small children. John loaded them into a two horse wagon and brought them back to Mississippi.

After 1838, John W. Amis came to Newton County and settled on a tract of land about halfway between Newton and Decatur, just north of a large plantation owned by Milton Blalock. John Woodson Amis died 1849 in Scott County and is buried in the Amis graveyard about five miles northwest of Conehatta in Newton County.

Freedmen Amis/Amos/Ammons Family

Haywood Amis was born enslaved in 1823 in Pittsboro, Chatham County, North Carolin,a. In 1880 Haywood Amis lived in the Beat 3 area of Newton County near Conehatta, Mississippi with his wife, Esther Amis, and possibly three of their children: Julia, age seventeen; Louisa, age fifteen and Walter, age ten. Living with Hayward and his family are two unidentified lodgers, Matt Amis and Vera Amis.

George Amis/Ammons was born enslaved in the state of Mississippi, possibly Newton County. George Ammons/Amis maintained an enslaved marriage with Sallie Vernon and during that period a daughter, Lizzie Amis /Ammons, was born. In 1868, George Ammons/Amis and Sallie Vernon legalized their marriage.

Elizabeth Lizzie Amis/Ammons married Oliver Toles, great grandfather of the author, in Mississippi and they had two stepchildren: Leona Toles and Ruby Toles. Two of the Toles children, twelve year old Leona Toles and ten year old Ruby Toles, were living with their parents in 1900 on a small farm near Conehatta. [Beat 3 area of Newton County, Mississippi]

Ruby may have died after 1900 and by 1910 only Leona was listed living in the Toles household. The second daughter Leona had a son, Essie Jay Toles. When he was seventeen years old Essie was killed in a saw mill accident. Lizzie died at age 76 on January 18, 1941 and is buried at the Conehatta Cemetery in Conehatta, Mississippi Newton County. (*In the Newton County court marriage records of 1868 Lizzie (Oliver) Toles signed her maiden name on her marriage certificate as* **Lizzie Amis**) (*See more on Oliver Toles*)

Native American Amiss/Amos Family

Sallie Amis was born in 1880 in Newton County. Lizzie Amos was listed on the Daws report with the Jack Amos family. Jack Amos was born in 1840 and Lizzie Amiss/Amos married Oliver Toles in Newton County, Mississippi and had two known children; Leona Toles and Ruby Toles.

The Anderson Family

Slaveholding Anderson Family

James Madison Anderson was one of the first White settlers who came to Newton County. A J Brown writes in his book, <u>The History of Newton County From 1834 to 1894,</u> James Anderson was probably among the first White settlers in Newton County. James M. Anderson came into Mississippi from Georgia in 1835, first to Lauderdale County and by 1850 to Neshoba County with five enslaved men, women and children. (*Information taken from the Anderson Family Genealogy*) J Anderson a slaveholding family member was born in South Carolina and relocated first to Georgia and later to Perry County, Alabama. He came into Mississippi in about 1835 and was listed in the 1860 census living in Newton County with his wife, Althea, and a daughter, Eliza Anderson. (*The Citing "United States Census, 1860", database with images, Family Search 30 December 2015, J Anderson*)

Freedmen Anderson Family

Moses Anderson and his wife, Elizabeth, were born in Georgia into slavery. Moses was born in 1804, and Elizabeth was born in 1824. The two may have been enslaved on the same Anderson plantation in Georgia or later in Alabama and Mississippi. While enslaved, Moses and Elizabeth lived together several years as man and wife in an arrangement known as a "Slave Marriage." Apparently the arrangement was with the permission of their slaveholders.

The census shows the couple had three children between the years of 1857 and 1867. Their daughter Elizabeth (Betsey) Anderson was born in 1857 while still living in Georgia. In 1860 a daughter Adeline was born in Mississippi. In 1867, it was lawful for Freedmen to marry and Moses and Elizabeth legalized their marriage. The marriage certificate issued by the Freedmen Bureau lists more children born to Moses and Elizabeth; a daughter, Matilda, born in 1853 and a son, Peter, both born enslaved. As of this printing no further information on Matilda and Peter was located in any historical documents. In 1870, Moses and Elizabeth Anderson were operating a farm near Hickory in the Good Hope Colored Settlement with a daughter, Elizabeth (Betsey) Anderson and a son, identified in the census as Harry Bennett along with Harry's four year old son, Robert Graham. By 1880, sixty five year old Moses Anderson and his family were operating a small farm in the Good Hope Colored Settlement.

John Anderson was born in Alabama. While enslaved he maintained an "enslaved marriage" with Betsey Johnson. Betsey Johnson was born enslaved on the Johnson plantation in Georgia. How, when and why she was in Alabama we can only guess. The ancestors had no answer and historical documents revealed nothing that would bring us to any solid conclusion, however slavery and it's patterns of selling and relocating unpaid labor as "they saw fit," would be a safe assumption.

Betsey was most likely sold by Johnson slaveholders to the Anderson slaveholders in Georgia and was taken to Alabama where she entered an enslaved marriage with John Anderson. John and Betsey may have had more children but as of this printing only one child, a daughter, Cherry Anderson, was located in historical records.

Cherry Anderson was born in 1843 in Henry County, Alabama. The Mississippi marriage records in 1868 show she married Cason Salter and they had several children. The 1870 census show them living in Jasper County, Mississippi. The family moved into Newton County by 1900 and worked a small farm in the Good Hope Freedmen Settlement. Cason and Cherry lived in the Good Hope community for many years. They were members of Good Hope Missionary Baptist Church and Cherry served the community as a midwife. Cherry Anderson Salter died in 1928 in Newton County, Mississippi and is buried in the Good Hope Church Cemetery. Research shows beginning in 1930 some of her children had left the community for the North. Soon after Cherry's death Cason relocated to Chicago where he lived with his children until his death.

Native American Anderson Family

Miko Phyliss J. Anderson was the first female "Miko" [Tribal Chief] of the Mississippi Band of the Choctaw Indians .(*from 2011 and as of this printing 2017*)

In 1920 and 1930, Oliver Anderson and Sallie Farmer were listed as Choctaw Indians living in Conehatta, Newton County, Mississippi. Oliver and Sallie had one known child who died on August 1, 1927 and was buried in Macedonia Indian Baptist Church Cemetery in the Conehatta community of the Mississippi Band of Choctaw Indians.

John Elijah Anderson married Telie Roberson Davis, the daughter of Thomas Roberson and Jane Davis. Thomas Roberson and Jane Davis were listed in Newton County vital records as Choctaw Indians. When Telie Anderson was twenty three years old she died on May 8, 1920 while giving birth to a still born child.

The Bates Family

Slaveholding Bates Family

Research discovered in the1860 Federal Census Slave Schedules: S G Bates held thirteen enslaved workers in Smith County, Mississippi and Lewis Bates of Clark County, Mississippi held four enslaved worker. As of this research period no Bates slaveholders were found in the adjoining county of Newton. Only a few Freedmen took the surname Bates in the Good Hope Freedmen Settlement.

The Freedmen Bates Family

Sarah Bates, was born in 1889 in Scott County, Mississippi. In 1910 she was a twenty one year old widow living in Newton County with three children: a daughter, Bessie; a son, Otis and one year old, Louise Bates.

Louise Bates, in later years, married Arthur Anderson and they had one known daughter, Elvira Anderson.

Elvira Bates married Albert Mc Donald and they operated a small farm in Jasper County, Mississippi. Albert and Elvira relocated to a farm in rural Hickory, Mississippi where they farmed for many years. Elvira died in 1941 when she was eighty one years old.

Cliff Bates was born in 1905 in Mississippi. The 1940 census shows Cliff Bates was a boarder in the home of Sylvia Walker Dawkins and employed as a sawmill worker. Cliff Beats died in 1977 in the Good Hope Colored Settlement.

The Beason Family

Slaveholding Beason Family

Joab Beason was born in Georgia in 1792. He lived in Alabama in 1826 and came into Mississippi to Kemper County and then to Jasper County. The 1860 Federal Census Slave Schedules shows Joab Beason of Jasper County, Mississippi had twenty one enslaved workers. A two year old Mulatto female was listed as a fugitive. In 1865, when the twenty one people he held enslaved were freed, some stayed on the plantation in Jasper County, others relocated to the Colored Settlement of Good Hope in search of land to farm.

Stephanie Beason a family history researcher wrote in the booklet she developed "Beason Family History Your Beginning" for the Beason family's first reunion in Sebastopol, Mississippi in May of 2006. "My belief of your beginning started with Classy Mosby born in Georgia, Classy gave birth to Liza in 1825. Since there is no further mention of Classy's birth or death we will never know if she came to Mississippi voluntarily with or without Liza. Liza a young slave became the property of the Chapmans' James or John. In that period of time the Chapman's were rich and owned many slaves in Newton/Jasper Counties.

So where did Liza get the name Beason? I believe being a slave Liza gave her children the name of the white person that impregnated her thenceforth came the name of Beason/ Beeson. Liza Beeson gave birth to her daughter, Eding in 1843. The father is unknown for all children born to Liza. Eding gave birth to Dock Beason around 1860. "

The Freedmen Beason Family

Dock Beason was born enslaved in 1859 in Alabama. In 1863, when he was five years old he gained his freedom. On February 16, 1882 in Newton, Mississippi he married Eliza Mosely, daughter of Classy Mosby. By 1900 Dock and Eliza had the following children: six boys; (Autina Beason, Groan), Clay, Ross, Bill, Judge, Newt and three girls; Hattie, Alencia and Ella. Dock Beason died before 1920. Eliza Beason died on September 18, 1926 when she was 101 years old. Both are buried in Mt. Zion Cemetery, Newton County. Informant: Autina Beason/Groan Auty Beason. These are all of the children mentioned in the 1900 census.

Autina/ Anthiny Beason was born in Mississippi to Dock and Eliza in 1876. By 1910, Autina Beason and his wife, Lillie Chapman, were living in Beat 4 of Newton County with three of their children: Henry age four, Glover age two and one year old Rilla. In 1920, Anthony/Autina had moved his family to the Good Hope Colored Settlement. More children were born Glover, Willie, Leroy, Minnie and Ethel.

Some of the children had moved out of the household between the censuses. In 1930, he owned several acres of farm land and worked the farmstead with his wife and a son, sixteen year old Leroy. Twenty two year old Glover worked in the Lumber Mill. Thirteen year old Minnie and nine year old Ethel attended school and helped on the farm. (*Beat 4 including Newton town – All of township 6 Range 11 South of Palto Creek in Beat 4 and sections 1, 2, 3 and 4 of township 5 Range11 and all east Newton and Garlandville public road.) Unsure of the spelling of Mr. Beason's given name (Autina)*

Ross Beason was born in Mississippi in 1886 to Dock and Eliza Mosby. In 1900, he lived in Newton County, Mississippi with his parents and several brothers and sisters. By 1910, twenty two year old Ross was single and continued to live on the farm with his parents in Newton County. In 1930, Ross married Fannie McCarty [the mother of Doris and Annie Johnson] the daughter of Frank and Nellie Mc Carty. Ross and Fannie had the following children: Clark, Vegie, Lula, Anloisie, Vertis, Opal, Romeo and Juliet. In 1940 Ross and Fannie relocated to Newton, Mississippi (*See Fannie McCarty) "United States Census, 1940," database with images, FamilySearch (https://familysearch.org/ark:/61903/1:1:VBS2-YTR : accessed 25 October 2016), Fannie Beason in household of Ross Beason, Beat 5, Newton, Mississippi, United States; citing enumeration district (ED) 51-22, sheet 1B, family, Sixteenth Census of the United States, 1940, NARA digital publication T627. Records of the Bureau of the Census, 1790 - 2007, RG 29 Washington, D.C.: National Archives and Records Administration, 2012, roll 2053.*

The Bogan/ Boggan Family

Slaveholding Boggan Family Anderson Boggan was born in North Carolina. He was listed as living in Jasper County, Mississippi in 1860 with five enslaved people: a thirty five year old male, a twenty five year old female, a twenty three year old female, a four year old female and a one year old female. All were brought in to Mississippi from North Carolina enslaved to Jasper County by the Anderson Boggan family.

The Freedmen Bogan/Boggan Family

Eli Bogan and Annie Bogan were born enslaved in Alabama. While enslaved they maintained an "enslaved marriage". Eli and Annie were legally married as soon as it was legal for them to do so. By 1880, they had three children: two daughters, Rose and Leah and a son, Lindsey Bogan. During this time the family lived on a Tenant farm in Northeast Jasper County in Mississippi. The Bogan may have had more children but at this printing only three have been discovered. In 1900, of the three known Bogan children only their son Lindsey was able to be traced.

Lindsey Bogan was the third child born to Eli and Annie Bogan. By 1880, eleven year old Lindsey was living with his parents and older sisters, Rose and Leah Bogan on a farm in Northeast Jasper County. Twenty years later Lindsay was married to Cornelia (Neely) Chapman, the daughter of Frank and Dilsey Chapman. Lindsey and Cornelia had the following children: Wilson, Sarah, Ella, Hilda and Ham Bogan. In 1910, the family was living in Township 5 Range 17 in Newton, Mississippi and more children were born to the couple. Hilda was born in 1902. She never married and lived with her parents on a farm near Newton. Hilda and her parents were members of the Good Hope Missionary Baptist Church. When Hilda was twenty-one years old she died of appendicitis and was buried in the Good Hope Church Cemetery. Their daughter, Ruby, married Mr. Posey his given name is not known. Wilson Bogan married Angie [maiden name not known] and had several children. The 1930 census listed six of their children: Clayborn, Carlene, Eugene, Lucile, Lorena and Carmelia. Except for Ham, Hilda, Ruby and Wilson no additional information was uncovered regarding the children of Lindsey and Cornelia Bogan. (*See Frank Chapman father of Cornelia Chapman spelled Boggan*)

Abraham/ Harry/ Ham Boggan was born to Lindsey and Cornelia (Neely) Bogan in 1901 in Newton County, Mississippi. In 1910, nine year old Ham was working with his parents on the farm and attended school when work allowed. In 1920, when he was eighteen years old Ham was still living with his parents and working with his father on the farm. Within the next four years Ham married Ludie Needim. The 1930 census shows Ham and Ludie living on a small rented farm near the town of Hickory, Mississippi with four of their children: six year old Leroy, five year old Ruby, three year old JD [female] and a one month old infant, Bonnie Jean Bogan.

Bonnie Jean Boggan married Thomas Ernest Johnson the son of Robert Johnson I and the grandson of Filmore Johnson. *(In the 1940 census Ham Bogan registered his given name as "Harry" and he spelled his surname "Boggan". Living with Harry and Luddie Boggan are six children: Leroy, Ruby, JD, Alfred, James and ten year old Bonnie Jean Boggan.)*

The Bolton/ Brown Family

Slaveholding Bolton/ Brown Family

Donna Bolton Brown, a slaveholder in Newton County, was the daughter of a slaveholder, William Bolton. Donna Bolton married G.K. Brown in 1857 in Sumter, Alabama. They had a son, Walter Brown. The 1860 Federal Census Slave Schedules of Newton County shows Donna Bolton Brown a twenty one year old widow held about ten enslaved workers in Newton County, Mississippi.

The Freedmen Bolton/ Brown Family

Jack Bolton was freed in 1863 and was listed in the 1870 census living in Newton County with his wife, Ann Bolton. Both Jack and Ann were born enslaved in Alabama. The couple had one known son, Hunter Brown. Hunter and his parents may have been part of the group of enslaved men and women brought into Newton County, Mississippi with C.K. Brown or other Brown/Bolton slaveholders. After Emancipation Proclamation the family worked as farm hands and lived in rural Hickory, Mississippi. The 1870 census shows Jack and Ann Bolton continued to live in Newton County with several unidentified household members: Elizabeth Bolton, Walter Anderson, Ella Jones, and Mary Thompson. When Jack Bolton died is not known. Ann Bolton died at the age of eighty nine in 1916 in Newton County.

Hunter Brown was held enslaved with his parents, Jack and Ann Bolton, on the Bolton/Brown plantation in Newton County. As a young man, while still enslaved, he took Rosetta a young woman who was living on the same plantation as his wife. Almost immediately after the Emancipation Proclamation was signed they legalized their slave marriage. Their son, W. J (Joe) Brown, was born soon afterward. Years later he w,as married and brought his bride, Maggie Missouri Petree, to live on the farm with his parents. When Hunter and Rosetta Brown died they were buried in the Good Hope Church Cemetery.

W. J (Joe) Brown married Maggie Missouri Petree, a daughter of Frank and Angelina (Walker) Petree. Maggie was very young when she married and had several children over the years. Some of their names were: Frank, Edger, Lucius, Olivia,

Lonnie, Sophie, Angel, Ottolee, Mattie Lee, Walter, Nancy and Sammy.

Frank Brown was born in 1893 and was named for his grandfather, Frank Petree II. From 1917 t,o 1919 a viral tuberculosis contagion appeared in the Brown family and it caused the death of several family members. Frank died of tuberculosis in 1918 when he was twenty six years old.

Edgar Brown was born in 1893. When he was nineteen years old he contracted tuberculosis and died soon after his brother.

Lucius Brown was born in 1894 and died in infancy.

Olivia Brown Gibson was born in 1897. At the age of fifteen Olivia married Willie Gibson. Willie and Olivia had one child, a daughter, Dorries Gibson. When Olivia was nineteen years old she contracted tuberculosis and died in 1919. (*See Gibson for more information*)

Joe and Maggie Brown continued to have more children throughout the years.

Lonnie Brown was born in 1899.

Sophie Brown was born in 1904. Years later she married Moses Pruitt and they had several children. (*See Moses Pruitt for more information*)

Angel Brown was born in 1906 and married Alonzo Johnson.

Mattie Lee Brown was born in 1911.

Walter Brown was born in 1914.

Nancy Brown was born in1915.

Sammy or Samella Brown was born in 1918.

After the tuberculosis epidemic Joe and Maggie Petree Brown continued to live in the Good Hope community for many years. They were core members in both the community and Good Hope Missionary Baptist Church. Maggie Missouri Petree Brown died in 1923 and was buried in the Good Hope Church Cemetery. (*More on Maggie Missouri Petree/Petry, a daughter of Frank and Angelina Petree I, in the Johnson Petry/Petree Story*)

Joe Brown married his second wife, Mattie Brown and they had the following children: Bertha, William, and Maggie Rea. Bertha married Alonzo Pruitt. Years later they relocated to Denver, Colorado with their family. Joe Brown lived to be seventy one years old and died in 1941.

Both Joe and his first wife, Maggie Petree Brown, were buried in Good Hope Church Cemetery. After Joe's death his second wife Mattie Brown relocated to Denver, Colorado to be with her daughter Bertha Brown Pruitt where she lived until her death.

Jerry Brown was born in Newton County, Mississippi in about 1873. On December 24, 1888 in Newton County, Mississippi he married Minerva Petree/Petry, a daughter of Frank and Angelina Petree. Jerry and Minerva had three children: Birdie, Willie and Thomas. (*More on Minerva Petree/Petry a daughter of Frank and Angelina Petree I in the Johnson Petry/Petree Story*)

Birdie Brown was born in October 1890.

Willie Brown was born to Jerry and Minerva Petree Brown in January 1892. Years later Willie married Willie Ann Ware. On July 9, 1923 Willie Ann Ware Brown died when she was thirty seven years old. Within the year Willie Brown was married to Lula Tramel.

Thomas W. Brown was born in May 1893.

Stephen Brown was held most of his life enslaved on a plantation in Newton County where he lived with Dora in an enslaved marriage on the same plantation. After the Emancipation document was signed they stayed on the same plantation and worked as sharecroppers. Some research shows Stephen and Dora had had several children however, only one son, John Brown was revealed during this research.

John Brown was born in 1877. When he was a young man he helped his parents, Stephen and Dora, with work on the farm. Later he married his childhood sweetheart, Eliza Stephens. They had two children: a son, Willie Brown and a daughter, Lizzie Brown. In about 1940, John took his family up to Joliet, Illinois to work with the Illinois Central Railroad. (*More on Eliza Stephens Brown see Eliza Stephens*)

Isham H. Brown was born into slavery in 1847 in Mississippi. In 1870, he was living in Newton County and chose Brown as his surname. As of this printing he had one known daughter, Bessie Brown. Bessie married Henry Mc Millan Bessie Brown McMillian, lived in rural Hickory in the early 1930s with her husband and a son, Claude. Horace Mc Millan, a boarder and possibly the brother of, was living with the family Not much more was discovered regarding Isham Brown. He may have been enslaved to AJ Brown, a slave holder in Newton County.

The Chapman Family

Slaveholding Chapman Family

The slaveholders Abel Edwards Chapman and Edward Edwards Chapman were two heads of the large Chapman family. Abel Edwards Chapman was a railroad surveyor and Edward E. Chapman worked mostly as a land surveyor. Both were farmers and slaveholders. Edward E. Chapman was the owner of six slave houses and held twenty nine people enslaved. Abel Chapman held twenty one enslaved workers.

The brothers lived in adjoining communities. Edward E. Chapman lived in the Bethel community and Abel Edwards Chapman settled five miles southeast of Newton near the small town of Hickory. (*Information researched from the book by AJ Brown History of Newton County*)

The Freedmen Chapman Family

Frank Chapman I was born enslaved in Mississippi. The 1870 census shows Frank Chapman and his wife, Dilsey [maiden name not known] living in Newton County, Mississippi with two children: two year old Ham Chapman and one year old Cornelia Chapman. Also living with the Chapman family is Angeline Chapman an unidentified six year old girl. By 188,0 Frank and Dilsey Chapman were farming in the Beat 5 section of Newton County with four more children: Lon, Frank II, Tildy and Martha Chapman. The 1900 census shows Frank and Dilsey living in Newton County with a granddaughter, Lecinday and six more children: Pleas, Eliza, Clinton, Green, Sylvester and Annie B. Chapman.

By 1920, the aging Frank and Dilsey owned their land and continued to operate the farm with the help of their daughter, twenty five year old Annie. Dilsey Chapman died between 1920 and 1930. In the 1930 census Frank is listed as an eighty nine year old widower living with his daughter, Cornelia (Neely) and son-in-law, Lindsey Bogan in rural Newton County. (*See Lindsey Bogan*)

Frank Chapman II was born in Mississippi in 1874 to Frank and Dilsey Chapman. Frank Chapman II married Margaret Chapman in 1894 and had the following children: George, Ham and Rebecca. By 1920, Frank and his wife were running a small farm in rural Hickory. The couple had four more children: Lillie, Floyd, Raleigh and Della Chapman.

The Cole Family

Slaveholding Cole Family

William A. Cole, the slaveholder, was born in 1789 in Georgia. In 1830, he relocated to Lowndes, Alabama where he held twelve people enslaved. By 1840, he had forty five enslaved workers and continued to live in Alabama until 1859. In 1860, William A. Cole had relocated to Jasper County, Mississippi with fifty five enslaved men, women and children. In 1863, the men, women and children he held enslaved were emancipated while living in Jasper County, Mississippi. William Cole died in 1868, and is buried in the Garlandville Cemetery Rose Hill, Jasper County.

The Freedmen Cole Family

Turner Cole was born in 1824 while his mother was held enslaved in the state of Alabama. He came into Mississippi with his slaveholders sometime after 1860. He lived enslaved on the Cole plantation in Jasper County until he was emancipated in 1863. After the War he continued to work as free man on the Cole plantation with his wife, Mary, until he was able to rent a little land for farming in Newton County. By 1889, he was living in Newton County in rural Hickory in the Good Hope Freedmen Settlement with several children: his daughter, Elizabeth born in 1879; a son, Price Cole born in 1884, and a daughter, Cora Cole born before 1890. His wife, Mary, died after 1890, possibly in childbirth.

Two years later the Newton County Vital Records show in 1892 Turner married twenty four year old Mildred Hayes. In 1893, a son, Elbert Cole, was born. In 1895, James was born. In 1897, Emma was born. Their youngest child, Neely, was born in 1899. The 1900 census shows seventy six year old Turner Cole was living in Beat 5 of Hickory Town, Mississippi with his twenty eight year old wife and six of his children: Price, Cora, Elbert, James, Emma and an infant Neely. Also living in the household were six of his brothers and sisters: Olis, Georgia, Lenora, Shelly, Lotta and Rassie.

Turner Cole died about 1906. After Turner's death Mildred Cole married Frank Jones, a farmer in the Good Hope Colored Settlement. By 1910, Frank and Mildred had two children: a son, three year old Shelly and a daughter, one year old Lenora. The 1910 census shows Frank and Mildred had settled on a larger farm adjoining Dan and Adeline Youngblood in the Good Hope Community *("United States Census, 1900," database with images,familysearch.org/ark:/61903/ 1:1:M9XLRM3 accessed 9 June 2016), Turner Cole, Beat 5 Hickory town, Newton, Mississippi, United States; citing sheet 17A, family 307*

Elbert Cole had married by 1920. Elbert and his wife, Mattie, settled on farmland in the Good Hope Community adjacent to the Frank Jones farm. *("United States Census, 1910," database with images,: accessed 12 June 2016), Elbert Cole in household of Frank Jones, Township 5 Range 17, Newton, Mississippi, United States)*

Price Cole worked several years with his father, Turner, on the farm. Some years later he married Eliza (maiden name not known). Eliza and Price's wedding ceremony may have been held at Good Hope Missionary Baptist Church where they were faithful members for many years. Early Good Hope Church records show Price served as Deacon and Eliza as Deaconess of the church.

Throughout the years they had a number of children. The 1920 census shows six of their children: Donny, Ida, Ora, William G. and Ethel Mae all living at home. Most of his children grew up in the Good Hope Community. Some married and relocated to other places. Many continued to live in the area. When Price and Eliza Cole died they were both buried in the Good Hope Church Colored Cemetery. Eddie Gibson was living with his grandparents, Price and Eliza Cole. In 1930 Clovis Gibson and his sister, Girtha Lee Gibson Hughes and John Gibson were also living with these grandparents in Good Hope Colored Settlement. This is the only information found regarding young Clovis as of this printing. *(Price Cole Beat 5, Newton, Mississippi born 1884 Head of Household, Liza Cole Beat 5, Newton, Mississippi born 1885 Wife , Children: Donny Cole born 1905 Son , Ida Cole born 1906 Daughter, Ora Cole born 1908 Daughter, William G Cole born 1910 Son, Ethel Cole born 1913 Daughter)*

The Cook Family

Freedmen Cook Family

Claiborne Cook of Hollys Spring, Mississippi married Eliza Petree, the daughter of Frank Petree I and his enslaved wife Mahalia Petree, soon after he was made free to do so. They had one child, a daughter, they named Rilla. *(See more on Eliza and Claiborne in the Frank Petry I Johnson Petry/Petree Story)*

Rilla Cook, the daughter of Eliza and Claiborne Cook, is a bit elusive. However, family lore proclaims Rilla Cook relocated to Newton, County from Hollys Spring, Mississippi. In 1910, she married John Hamilton and had two daughters Eliza and Emma. The families were members of the Good Hope Missionary Baptist Church. John Hamilton died in 1941 and is buried in Good Hope Church Cemetery. After he died Rilla and her daughters relocated to Meridian, Mississippi. (*See more on Rilla in the Frank Petry I Johnson Petry/Petree Story*)

The Croft Family

Slaveholding Croft Family

MA Croft was a slaveholder in Mississippi. He held 50 people enslaved in Lauderdale, Mississippi. In 1860, John Croft held 36 enslaved workers in Alabama. By 1870, John Croft was living in Jasper County, Mississippi. Family members state that the Crofts of Newton and Jasper counties came into Mississippi with MA Croft or John Croft or both.

The Freedmen Croft Family

Ollie Croft was born in 1810 in Alabama and was thought to be of Cherokee or Chickasaw descent. She lived most of her life enslaved. In 1866 and 1870, Ollie lived in Jasper County possibly on the Croft plantation. The 1900 census shows Ollie Croft as a seventy year old widow living with a daughter, Hannah Garner and her husband, Julius Garner and three unidentified residents with the surname, Garner: Lucinda Garner age 18, Willis Garner age 16 and six year old Massuletta Garner. The 1910 census shows one hundred year old Ollie Croft continued to live in the Good Hope Settlement with her family.

Soon after her 100th birthday Ollie Croft died and is buried in the Good Hope Baptist Church Cemetery. (*More on Hannah Garner and her husband Julius Garner see The Salter of Good Hope Colored Community*) (*Ollie Croft the 2nd maternal great grandmother*)

Hannah Croft was born enslaved in 1832, to Ollie an enslaved women and thought to be a Cherokee or Chickasaw Indian. In the 1870 census thirty eight year old Hannah Croft Garner was living in Jasper County, Mississippi with her husband, Julius Garner, their three year old son, Luke Garner and a daughter, seventeen year old Dora Garner Salter [maternal great grandmother of the author] who was living with her husband, Frank Salter, son of Hardy and Louisa Salter of Jasper County, Mississippi.

In 1880, Hannah and her husband, Julius, had relocated to rural Hickory, Mississippi. They were farming in the Good Hope Community with their children: fourteen year old Luke, twelve year old Hasty, nine year old Ralph, five year old Mary and one year old James. From 1900, until their death Hannah and Julius farmed in Jasper County near Garlandville, Mississippi. Both Hannah and Julius Garner are buried in the Good Hope Church Cemetery. (*More on Dora Garner Salter see The Salter of Good Hope Colored Community*)

Native American Croft Family

Ollie Croft was born in 1810, in Alabama and thought to be Cherokee or Chickasaw. She lived most of her life enslaved; first in Alabama and later in Mississippi. (*More on Ollie Croft see The Salter of Good Hope Colored Community*)

The Curry Family

Slaveholding Curry Family

James Curry and John T. Curry were slaveholders in Newton County. In 1860, James Curry held six enslaved workers and John T. Curry held five.

The Freedmen Curry Family

John Curry I was born in 1886 ,in Newton County, Mississippi. In the early 1900's, he met and married Viola Evans. They settled in Newton County and worked on a rented farm in the Good Hope Freedmen Settlement. John and Viola had ten children: Leroy born in 1902, Lelia 1904, Charles 1905, Lamar 1906, Grady 1910, John and Frances were born in 1914. Frances died three days later and was buried in the Good Hope Church Cemetery. A daughter, Katie, was born in 1916, and a son, Clifton, in1920. In the late 1920s John Curry had purchased a farm in the community. In 1930, John, Viola and three of their ten children; seventeen years old John Jr., twelve year old Clifton and nine year old Willa, were living and working on the farm.

The Dawkins Family

Slaveholding Dawkins Family

David Dawkins was a slaveholder in Newton County. He was born in 1793, in South Carolina and was listed in the 1850 census living in Choctaw, Alabama with his wife, Winford, and a son, W.D. Dawkins.

In 1860, the slaveholding Dawkins family was living in Jasper County, Mississippi. Living with the couple is an unidentified man, thirty four year old George Kidd born in Alabama.

In 1910, seventy six year old Williams D. Dawkins was living in rural Newton County with his son- in- law, Kelly W. Parks, and daughter, Littie Dawkins Parks. The Dawkins came into Mississippi from South Carolina by 1860 with five enslaved people: two adult women, two female children, ages eight and two and one male infant.

The Freedmen Dawkins Family

Claud Dawkins *Claude [spelled Claud in the census]* was born in 1874 to enslaved parents. Claud and his wife Sylvia Walker was one of the pioneer residents and farmers in the Good Hope Freedmen Settlement. By 1910, Claud and Sylvia Walker had seven children: Sportier Dawkins, born in 1895, Classie Dawkins 1897, Vergie Dawkins 1899, Lillie Dawkins 1901, Jolene Dawkins 1904, Cherry Dawkins 1906 and Costeller Dawkins was born about 1909. Claud and Sylvia were stellar community and church members until their death. Both were buried in the Good Hope Church Cemetery. Cherry Dawkins, daughter of Sylvia Walker Dawkins, was born in Mississippi. Cherry died on March 28, 1915 when she was eleven years old and was buried in Good Hope Colored Church Cemetery in 1915. (*Costeller/ Costello, Costella all are spellings in the census, however in later years, Costeller used this spelling for his given name.)(In genealogy tracing female family members into adulthood is not always possible. The primary problem is that women usually changed their surnames once married and living in another household or if they had died between the years of the census The census is of no use without a surname.*)

Classie Dawkins married Preston Johnson II, the son of Filmore and Elizabeth /Bettie Johnson. The1930 census record shows that Preston and Classie Johnson owned and operated a small farm in the Good Hope Colored Settlement near the Claud Dawkins family farm for many years. After Classie died Preston relocated to Illinois with relatives. (*More about Preston Johnson in the Johnson Petry/Petree Story*)

Costeller Dawkins was born in 1909. While growing up he worked on the Dawkins family farm and attended Good Hope Colored School. Costeller's first wife was Ottolee Brown, the daughter of Joe Brown and Maggie Missouri Petree. They had a son named Charles. Charles was the couple's only child. Charles died and is buried in the Good Hope Church Cemetery.

Costeller's second wife was Ada Crosby Paige, a widow with two children: Oskar Lee and Elvin Paige. Ada and Costeller had four children: Alice, Claud, Don and Laura Dawkins. Ada was a strong Christian and was considered to be a loyal member of the Good Hope Missionary Baptist Church. The family attended church most every Sunday.

Later in his life Costeller became an avid worker in the church and he held the job as Church clerk for many years. The Dawkins children were active in Sunday service and sang in the choir. Costeller and Ada continued to live in the Good Hope Community where they purchased timber and farming land. When Costeller and Ada died they were buried in Good Hope Church Cemetery.

The Native American Dawkins Family

Kimberly, a Dawkins descendant, wrote, regarding Viola Dawkins Evans, "I am looking for information about the Choctaw Indian history of my great grandmother. Her name was Viola Dawkins. Her mother's name was Sarah and was believed to be a midwife/ medicine woman. They are originally from Newton County, Mississippi."

The Dyes Family

Slaveholding Dyes Family

The 1860 Slave Schedule shows John Dyes, Emely Dyes, Collins Dyes and Joshua Dyes were cotton planters in Newton County and together held ten workers enslaved. In 1830, Frank and Harriet were born on the Dyes plantation in Newton County in Mississippi. As of this research the exact Dyes plantation has not been identified.

The Freedmen Dyes Family

Frank Dyes was born in1830 in Mississippi into slavery. He lived most of his young life enslaved on plantations in Jasper and Newton counties in Mississippi. During the time of enslavement he maintained a marriage relationship with Harriet Walker, an enslaved woman. In 1858, a daughter, Adeline, was born and a son, Matthew, was born in 1861. [It is possible that Frank and Harriet had more children but none were discovered as of this printing.] When the Emancipation document was signed and he was free to do so, Frank legalized his marriage relationship with Harriet Walker. Frank and Harriet settled on a small farm in rural Hickory, Mississippi.

Adeline Dyes was born enslaved in 1858, and may have been Frank and Harriet Dyes' oldest child. In 1863, Adeline was seven years old when she was freed from slavery. Like most newly freed children she worked on the former slaveholder's farm with her parents. When her father had money enough to buy his own farm they relocated to an area near the Good Hope Colored Settlement. When she was seventeen years old Adeline married Mr. Nixon [First name not known]. Mr. Nixon was a railroad man by trade and followed the rails from coast to coast.

By 1880, twenty two year old Adeline Dyes Nixon was listed as head of household living in Fort Worth, Texas with her brother, Matthew Dyes. (*Adeline may have been a widow or Mr. Nixon may have been counted in the 1880 Railroad Census) [The Dyess/ Dyes/ Dais is spelled several ways in the census but will be spelled Dyes in the book]*

Matthew Dyes was born in 1861, enslaved to Frank and Harriet on the Dyes plantation. After Emancipation Proclamation he settled with his parents in rural Hickory and worked with his father on the farm. Matthew left his parents' farm when he was nineteen years old and took a job with the railroad. The 1880 census report listed Matthew living in Fort Worth, Texas with his sister, Adeline Dyes Nixon. In the late 1880's, Matthew left Fort Worth, Texas and returned to Newton County. Soon after his return he married Lucinda Hughes. Matthew and Lucinda had sixteen children over the years. In 1886, Harriet was born and Minnie also in 1886 (they may have been twins),Goldie-1888, Nora-1889, Viney-1893, Geneva-1894, Imogene-1900, Ida, Annie Jane, Bessie Pearl, Cleona, Susan and Adeline plus three sons; Thomas-1896, Daniel-1898, and June. Four of the sixteen Dyes children died during the Tuberculosis epidemic in Newton County. The Dyes' first losses began in 1914 with the death of their son, Thomas.

In 1916, Goldie Dyes Gage, a married daughter, died in Chunkey. Nora died in 1918, and in 1919 a daughter Susan died. The couple made their home first in rural Hickory near the Good Hope Colored Settlement and later relocated to a farm Matthew had purchased in rural Lauderdale County.

Matthew and Lucinda Dyes relocated in 1920 to the Chunkyville area. Matthew himself was also ill with the dreaded disease and four years after the death of their children Lucinda lost her husband. Sixty four year old Matthew died on January 23, 1922 and was buried in the Chunkyville Cemetery. After Matthew died, Lucinda continued to live on the farm in Chunkyville with three of her children: two daughters, Annie Jean and Adeline and a son, June. Also living with Lucinda were two grandchildren: a boy, eleven year old Edd Croft and a girl, nine year old Eddie M. Easter. In 1929, Lucinda enrolled her granddaughter, Eddie M. Easter, in the Community School as Eddie M. Dyes, age eight years.

After interviewing Nannie Youngblood Edison, the eighty nine year old granddaughter of Matthew and Lucinda Dyes, along with extensive research done regarding the remaining children of Matthew and Lucinda Dyes: Harriet, Minnie, Cleopa, Imogene and Geneva; nothing was uncovered to document their lives after 1940. Of the sixteen children twelve were daughters. In 1940, seventy two year old Lucinda Dyes was listed in the census living with her son, June Dyes and his wife, Vertis. Nannie Youngblood Edison said in an interview, "My grandma Lucy [Lucinda Dyes] lived to be ninety years old." Research uncovered a variety of information on Matthew and Lucinda Dyes' seven remaining children Some married and had children and continued to live in the community while some moved to other counties and states.

Thomas Dyes was born in 1896. When he was a young boy he worked on the farm with his father and attended school whenever possible. Tragedy first struck for the Dyes when Thomas died. Thomas had not reached the age of fourteen when he became very sick with tuberculosis and died in 1914.

Nora Dyes was born on April 18, 1889. While growing up she worked with her parents on the farm and attended school in rural Hickory. Nora never married. She became a teacher and taught in the Good Hope Colored Settlement School. In 1917, she contracted tuberculosis and died in 1918.

Nora may have been infected with the dreaded disease by her students. It was discovered by health officials in 1916, that many children infected by the disease harbored the signs of the illness for many years before becoming ill. Consequently the disease spread rampantly and many parents, teachers and other adults died of the illness.

Susan Dyes the third child to die had possibly contracted the illness from her sister, Nora. She died in 1918, when she was eleven years old. (*The state's concern for the Negro tuberculosis problem arose because many Negroes worked intimately within white households thus the disease could be spread to both white and the Negro populations. Tuberculosis was a major problem within the Colored community and the Negro tuberculosis mortality rates were always larger than the mortality rates of the white community.*)

Viney Dyes married at an early age to a Mr. Croft [first name not known as of this printing]. They had two children: a daughter, Leona Croft and a son, Edward Croft. Viney Dyes Croft was widowed at an early age. In the late 1920's, after her husband's death, Viney returned to her parent's farm in Newton County where she registered her children in Newton County (Beat 5) school district. In 1940, her children were living with her brother, June and his wife, Vertis in rural Hickory, Mississippi.

Ida Dyes married George Youngblood II, the son of Sylvia and George Youngblood I and had sixteen children: Thomas, West, Warren, Lucinda, Daniel, Francis, Nannie Mae, George III, Virginia, Otha, Matthew II, Pete, Ida Jean, Ruby, and Connie. (*See Youngblood Family an interview with Nannie Youngblood, daughter of Ida Dyes and George Youngblood II*)

Annie Jane Dyes grew up on the farm with her parents. She attended school in the community. Annie Jane never married. In the 1940 census Annie Jane was listed living on the farm in the community with her widowed mother, Lucinda Dyes and some of her younger siblings.

Bessie Dyes a daughter of Matt and Lucinda, was born in 1900, and died in Hickory, Mississippi in 1972. (*As of this printing little is known regarding Bessie Dyes.*)

Adeline Dyes the youngest daughter of Matt and Lucinda never married. Adeline died in Missouri in 1991, at the age of seventy five.

Daniel Dyes the second son of Matt and Lucinda married Mary Clay and lived for a while in the Good Hope Settlement. On January 21, 1914 they had a son, S. T. Dyes. The infant died in April of that same year with Whooping Cough and was buried in the Good Hope Church Cemetery.

June Dyes married Vertis in 1933 (maiden name not known), and in 1934 their first child, Bessie Pearl, was born. The following years June and Vertis had more children: June Harris was born in 1936, Eldora in 1938, and Ralph in 1940. In 1940, June and his wife, Vertis, Ed Lee and Eddie Croft ,the children of his sister Viney Croft, were all living in rural Hickory, Mississippi.

John Dyes I (possibly) the brother of Frank Dyes and John II, Sonny, Joe and Prince Dyes, were land owners in the community as early as 1868. Along with John Dyes I, they all had served in the Civil War with the Union and subsequently was awarded a small amount of land for their service during the War. (*Read more on Dyes Rebellion of Newton County' in Appendices*)

Henry Dyes I was born into slavery in 1862. His parents' names are not known as of this printing. Henry and his brother, Orang, may have been born on the Dyes plantation. Once they were freed, Henry and his brother may have worked for a time on the Dyes plantation as tenant farmers. In 1880, when Henry was eighteen years old he took his fourteen year old brother, Orang, and they worked as hired farm laborers for the planters in the area in hope of saving enough money to buy farmland for themselves. During Reconstruction he was able to purchase land enough for a small farm. By the early 1900s, with the help of his brother, Henry was able to purchase more land near the Good Hope Colored Settlement. In 1883, Henry Dyes married Mary Francis Salter, the daughter of Frank and Dora Salter, and settled in the Good Hope Freedmen Settlement. Henry and Mary Francis had their only son, Thomas Dyes, in 1891. Four years after the birth of their son, Mary Francis Salter Dyes died.

Henry married Louise [Babe] Salter, the sister of his late wife in 1895. The family remained in the Good Hope Settlement and worked a small farm. Henry and his wife, Louise, had their first child, Carrie Dyes, in 1896. Henry and Louise Dyes continued to live in the settlement and operated a small farm. Their second child, Frank Dyes II, was born in 1905. On August 13, 1914 a third child, Frances Rebecca Dyes, was born. Frances Rebecca Dyes died five days later and is buried in the Good Hope Colored Cemetery. In 1917, a fourth child, Sophie Dyes, was born. By 1910, census their daughter Carrie is no longer in the home and as of this printing she was not located in the census for various reasons. Carrie would have been fourteen years old and may have been married with an unknown surname or had died before 1910.

Sophia married Jim Mitchell and they had a daughter, Theresa. Theresa married Will Chapman in 1952, in the Good Hope Settlement. In 1955, the couple relocated to Denver, Colorado. There they had five children: Ouida, Willie, James, Percy Lee and Nyla. Will died first and then Theresa died later in 2016 in Denver, Colorado.

Sixty three year old Henry and forty three year old Louise had lived in the settlement for many years. They had raised both their children and their grandchildren. Henry died sometime before 1930. When Henry Dyes I died Louise married her second husband, Frank Petree II. Frank and Louise continued to live on the Dyes farm in rural Hickory, Mississippi near the Good Hope Colored Settlement until 1940. The 1940 census lists one hundred and three year old Frank and eight three year old Louise living with a granddaughter, Lucy Dyes Johnson near Hickory, Mississippi. (*Citing this record "Mississippi Enumeration of Educable Children, 1850-1892; 1908-1957," database, Babe Dyes in entry for Sofia Dyes, 1933; citing School enrollment, Newton, Mississippi Department of Archives & History, Jackson)A child Ray Dyes born in 1924 was listed in Newton County school records as child of Babe Louise Dyes, Newton County, Mississippi School records in 1933 shows the Enumeration of Educable Children listed as educable children are the children and grandchildren of Louise Babe Dyes; a son Frank Dyes, daughter Sofia Dyes and grandson eight year old Ray Dyes.*)

Lucy/Lucile Jones was listed in 1940 as head of household living in Beat 5 of Newton County, Mississippi with her fifteen year old son, Ray and her grandparents, one hundred and three year old Frank Petry II and his eighty three year old wife, Louise Salter Petry.

Thomas Dyes was born 1891 in the Good Hope Settlement, the son of Mary Francis Salter Dyes and Henry Dyes. Mary died soon after giving birth. In the 1910 census nineteen year old Tom Dyes was listed as a boarder living on the Thomas and Lillie Petry/ Petree farm in Good Hope Colored Settlement. In 1916, Tom relocated up North to Freeport, Illinois where he lived on Sherman Ave with a relative, Josephine Hayden Ligon. In 1917, during World War I he registered for military duty in Stephenson County, Illinois. After the War Tom returned to Freeport and worked as a laborer on the Illinois Central Railroad. However, by 1930, when he was thirty nine years old, Tom returned home to the Good Hope Settlement where he lived with his Uncle Henry Dyes and other relatives until his death in 1972. (*See The Salter of Good Hope Settlement*)

Lucy Dyes was born enslaved in Mississippi. After Lucy was made free and able to do so, she legally married her enslaved husband, William Johnson. The couple lived in the settlement as early as 1880 with their sons: Robert, Mauley, Frank and Francis Walter. Listed living in the household was twenty year old Henry Dyes and eighteen year old Sophia Dyes. *(The Johnson Petree Story regarding Williams Johnson)*

The Edison Family

The Freedmen Edison Family

Allen Edison was born in 1871 in Mississippi, possibly in Jasper County. Allen married Mattie and had the following children: Nancy, Kheva, Eddie, Virgie, Willie, Dora, Doby, Ben, William and AC/ Aaron C Edison.

Mattie Edison was listed in the census of 1930 as a widow and living in Beat 4 of Newton County with three of her children: Aaron C, William and eight year old Massas Edison. The 1940 census shows Mattie at age seventy living in Newton, Mississippi with her sons, AC and William Edison.

Edd Edison the son of Allen and Mattie Edison married Lela Johnson, the daughter of Filmore and Bettie Johnson, and had eight children. Edd and Lela were farmers in the community and owned their own land. Edd died in 1959 and is buried in the Good Hope Church Cemetery. Once the children were raised to adulthood Lela relocated to Illinois. While in Illinois she lived in Chicago with her sister, Sallie Johnson Salter, and in Freeport, Illinois with her daughter, Maudie, and a son, Johnnie and his wife, Nannie Youngblood and their children, Johnnie and Gary. Lela lived to be ninety nine years old. She died in 1990 in Freeport, Illinois *(More on Lela Johnson– The Johnson Petree Story)*

Ardell Edison the eldest son of Ed and Lela Johnson Edison married Clatie Bell Patrick in 1948. Ardell and Clatie Bell became the back bones of the community and the pillars of the settlement church. Ardell was a Deacon and Sunday School Superintendent for forty years at the Good Hope Settlement Church. Ardell registered for the draft during WW II in Newton County, Mississippi. Ardell died and is buried in the Good Hope Church Cemetery. Clatie Bell continue to live in the settlement. Ardell and Clatie Bell had six children. After living sixty six years in her home that her husband built for her in the Good Hope Settlement, Clatie Bell now lives in St Louis, Illinois. *(Clatie Bell Edison is the woman on the right on the cover of the this book)*

Percy Edison died at a young age.

Maudie Edison was born in Good Hope, Mississippi in 1921. She attended the Good Hope Settlement School. Later she was hired as one of the teachers in the little two room school in the Good Hope Community. In 1940, she relocated to Freeport, Illinois where she met and married Roger Massey. Maudie died in 2005 in Freeport, Illinois. Maudie and Roger Massey had no children.

Chester Edison married Vergie and relocated up North. They were childless.

Clifton Edison after joining the Army left the Good Hope Settlement. When the war ended Clifton married Rena Mae Edison, the daughter of Aston and Tettie Morris. For many years they farmed up North. After Clifton retired he returned to the Good Hope Colored Settlement and as of this printing, at age ninety years old, Cliff continues to live in the area. Rena Mae died and is buried in Good Hope Church Cemetery. Clifton and Rena Mae Morris Edison had four children.

Earlene Edison following the example of her brothers, migrated up North to Freeport, Illinois. Like her brothers she also returned home to Good Hope. Earlene was proprietor of a restaurant and was famous in all of Mississippi for her wonderful food. When Earlene died she was buried in the Good Hope Church Cemetery.

Johnnie Edison I was born in 1927, in the Good Hope Settlement. He worked with his father and attended the settlement school. He married Nannie Mae Youngblood and moved up to Freeport, Illinois. Johnnie died in 1990. Nannie continues to live in Freeport. Johnnie and Nannie Youngblood Edison had two children.

Oliver James/ OJ Edison was born in Good Hope, Mississippi. He migrated to Freeport, Illinois where he met and married Maxine Cain. They lived many years in California. Years later Oliver James was called to preach and pastored a church in Des Moines, Iowa. When he retired he returned to the Good Hope Settlement where he served as the Associate Minister at the Good Hope Baptist Church. Maxine died and is buried in the Good Hope Cemetery. Reverend Edison continues to live in the Good Hope Community area. Oliver J. (OJ) and Maxine Cain Edison had four children.

Edward Edison died at an early age and is buried in Good Hope Cemetery.

The Ford Family

The Freedmen Ford Family

Samuel Ford was born in 1879, in Mississippi. He lived with his parents on a farm in Beat 5 Chunky Village in Newton County. He married Julia [no maiden name] in 1894. Their first child, Pinckney Ford, was born in 1897; then a son, George Ford, was born in 1898; a third son, Nathaniel Ford, was born in 1900. Living with Samuel Ford and his wife Julia in 1900 in Newton County were three young people: seventeen year old Mary Ford, fifteen year old Roxy Ella Ford and nineteen year old David Ford. They are all listed as the stepchildren of Samuel Ford. In 1910, thirty eight year old Samuel Ford and thirty one year old Julia Ford were living in Beat 2 Jasper County, Mississippi. Living in the household with Samuel and Julia are five children: Joe P. Ford, Bettie Ford, Charlie Ford, Olivia and Beatrice Ford.

In 1920, forty two year old Julia Ford is listed as a widow and her son twenty-two year old Joe P. Ford is listed as head of household. The family continued to live in Northeast, Jasper County on Hickman and Enterprise Road. Living with Joe and his mother are his brothers and sisters: Bettie, Charlie, Olivia, Helen, Beatrice, Tommie, Roosevelt and a nephew, three year old Robert Ford. In 1940, sixty five year old Julia Ford was listed as head of household in Jasper County with her son, Tommie and a daughter-in-law, Mary Ford.

George Ford was born May 1898, in Beat 5, Newton County, Mississippi to Julia Ford.

Dave Ford was born in Mississippi in 1882, to Julia Ford and was listed living in Beat 5 Newton County, Mississippi. By 1910, Dave had married Caroline Davis. [Caroline Davis picture on the back cover of the book] They had two daughters, Ida Mae and Julia Ford and continued to live in Newton County, Mississippi. In 1920, Dave and Caroline Davis Ford were settled on a small rented farm in Newton County with six children: twelve year old Ida Mae, ten year old Maggie, nine year old Junior, seven year old Sam, five year old Carter and one year old Rufus.

Rufus /Ed Ford was born to Dave and Caroline Davis Ford on June 19, 1919 in Newton County, Mississippi. He worked with his father and brothers and sister on the farm and attended school whenever possible. In 1935, he married Opal Johnson. Opal was one of the daughters of Reverend Daniel and Lilia Johnson of the Good Hope Settlement. Over the years Opal and Ed/Rufus had thirteen children. (*More on Opal Johnson in The Johnson Petree Story*)

Green Ford was born on November 24, 1913 in Newton County and at only 5 days old he died, November 29, 1913, and is buried at Good Hope Cemetery.

Mack Ford was born to George Ford on December 25, 1887 in Newton County. Mack may have lived with his family in Union, Mississippi. At an early age Mack began working for J R Buckwalter Sawmills. Like many young men who worked the lumber and sawmill industries during this period, Mack Ford contracted pneumonia. In 1918, when he was thirteen one years old he died of pneumonia. Mack was buried at Spring Hill Cemetery. Informant: Jasper Ford of Union.

Oleana Ford and Harris Brown were the parents of James Brown. James was born in March of 1925 in Jasper County. Eight months later on November 15, 1925 James Brown died of influenza and was buried in Good Hope Colored Baptist Church Cemetery. Informant: Henry Clayton

The Fielder Family

Possible Slaveholding Family

Henry D. Jones brought Annabella into Newton County. According to the 1860 Slave Schedule, Henry D Jones held nineteen people enslaved in three slave houses in Newton County. "Colonel W N Raines was very instrumental in bringing the railroads to Newton County. He was a large slave owner (from Virginia) and went back to Virginia to purchase slaves to work on the Newton County railroad. My family's matriarch Annabella Jones-Fielder we believe was purchased at this time by either Mr. Raines or Henry D Jones. We lean toward Henry D Jones.

She had some kids by Levi Jones, son of Henry D Jones". Annabella's grandson *Darrell Fielder 2014 Darrell Fielder wrote* "*My family matriarch Annabella Jones-Fielder we believe was purchased at this time by either Colonel WN Raines or Henry D Jones. We lean toward Henry D Jones.*"

The Freedmen Fielder Family

Joshua Fielder was a domestic servant for Alfred Raines (son of Colonel W N) in the 1910 census. Our oral history indicates he was accused of having an affair with one of Alfred Raines' daughters. As a result, he was killed by the Klan and buried in Potterchitto swamp in Hickory. His body has never been recovered. Information acquired from the book In search of Annabella's Children (A history of the Fielder family in Mississippi and beyond) **by Darrell Fielder.**

William Estell Fielder was born in 1853 in Newton County, Mississippi. Some years later he married Annabella Jones and they had eleven children: Redie, Docia, Marion, Joseph, Benjamin Franklin, Curtis and Mirtis, Rita, Scotia, Calhoun and Margret. (*See Annabella Jones*)

The Gaddis Family

Slaveholding Gaddis/Gaddice Family

The 1840 United States Census shows Warren J Gaddis (spelled Gaddice) was living in Coweta, Georgia with only one enslaved person. By 1850, Warren J Gaddis had relocated to Lauderdale County, Mississippi with his wife, Mariam, and several children, including two year old Peter M. Gaddis. In 1860, Warren J Gaddis moved once again to Scott County in Mississippi. This time he moved with three of his children and thirteen enslaved workers. Research reveals when Warren J Gaddis died Peter Gaddis inherited from his father the thirteen enslaved workers and relocated with his family to Newton and Jasper Counties in Mississippi. After Emancipation Proclamation the Gaddis Freemen settled in Leaks, Jasper and Newton Counties in Mississippi.

The Freedmen Gaddis Family

Jacob Gaddis was born in 1820, enslaved in South Carolina. He was the patriarch of the Gaddis family. Jacob was possibly one of the thirteen enslaved men, women and children brought into Newton County, Mississippi by the slaveholding Gaddice/Gaddis family. In 1866, when Jacob was free to have a surname he chose for his family the surname of his former slaveholders "The Gaddice family." [He spelled it Gaddis] In 1870, Jacob was married to Fannie [maiden name not known]. Fannie was born in 1848 into slavery in Tennessee.

The 1880 census lists sixty year old Jacob Gaddis living in Newton County and married to thirty two year old Fannie Gaddis. Over the years Jacob and Fannie had several children: Hubert, Jake, Morris, Philadelphia, John and Peter plus two daughters, Marcy and Scilla. After extensive research done on the Gaddis family the census and historical records revealed information pertaining to only four of the eight Gaddis children: sons Jake, Moses and Peter and a daughter, Scilla Gaddis.

Jake Gaddis was born in Mississippi in 1871 to Jacob and Fannie Gaddis. In 1895, he married Sylvia Quince, the daughter of William and Martha Quince. Jake and Sylvia had five children: four daughters; Lillie Mae, Abbie, Savannah and Dilly Ann and one son, William. From 1900 until 1910, the family lived in Newton County, Mississippi. Afterward Jake relocated with his family to Jasper County, Mississippi. By 1910, his wife, Sylvia, had died and he was living with his younger brother, Peter, in Jasper County. Jake and Peter worked at a sawmill operation near Hickory, Mississippi. The 1920, census showed Jake Gaddis as a widower and was married a second time to thirty nine year old, Docia [maiden named not known]. In 1923, at the age of fifty one Jake Gaddis died of tuberculosis and was buried in Hickory, Mississippi. The census records and other researched documents uncovered information pertaining to two of Jake's children: Dilly Ann and William. Nothing was revealed regarding Lillie Mae, Abbie or Savannah.

Dilly Ann Gaddis was the fourth child born to Jake Gaddis and Sylvia Quince Gaddis. In the early years Dilly Ann and her siblings farmed with their parents and attended the Good Hope Settlement School in rural Hickory, Mississippi. In 1918, Dilly Ann Gaddis married Dutch McLaurin and had one known child, John Wesley McLaurin.

William Gaddis married Eunice McGee. They had one known daughter which William named Savannah in honor of his sister, Savannah Gaddis. Research did not uncover further information pertaining to young Savannah Gaddis II.

Peter Gaddis was the youngest son born to Jacob and Fannie Gaddis. In the 1910 census Peter was living in Hickory, Mississippi with his older brother, Jake. No other information was found regarding Peter as of this printing.

Scilla Gaddis the daughter of Jacob and Fannie Gaddis died at an early age and is buried in Newton County. (*Newton County Death Record*)

James Gaddis was born in Mississippi and lived in the Good Hope Settlement where he owned land with his wife, Jeanette (Nettie). The couple had nine children: four sons; James Paul (J P), Henry, Bohen and Mason and five daughters; Easter, Ruth, Hettie, Lula and Lorabell. The Gaddis family lived and worked and attended school in the Good Hope Settlement for many years. However, the family was not members of Good Hope Baptist Church. James and Jeanette chose for themselves and their children the membership in Wesley Chapel Methodist Church in Hickory, Mississippi.

In 1920, James Gaddis relocated for a time to Freeport, Illinois for work with the Illinois Central Railroad. While in Freeport James acquired a job with the railroad and lived with relatives: a cousin, Broomsy Norman, and his wife, Nellie Salter Norman. By 1930, Henry had returned to the Good Hope Colored Settlement. The 1930 census shows he was farming in the settlement with his wife, Nettie, and their sixteen year old son, Mason, and three daughters: Nettie, Lula and Lorabell. By 1940, all of the Gaddis children had relocated up North to Chicago. (*The 1930 census lists Henry Norman, widower as step father to head of household James Gaddis*)

James Paul Gaddis was the eldest son (JP as he was known), joined the Navy during World War II and achieved the rank of Chief Petty Officer. After the war he returned to Chicago where he met his wife, Magdalene Roberts. The couple was childless. He worked for Pullman Company until he retired.

Henry Gaddis moved up to Chicago with his sibling and had several businesses. In his later life he married a home town young woman, Amie Lee Johnson they had one son, Lacy Gaddis. (*More on Amie Lee Johnson see descendants of Filmore Johnson*)

Bowen Gaddis relocated to Median, Mississippi.

Harry Gaddis died in Newton County in 1918.

Moses Gaddis died in Newton County in 1922.

The Garner Family

Slaveholding Garner Family

Burgess Garner of North Carolina and Georgia in 1860 was living in Newton County, Mississippi where he held seven people enslaved. After 1863, Burgess Garner freed his enslaved workers. When the former enslaved men and women were free to do so they registered in the 1866 Mississippi State Census and took the surname Garner. Conceivably Mariah Garner, Julius Garner and other Garner family members were included in the group of freed men and women.

The Freedmen Garner Family

Mariah Garner was born in North Carolina in 1820, enslaved. Mariah was possibly brought into Mississippi while enslaved by the Garner family of North Carolina and Newton County, Mississippi. The 1870 census documented Mariah living with her nineteen year old son, Thomas Garner, a Mulatto in rural Hickory, Mississippi in Newton County.

Julius Garner [2nd maternal great grandfather of the author] was born enslaved in 1833 in North Carolina and was living in rural Newton County in 1870. Living with Julius was his wife, Hannah Croft Garner. Hannah was born enslaved in 1832 in North Carolina to Ollie Croft. In 1853, a daughter, Dora Garner, was born and a son, Luke Garner, was born a free child, in Newton County Mississippi in 1867. The family continued to live in rural Newton County and in the following years they had more children: Hasty was born in 1868, Ralph was born in 1871, Mary in 1875 and James in 1879. Also living with the family was Julius' seventeen year old sister, Indiana Garner.

In 1900, Julius relocated with his family to a farm in nearby Jasper County. While living in Jasper County three more children were born to the Garners. A daughter Lucinda was born in 1882, a son Willis in 1884 and Masalee in 1893. Also living in the household was Hannah's seventy year old mother, Ollie Croft. [The 3rd great grandmother to the author]

In 1910, Julius and Hannah Garner returned to the settlement and attended Good Hope Settlement Church. Mary and Masa L. Garner were still living with their parents plus one hundred year old Ollie Croft and as some elders claim she was "still working on the farm." (*See Ollie Croft*)

Sarah Garner was born in North Carolina in 1805. As of this printing nothing more was uncovered regarding Sarah Garner.

Ellen Garner was born in Mississippi, the daughter of Henry and Mary Bennett Garner. Ellen married Joe Garner and lived in Union, Mississippi. Ellen died in 1938 of a heart attack at age sixty and was buried at Enterprise, Mississippi.

Juno Garner was born in 1836, and died a widow at age eighty five on April 19, 1921. She is buried in Hickory. Parents' names were not given. Informant: Roan Garner. *(More about Garner Family See the Salter family of Good Hope Colored Settlement) for more on Frank and Dora Garner Salter see The Salter of Good Hope Colored Community) (More on Hannah and Julius Garner see The Salter of Good Hope Colored Community) (A number of descendants of the Garner remained in the Good Hope Settlement. Indiana Garner, Jack Garner, Lucinda Garner, Luke Garner, Mariah Garner, Margaret Garner, Thomas Garner, Frances J Garner, Josephine Garner, Alfred Garner, Susan Garner, Jeremiah Garner and George Garner.)*

The Native American Garner Family (See Ollie Croft)

The Gibbs Family

Slaveholding Gibbs Family

In 1850, Edward Gibbs lived in Neshoba County, Mississippi where he held five people enslaved. Henry D. Gibbs and Wilmont Gibbs each held twenty five people enslaved in Hinds County. Any of the three slaveholders may well have been the men and women that held the Freedmen Gibbs family enslaved.

The Freedmen Gibbs Family

Barbara Gibbs was listed in the census with her sons: George, Jeremiah, Esquire, Ham, Thomas, Daniel and Warren. After they were freed Barbara Gibbs and her sons settled on a little piece of land in the Colored Settlement of Good Hope. As of this printing little is known regarding her children with the exception of her sons, Esquire, Daniel, Warren and Jeremiah.

Esquire or Squire Gibbs married a young woman named Sweet Salter on October 3, 1889 in Newton County. Sweet was the daughter of Cason and Cherry Anderson Salter. Over time Esquire and Sweet had nine children: Ham, Abb, Eugene, Warren, Daniel, Mary, Em, Tommie and Alice. Esquire and his wife and children worked a farm in the Good Hope Colored Settlement. His wife died in the early 1900s.

Squire died soon afterward on November 25, 1915 at age sixty two. He was buried in Good Hope Church Cemetery. Ham Gibbs of Hickory, Mississippi, the son of Esquire, was listed as the informant on his death certificate. (*More on Sweet Salter See the Salter of Good Hope Colored Settlement*)

Daniel Gibbs son of Esquire and Sweet Salter Gibbs was born in 1897 in Newton, County. He married Emma (maiden name not known). Like many others Daniel left Newton County before World War 1.

His destination was to migrate up North. Daniel and Emma relocated to East St Louis, Illinois. While in East St Louis he registered for theWW1 Draft. After the war the family continued to live in St Louis.

Warren Gibbs followed his brother to East St Louis after the War. Three years after the death of their father, Esquire Gibbs, Sweet Gibbs joined her sons in East St. Louis. (*See more Sweet Salter Gibbs, the daughter of Cason and Cherry Salter the Salter of Good Hope Colored Community*)

Jeremiah Gibbs was born enslaved in 1853 in Mississippi. After he was freed he stayed on in Mississippi. The 1930 census shows seventy year old Jerry living alone in Hickory, Mississippi.

The Gibson/Gipson Family

Slaveholding Gibson Family

Henry Gibson was a slaveholder. He and his wife, Nancy Miller, were wealthy plantation owners in Harris County, Georgia and held forty three people enslaved. Their daughter Susan married Cicero Johnson while living in Georgia. In 1857, Henry Gibson migrated to Alabama along with his daughter, Susan and son-in-law, Cicero Johnson. Henry Gibson and Cicero Johnson settled for a time with their families in Alabama. After 1860, the family migrated into Mississippi along with the workers they held enslaved and settled in rural Hickory, Newton County, Mississippi near the Jasper County border.(*Slaveholders Henry Gibson and Cicero Johnson are buried in the old Good Hope Baptist Church Cemetery where the original "White Good Hope" was first built before 1855 about fifteen feet from and area posted "Colored Cemetery" where the early Johnson Petry/ Petree and Gibson were laid to rest most were members of the church*)

The Freemen Gibson/ Gipson Family

Richmond Gibson was born enslaved in Harris County, Georgia in 1838. While he was enslaved on the Gibson plantation in Alabama, Richmond was allowed to enter into an "enslaved marriage" with a young enslaved woman named Susan. Richmond and Susan had three children during the time of enslavement: Litha, Sarah, and James. Richmond and his wife, Susan, and their children are thought to have traveled with their slaveholders into Newton County, Mississippi in about 1854. After the time of enslavement Richmond and his family worked on the Gibson plantation in the Good Hope Fellowship area in rural Hickory, Mississippi. For many years Richmond and his family were members of the original Good Hope Baptist Church on Fellowship Road ("The Master's Church") and attended church services along with their slaveholder, Henry Gibson and his family.

After freedom from 1865 until 1870, Richmond and Susan Gibson were working a small farm on the Gibson plantation with a number of their children. Also living in the household with the Gibson family in 1870 was a young woman, Amanda Johnson [possibly the sister of Filmore Johnson] and Amanda's daughter, four year old Sarah Johnson. By 1880 Richmond Gibson had acquired a few acres of farmland near the Good Hope Freedmen Settlement.

The 1900 and 1910 Mississippi Census shows Richmond and Susan continued to work the small farm in the settlement. More children were born to the Gibsons between 1900 and 1910: Dora, Mira, Epie/Exie, Mariah, Susan and Elsie. Two granddaughters, twenty year old Ida Gibson and fifteen year old Anna Wash, were living with the family during this period. Richmond Gibson died in 1918, and is buried on the Southwest portion of the old Good Hope Regular Baptist Church Cemetery posted "Colored Cemetery". Both Richmond and Susan Gibson graves are less than twenty feet from the "White Cemetery". After Richmond died Susan lived with their daughter, Epie/ Exie and her husband, Ben Wash, until her death. (*Richmond Gibson died at age 77*)

Very little information as of this research was uncovered pertaining to Litha, Sarah and James, Mira, Mariah, Susan and Elsie, the children of Richmond and Susan Gibson. However, assorted bits of information were discovered regarding their daughters: Dora and Epie/ Exie Gibson.

Epie/Exie Gibson was born in 1885. She married Ben Wash and lived in the Good Hope Freedmen Settlement on a farm adjacent to her parents, Richmond and Susan Gibson. Epie/Exie and Ben had one child who died at birth. They may have had other children but none were discovered during this printing. In 1925, Epie/ Exie died during the tuberculosis epidemic in Newton County and is buried in the Good Hope Church Cemetery.

Dora Gibson was living in the Good Hope Colored Settlement in 1920, with her sister, Epie/Exie and her sister's husband. After Epie/ Exie died Dora was no longer listed in the Wash household.

Frances Gibson was born in 1868 [parents unknown]. However they may have been a part of the Gibson group of enslaved people brought in by Henry Gibson and Cicero Johnson. In 1870 two year old Frances was living with Daniel Johnson I and his wife, Frances [unknown maiden name, may have been Gibson] Also living in the household was his younger brother, thirteen year old Filmore Johnson. (*More on this family in The Johnson Petry/Petree Story*)

Esther Gibson lived in the area near the Good Hope Colored Settlement in the early 1900s with four daughters: Mary Jane, Vera, Zilphea, and Mae Francis Gibson. As of this printing no other information has been uncovered regarding the women of this family. (*In genealogy tracing female family members into adulthood is not always possible. The primary problem is that women usually change their surnames once married and lives in another household.*)

Anderson Gibson was listed in the 1880 census with his wife, Catharine; her maiden name was not listed. Anderson and Catharine were living on a farm in rural Newton County with their six children: two sons, Philip, age seventeen and Richmond, age two years; four daughters, Francis, Bama, Louisa and Lilly. (*Anderson Gibson may have been a son of Richmond Gibson*)

William/ Willie Gibson was born enslaved in 1839, in Georgia. During the time of enslavement he and Elizabeth/ Betsy, an enslaved woman born in Virginia, had several children: John (born in 1860), George W. Gibson, Willie, Ed, Smith, Jasper, Letha, and Rodia.

George W. Gibson was born in Mississippi on June 1863, the son of William and Elizabeth Gibson. In 1874, he married Jennie Hall. Between the census years of 1890 and 1910 George and thirty five year old Jennie had twelve children. Their first child was Attie, next Cora, was born in 1890. Martha, was born in June of 1891. Pearl, Ida Bell, and Raleigh a son, Green Gibson, were born after 1893.

Four more children were born after 1898: Eddie, Nathaniel, Willie Lee, Walter, were all born in the 1900s. Luther and the youngest children: Otha, Sam and Joe, were born between 1900 and 1910. After giving birth to all of her children Jennie Gibson died. That same year George married Minerva Petree/Petry, the daughter of Frank Petree/Petry II and Angelina Walker. Minerva and George operated a farm in the Good Hope Colored Settlement for several decades. Both were considered pillars of the church and the Good Hope Settlement.

Years later with the help of their two grandsons, nine year old James Brown and six year old Roy Evans, the elderly couple continued to work their small farm. Each Sunday morning George and Minerva would ride to church in their spring board wagon to attend services at the Good Hope Colored Baptist Church. When George and Minerva died they were buried in the Good Hope Colored Church Cemetery.

Cora Gibson was a daughter of George and Jennie Gibson. She attended the Good Hope Colored Settlement School in the community and worked with her family on the farm. Cora never married. In 1923, she contracted tuberculosis and died on September 2, 1924, at the age of twenty five and was buried at Good Hope Church Colored Cemetery.

Luther Gibson was born in 1903, to George and Jennie Gibson. Worked on his father's farm with his brothers and sisters and attended school whenever he could be away from his farm chores. Some years later Luther married Julia, a women he met in the community. In 1920 and 1930, Luther and Julia Gibson were farming a small plot of land in rural Hickory near the Good Hope Colored Settlement.

Joe Gibson was born to George and Jennie Gibson. Like his brother Luther, Joe worked with his family on the farm and was only able to attend school whenever he could be away from his farm chores. As a young man Joe married Mattie. Mattie Blaylock was the daughter of Allen Blaylock. After Joe and Mattie were married they worked as share cropper farmers in an area known as Stout Hill. Joe and Mattie Gibson had several children.

"At a Gipson/Gibson Family Reunion in 2005 in Tunica, Mississippi the elder Matriarch of the Gipson/ Blalock family Mattie Blalock Gipson was honored with words and deeds. One family history writer wrote of the Matriarch, "The Gipson and Blalock families can only be traced back to the slave era in the1800's. Both family names were given by their slave masters.

The families had struggled with many hardships down through the years to arrive at this point in time. We," the writer continued, " have endured from generation to generation due to love, strength, dedication, and the grace of God. The family tree starts with Willis Gipson. Willis Gipson married Betsy (unknown). From this union eight children were born; six sons and two daughters. The names of these children are: George Washington, Willie, John, Ed, Smith, Jasper, Letha, and Rodia. George Washington Gipson was born in 1860. He grew up to be a man with many talents. He was a farmer, a basket maker, and he was known for his skill in making bottoms for chairs.

George Washington Gipson married Jennie Hall and they became the proud parents of fifteen children. Their names are: Attie, Cora, Martha, Pearl, Ida Bell, Raleigh, Green, Eddie, Willie Lee, Nathaniel, Walter, Luther, Otha, and the twins Sam and Joe. Joe Gipson and Mattie Blalock were united in holy matrimony, February 3, 1929. They were married in the home of Mattie's parents by Rev. Jones Moore. Joe started working at the Newton Saw Mill when he was fifteen years old. He had several jobs during his life time. The jobs included logging pulpwood and sharecropping. He also worked at the Eagle Chemical Plant in Joliet, Illinois. Mattie was a housewife during the early years. After the children were older she worked as a domestic."

The writer quoted Psalms 127:3 ' lo, children are an heritage of the Lord; and the fruit of the womb is his reward.' "The fruitful heritage of Joe and Mattie included: George, Mattie Maude, Annie, Mildred, Minnie Ruth, Eleanor, Fred, Floyd, and Arstralia. The children were raised in a Christian home. They grew up attending the Good Hope Baptist Church."

Orea Gibson is listed as the eleven year old granddaughter of Joe and Mattie Brown. Orea was living with the Brown family in 1930 in the Good Hope Colored Settlement.

Jessie Gibson lived in Township 5 Range 17, Newton County, Mississippi.

Frank Gipson in 1920 was living in Northwest Jasper, Mississippi on Enterprise and Garlandville Road with his grandparents, Frank and Nellie McCarty.

Native American Gibson Families

Isham Gibson, Frank J. Gibson, Martha Gibson, Mary Gibson, Nancy Gibson, Eliza and Jack Gibson, Gilmore Gibson, Jan Gibson, Squire Gibson, Tom Gibson and Winnie Gibson

George Gibson and Cilli Smith, residents of Conehatta, Newton County, were listed as the parents of nine year old Sampson Smith Gibson. Sampson died of tuberculosis in 1923, and is buried in the Choctaw Cemetery in Conehatta.

The Graham Family

The Slaveholding Graham Family

The Graham family of Clark, Jasper, Leake and Scott Counties in Mississippi held a large number of enslaved workers. The enslaved workers held by the Graham slaveholders are the ancestors of the Freedmen Graham family in Newton County, Mississippi.

The Freedmen Graham Family

William Graham was born into slavery in North Carolina. He may have been brought into Mississippi sometime in the early 1840s by the Graham slaveholders. After he was freed he operated a small farm perhaps on the Graham plantation in Newton County. In 1870, William was living in the Good Hope Freedmen Settlement adjacent to the Eliza Griffin farm.

The Griffin Family

The Slaveholding Griffin Family

The Griffin family was held enslaved in Georgia and was possibly brought into Mississippi by the Griffins of Newton County. There is no proof of this at the time of printing. George Griffin and others may have signed a mandatory labor contract and were sent out to work on the Griffin farm.

The Griffin families were not documented in the Federal Census until 1870. Some research shows the Griffin family was listed in the 1870 census living on the Griffin farm in Jasper County and working as farm laborers.

The Freedmen Griffin Family

George Griffin was born in 1835 in Mississippi possibly on the Griffin plantation. However, in the1900 census sixty five year old George was listed as a "servant" in residence on the Walter and Winnie Dixon Wall plantation in rural Hickory, Mississippi.

The Gully Family

The Freedmen Gully Family

James Gully was born in 1875 in Mississippi. In 1902, he married Agnes Johnson. In 1908 a daughter, Lena Gully, was born. In 1910, James and Agnes Johnson Gully and their daughter, Lena, were living on rented farmland in Township 5 Range 17 of Newton County, in Mississippi. In 1920, James, Agnes and their nineteen year old daughter, Lilia Anderson, were living in the Good Hope Colored Settlement. James Gully died sometime after 1920. Agnes and her daughter, Lena Anderson and Lena's children; Lelia, Frank, Jessie and Willie C. Anderson continued to work the farm. In 1929, Lena gave birth to a daughter, Louisa, and she died in child birth. *(More on Agnes Johnson Gully see Harriet Johnson)*

The Hall Family

The Slaveholding Hall Family

Elijah Hall held six people enslaved in Jasper County. Peter and Sarah Hall may have been held enslaved on the Elijah Hall plantation in Jasper County or held by Ezekiel Hall in Scott County, Mississippi. No documents were discovered to prove information as of this printing.

The Freedmen Hall Family

Peter Hall and Sarah lived together as man and wife in an "enslaved marriage" for several years while held enslaved. Soon after they were emancipated Peter and Sarah left the plantation of their former slaveholders seeking new living quarters. Peter and Sarah legalized their marriage and established themselves on a small rented farm in the Good Hope Colored Settlement. They had the following children: Walter Georgia Gene and Jennie Hall. Years later Jennie married George W. Gipson. Peter died in 1910. On August 14, 1921 Sarah Hall died at the age of 104.

Both Peter and his wife, Sarah, are buried in Good Hope Church Cemetery. *(The Black Codes for the state of Mississippi demands if newly freed couples preferred to continue to live together as man and wife they must marry according to the new laws.)*

The Hamilton Family

The Freedmen Hamilton Family

John Hamilton was born in Copiah County, Mississippi to Rebecca [her maiden name is not known]. When they came to Newton County is not known nor who held him enslaved during that period. Once freed John commenced farming in the Good Hope Colored Community and married Rilla Cook, the daughter of Eliza Petry and Cornelius Cook. John and Rilla had two daughters; Eliza and Emma . The family were members of Good Hope Missionary Baptist Church. John Hamilton died in 1941, and is buried in Good Hope Church Cemetery. After he died Rilla and her daughters relocated to Meridian, Mississippi. *(More about Rilla Cook Petry in The Johnson Petry/Petree Story)*

The Hardy Family

The Freedmen Hardy Family

Thomas Hardy was married to Eady [no maiden name] and were both listed as Mulattoes in the 1870 census living near the Good Hope Settlement. Hardy and his wife, Eady, owned their farm valued at nine hundred dollars and personal property worth two hundred and fifty seven dollars. Working on the farm with them were six of their children: Lana, Anor, Horace, Amanda, Jennette and Jasper. *(Research did not uncover more information on the Hardy family)*

The Johnson Family

The Slaveholding Johnson Family

Cicero Johnson/ Henry Gibson

Cicero Johnson the planter, who may have held Filmore Johnson and his family enslaved in Newton County, was the son of Samuel Johnson and Frances Corney Johnson. Samuel and Frances were married December 3, 1829 in Putnam County, Georgia. They had three children. One son, Cicero, was born in 1831 in Georgia. His father, Samuel Johnson, died when Cicero was only sixteen years old. Soon after his father's death his mother remarried John Wright, a large plantation owner in Georgia. That same year he was betrothed to young Susan Gibson, the daughter of Henry Gibson.

Henry Gibson was a wealthy plantation owner in Harris County, Georgia. He held large amounts of land and forty three people enslaved. On his eighteenth birthday Cicero Johnson inherited his portion of his father's estate and on December 5, 1850, he and Susan were married at her family home. Seven years later in 1857, Henry Gibson had migrated to Alabama and then into Newton County, Mississippi along with his daughter, Susan, and son-in-law, Cicero Johnson, and forty three people they held enslaved. (*Henry Gibson lived in Valley Plains, Georgia, in 1850. Age: 51 a daughter was born in Alabama in 1857. In 1860 lived in Hickory, Mississippi*)

The Freedmen Johnson Family

Daniel Johnson I the elder was born in 1845, to Mary Johnson Kirby enslaved. After he was freed he married Fannie [maiden name not known]. She may have been enslaved by the Gibson family. In the 1870 census Daniel Johnson I was living in Jasper County on several acres of land and had personal property worth one hundred and seventy dollars. The 1880 census shows Daniel living in Northeast Jasper County with his wife and six year old daughter, Barnah Johnson. Additional information pertaining to Daniel and his daughter, Barnah, was not found and very little information regarding his wife, Fannie, was uncovered. (*More on Daniel and Fannie Johnson in The Johnson Petry/Petree Story*) An article published in the *Meridian Mercury on February 1868 declares; (From the perspective of the reporter in 1868). Daniel Johnson was in the Sunday fight and had been arrested and committed to Jasper County jail. "A certain restless Negro [Possibly Daniel Johnson] who is well known in Newton County has on several occasions shown a disposition to incite his people to violence, was out early on Wednesday morning.)*

Preston Johnson I the second son, married Harriett and they had a daughter, Agnes, in 1861. In 1863, when the family was made free after the signing of the Emancipation Proclamation, three year old Agnes and her parents left the plantation to start life anew. In 1870, the family was operating a small farm in the Freedmen Settlement of Good Hope. In 1902, Agnes Johnson married James Gully. Agnes and James stayed on for a while with her parents and worked a farm together in the settlement. In 1908 their only daughter Lena was born. In 1910, James and Agnes Johnson and their nine year old daughter Lena left the Good Hope Freedmen Settlement and rented farmland in Township 5 Range 17 Newton County. James Gully died sometime after 1920. Agnes and her daughter, widowed daughter Lena Anderson, and her children; Lelia Anderson, Frank Anderson, Jessie M. Anderson, Willie C Anderson continued to work the farm. In 1929, baby Louisa Anderson was born and Lena died in child birth. Agnes' father, Preston Johnson, died soon after in 1930. After the death of her father Agnes took her mother to live with her and the grandchildren. Harriett Johnson died in 1935.

Agnes Johnson Gully never remarried and spent her widowhood living with relatives. In 1940, seventy eight year old Agnes Gully was living with her granddaughter Lela Anderson in Newton, Mississippi. (*More on Preston Johnson in The Johnson Petry/Petree Story*)

Amanda Johnson was living with Richmond Gibson and his wife and their children and with her four year old, Sarah Johnson. [Amanda may possibly be the sister of Filmore Johnson](*The Johnson Petry Family History)*

Dock Johnson was born into slavery in 1843, possibly in Jasper County, Mississippi. When Dock and his parents were freed they managed to buy a small piece of land for farming. His father died before 1880. His mother, Hager Richardson, was listed as a widow in the 1880 census. Hager was living on the farm with her son, Dock Johnson, and his wife, Catherine, and their children: Martha E., Lamer and Judge. Also living with the family was Laura Gibson Dock's fourteen year old niece. According to family research writer Darrell Fielder, Dock Johnson was married four times. In 1885, Dock enrolled his children in the Good Hope Freedmen Settlement School. Dock and his family were living adjacent to George Youngblood and the Preston Johnson I farms. The 1910 census shows sixty seven year old Dock Johnson was married to thirty two year old Louisa Fielder.(*Nothing more was uncovered as of this printing date in reference to Laura Gibson.)*

Lucy Johnson was living in the Good Hope Community in 1940, with her grandparents: one hundred and three year old Frank Petree II and eighty three year old Louisa Salter Petree. (*The Johnson Petry Family History more on Louise Salter in the Salter of Good Hope Colored Community)*

William Johnson was born in 1908 [parents unknown]. In 1920, when he was twelve years old he was listed in the Mississippi Census living with his aunt Rilla Cook Johnson in the Good Hope Colored Settlement. (*The Johnson Petry Family History)*

Henry Johnson married Betsy Anderson, daughter of Moses and Elizabeth Anderson. They had a daughter, Cherry Johnson. Cherry married Cason Salter and had several children. Cason and Cherry lived in the Good Hope Settlement for many years where she served the community as a midwife. Cherry died of heart lesion in 1928. Research shows beginning in 1940 some of her children had left the community for the North. Sometime after Cherry's death Cason relocated to Chicago where he lived with his children until his death. (*More on Cason Salter see The Salter of Good Hope Colored Community)*

Milton Johnson was born in Georgia enslaved. By 1870, Milton was living in Beat 5 of rural Hickory in Newton County, Mississippi. Living with Milton was his wife, Sarah, and six children who were working with him on a small farm. (*Nothing more was uncovered as of this printing date in reference to Milton Johnson that connect him to the Petry/ Johnson line*)

Frank Johnson in 1880, was listed as head of household living in the Good Hope Settlement with his wife, Jane Blalock, and an infant son, William Johnson. William was born on February 8, 1880. *Nothing more was uncovered as of this printing date in reference to Frank Johnson that connect him to the Petry/ Johnson line)*

Emma Lee Johnson was listed in the 1880 census documented as a widow living with her brother, Seaborne Lee I in the Good Hope Settlement with her children: Willie Johnson, age 11 and 9 year old Archie Johnson. Additional information pertaining to Willie and Archie Johnson was not found during this research period. *(See more on Seaborne Lee I The Salter of Good Hope Colored Community The Johnson Petry Family History)*

The Jones Family

The Slaveholding Jones Family

Levitt L. Jones (White male) was born on November 19, 1842, and died on January 7, 1919, and is buried in Chunky Newton County. Levitt parents were Henry Jones and Frances Dorrouch. Cause of death: paralysis. Informant: Miss Sallie Jones. Henry D. Jones held nineteen people enslaved and had three slave houses.

Cofield Ellis was born in 1822, and came into Mississippi possibly to Lauderdale County in about 1845. His son, Eli W. Ellis, came to Clark County, Mississippi in about 1920 with his wife, Mary, and four children. Living with the family was Edd Jones, born in 1864, listed as a single White servant. (*Ed Jones was born in 1864. The 1910 census shows forty six year old Ed Jones listed as "White" and was living in Enterprise, Clark County, Mississippi with Eli W. Ellis, his wife, Nancy and their four children. Relationship to head of household was shown as "Servant.")*

The Freedmen Jones Family

Britta Pruitt a family member wrote *"Ed Jones was the father of Sam Jones, Henry Jones and Mary Jones and Jo, Francis Jones Ellis. His first wife was Vina Kirby Jones. Vina Jones was of Indian descent. She had many children and appears on the census up until 1900. After that, she disappears. It is not known if she died or just went back to live on a reservation. Ed Jones's mother was black, but I think his father was white. I have a hunch that his father might have been a man named Levitt L. Jones, but I am not for sure"* (Britta Pruitt wrote more- see information on the Pruitt of Newton County)

Anabella Jones was born enslaved in 1844 in Virginia to a woman born in Virginia and to a father [no names shown] born in Africa. (*Information listed in the 1870 census*) By 1870, Anabella Jones was listed living in rural Hickory, Mississippi. Living in the household with Anabella was four of her children: nine year old Ida Jones, eight year old Matilda Jones, six year old Ed Jones I and four year old Wiley Jones. All were listed as Mulattoes. Also in the residence was an unidentified young man, seventeen year old William Fielder. (*See William Estell Fielder*)

According to family, Annabella Jones was a domestic servant to Henry and Frances Jones and allegedly had children by Levi Jones, son of Henry and Frances Jones. Some years later she married William Fielder and had several children. (*See William Estell Fielder*)Family members believe twenty six year old Anabella Jones, a Mulatto woman, was ravished by the slaveholder when she was very young. Over the years she had four Mulatto children: Ida Jones, Matilda Jones, Edward Jones, and Wiley Jones. Anabella's daughter, Matilda Jones, ten years later, experienced the same ill treatment at age sixteen as her mother. (*"I know these facts will seem too awful to relate," warns former enslaved man William J. Anderson in his1857 narrative, "... as they are some of the real dark deeds of American Slavery."*)

Matilda Jones the daughter of Anabella Jones, a Mulatto woman, was born in Mississippi into slavery in 1862. She was freed the following year after President Lincoln signed the Emancipation Proclamation of 1863. The 1880 census shows eighteen year old Matilda's residence as Newton, Mississippi and working as a "servant." Living with Matilda was her son, two year old Ed Jones II, born in 1911. (*Listed in the 1880 census*)

Ed Jones I, the son of Anabella Jones, was born in 1864, and lived at home with mother until he was twenty one years old. The 1900 census shows Ed Jones was married to Vina Jones in 1885.They had eight children listed: beginning with fifteen year old Rachel, followed by fourteen year old Mack, fourteen year old Anna Bella, thirteen year old Robert, twelve year old Matilda, eleven year old Josephine, five year old Emma and lastly four year old John M. Jones. The 1900 census shows Ed Jones and Vina Jones had been married for fifteen years and were living in rural Hickory in Newton County.

J Ed Jones II was born in 1870. The 1910 census shows Ed Jones was married to Emma Jones. J Ed Jones and Emma over the years had ten children: five daughters; Matilda, Josephine, Emma, Edna and Carrie plus five sons; Mack, Robert, John, Otis and Charles. The 1930 census shows fifty year old Emma and sixty year old Ed were living in rural Newton County and owned and worked his farm with his two grandsons: eighteen year old Willie Jones and sixteen year old James Jones. Emma worked as a washerwoman in the community. Emma Jones died three years later on April 8, 1933 and is buried in Newton, Mississippi. (*Emma China was born in 1875 to Tom and Ella China*)

Willey Jones The son Of Annabella Jones was born in 1868. He married Ina/ Hanner Davis [exact name not known] and they had a daughter, Judy. Judy Jones married Simon Pruitt of Jasper County, Mississippi and they had a daughter they also named Judy. Judy Pruitt married Will Salter and relocated to the Good Hope Colored Settlement. Will and Judy Pruitt Salter had five daughters and one son. (*More on Will Salter see the Salter of Good Hope Colored Settlement*)

Mack Jones was born in 1887 in Mississippi. Mack married Margret Jones and they lived and farmed in the Beat 5 area of Newton County, Mississippi. The 1940 census only shows some of the Jones children living in their father's household: Mary, a son Mack Jones II, Lewis, Clarence, Argimae, Edna and Bobbie J.

Sam Jones was born in 1890 in Mississippi. In the 1930 census he was married to Josephine Jones with six daughters: Bertha age sixteen, Annie age fifteen, Francis ae fourteen, Maud age twelves, Lucy age ten and Mary Jones age six.

Mary Jones married Charlie Watkins. (*Brita Pruitt wrote*)

Lucy Jones lived in Newton, Mississippi on Jones Street. Family member Britta Jones attests that she may not live in her home now, "but I was told by my aunt Mary Lois, the sister of Jo Francis, that Jones Street in Newton, Mississippi was named after her because it was the only house on the block." (*Brita Pruitt wrote*)

Emma Jones was born in 1880. (*Brita Pruitt wrote*)

Ned Jones was born to Amy Jones. He married Eliza Jones. (*Brita Pruitt wrote*)

Frank Jones married Mildred Cole, a widow, in 1906. Frank and Mildred had two children. By 1910, their son, Shelly, was three years old and daughter, Lenora, was a one year old. The 1910 census shows Frank and Mildred had settled on a larger farm adjoining Dan and Adeline Youngblood in the Good Hope Community. (*See Turner Cole- Mildred Cole)*

Mack Jones was listed in the 1910 census married to Georgia Robinson. Mack and Georgia had been married two years and was living in Township 6 Range 17 in Newton County. On June 27, 1918 Newton County death record shows a still born baby boy was born to the couple. Mack and his wife, Georgia, buried their unnamed child in Shiloh Cemetery in Hickory, Mississippi. (*Newton County death records)*

Britta Pruitt wrote: "Does anyone know of or has any information about people with the names of Pruitt or Jones in Newton County, Mississippi? Specifically I am looking for any information about Sam Jones, Josephine Jones, Ed Jones, Emma Jones, Vina Kirby and Margaret Davis around 1880-1930. All of these people are African-Americans or part Indian. I checked most of the information about Newton County and information for African American records are sparse to nil. Some other surnames connected to this family is McDonald and Watkins. Any information is greatly appreciated." Britta Pruitt

Native American Jones Family

(This Jones family is African-American of Native American lineage who lived in Newton County from 1880-1930. As of this printing information regarding African American Jones family in Newton County are sparse to nil. Some other surnames connected to this family are Davis, Kirby, McDonald and Watkins.) Britta Pruitt

Vina Kirby Jones was of Indian descent. She had many children and appears on the census up until 1900. After that she disappears. It is not known if she died or just went back to live on a reservation. *Britta Pruitt*

The Kirby Family

The Slaveholding Kirby Family

See Mary Kirby Story

The Freedmen Kirby Family

Doctor Kirby was born into slavery in North Carolina. He came to Newton County with his slaveholders. When he was freed he left the plantation and settled in the Good Hope Settlement with his wife, Salina, a washerwoman. Census record reveals Salina was born in 1830 in Alabama, enslaved. Nothing more is known of how and when she arrived in Newton County.

The Kidd Family

The Freedmen Kidd Family

Henry Kidd was born July 12, 1882 in Newton County. He married Bessie while living in the Good Hope Colored Settlement. Henry and Bessie had several children. One son, Jessie Kidd, was born on November 28, 1913 and died at age four months and was buried in Good Hope Cemetery. *(See more on Henry Kidd Moving up North)*

The Lee Family

Slaveholding Lee Family

The slaveholding Lee family had several plantations in North Carolina. Years later the slaveholding Lee family, along with their many enslaved workers, migrated to Georgia. Then the slaveholding family relocated again to the state of Mississippi in search of good fertile land as early as 1840.

Freedmen Lee Family

Jack Lee and Annie Stratton maintained a "slave marriage" while enslaved possibly on the Lee plantation in North Carolina. In 1827, a son, Seaborne Lee I, was born. The slaveholding family then relocated with Jack and Annie and young Seaborne I to the state of Mississippi in 1840. After he was emancipated, like other freedmen in the county, Seaborne I stayed on the plantation and worked; "just like we did in the real slavery days" he said. However, not long after the time of enslavement he began looking for land to homestead in the Colored Settlements.

Then thirty four year old Seaborne Lee I legalized his marriage to seventeen year old Harriett; the woman he had lived with during the time of enslavement. Seaborne I and Harriett had two sons and three daughters. In 1865, their first son, Liston, was born and by 1874 their second son, Seaborne II, was born and in 1876 a third child, Adeline, was born.

 In 1900, Seaborne I and Harriett had begun farming in the Good Hope Colored Settlement with four of their five children: Liston the eldest son and three daughters: Leona, Adeline and Willa. Seaborne II had married and no longer lived on the family farm. In 1910, eighty eight year old Seaborne I and sixty five year old Harriett continued to live on the farm with their son, Liston, and his wife, Frances Youngblood Salter and three of Frances' children by her late husband, Emmanuel Salter. Harriett died at age eighty five on April 14, 1923. Seaborne I, at age one hundred and three years old, died four months later on July 3, 1923. Both were buried in Good Hope Church Cemetery. *(Harriet Lee, resident of Hickory and wife of Sebron Lee age 85, born in Alabama, died April 14, 1923 and buried on May 15, 1923 at Good Hope. Father's name not given and only her mother's given name "Hannah" was on the death certificate. Hannah was born in Alabama. Cause of death: chronic nephritis.)*

Liston Lee was born in 1865; the first child born to Seaborne I and Harriett Lee. Liston was born during the time of Emancipation Proclamation. He had no recollection of the horrors of slavery days. Liston lived a few years on the Lee plantation with his parents until his father relocated to the Good Hope Freedmen Settlement. In 1910, Liston married Frances Salter, the widow of Emmanuel Salter who had died sometime before 1910. After Liston was married he stayed on and worked the farm with his parents. The 1910 census reports several generations of family members were living in the home with Liston and Frances. Included in the residence were the children by her late husband, Emanuel Salter: George Salter, age seven and Will Salter, age five and Moses. Also included in the home were Liston's elderly parents, Seaborne I and Harriett Lee, plus a young girl, Alice Salter age nine and a young woman, Nella, and her daughter, Ocie age two.

Seaborne Lee II was born in May 1874 in Mississippi. He was the second child born to Seaborne I and Harriett Lee. When he was 20 years of age, he left his father's farm and rented 14 acres of land from his father's former slaveholders and began farming. In 1897, when Seaborne chose a wife, like most of the young men, he married one of the young women in the community that he may had met at church or some other event.

He met and married Fannie Johnson, the daughter of Filmore and Bettie Levy Johnson. Fannie and Seaborne II had a son Fannie named Daniel in honor of her brother Reverend Daniel Johnson II. *(See more about Fannie in Family Legends and Lore The Complex Story of Filmore Johnson-Petry)*

Fannie Johnson Lee was born in August 1874, to Filmore and Bettie Levy Johnson She married Seaborne Lee II in 1897. They had one child during their marriage. Daniel Lee was born in May of 1874, in the Good Hope Settlement. Fannie died in Chicago, however, she was buried in the Good Hope Church Cemetery *(More about Fannie Johnson Lee in The Johnson Petree Story)*

Annie Lee was born in 1887, to Seaborne I and Harriett Lee. In 1900, twelve year old Annie was living in the Good Hope Settlement with her parents and two sisters, Leona Lee and Willa Lee. Years later she married Robert Johnson I, the son of Filmore and Bettie Johnson. *(More about Annie Lee and Robert Johnson in Johnson Story)*

Daniel Lee was born in January 1900 in rural Hickory, Mississippi in the Good Hope Settlement to Seaborne Lee II and Fannie Johnson Lee. While living in the Good Hope Community Daniel Lee married Missouri Christine Allen. They had a son, Felix Raymond Lee. Felix was born on April 4, 1918 in the Settlement. During the Great Migration Daniel relocated up North to Chicago, Illinois with his family. After the death of his father Seaborne II, Daniel moved his mother up to Chicago.

Fannie lived many years in Chicago mostly with her sister Sally Johnson Salter. Fannie died in Chicago and was buried in the Good Hope Church Cemetery in Mississippi. Daniel lived in Chicago for many years and died in Chicago. Missouri Christine died on July 4, 1995 in Chicago at the age of ninety four. Felix Lee continued to live in Chicago and had several children. As of this printing Felix had two known daughters, Lillian and Christine. Felix Lee died on September 9, 2000 in Chicago, Illinois, at the age of eighty two.(***Daniel Lee*** *was born in January 1900 in Good Hope Colored Settlement near Hickory, Mississippi. Daniel Lee married Missouri Lee in Mississippi and moved up to Chicago. Missouri was born on April 12, 1901 in Mississippi. She died on July 4, 1995 in Chicago, Cook County, Illinois. He died on September 26, 1989 in Chicago, Cook County, Illinois.)*

The Mc Carty Family

Slaveholding Mc Carty Family

The Family originally came from Stafford, Virginia with John Kelly in Pike

County, Mississippi.

Freedmen Mc Carty Family

Olive Mc Carty married Samuel Johnson. John A Mc Carty is listed in the 1920 census as Claud Dawkins grandson.

Peter Mc Carty was listed in the 1880 census living with Hardy Salter and was listed as Peter Salter, however, there was a line drawn through the name Salter and Mc Carty was added as his surname. *(See the Salter of Good Hope Colored Settlement)*

The McCune Family

The Freedmen McCune Family

Wade McCune and his wife, Mary Jefferson McCune, were born in Newton County. They were listed as parents on a death certificate of John McCune, a male child, age six, born in Newton County and died on February 13, 1920, and is buried in Good Hope Cemetery. Cause of death: pneumonia.

The McMillian Family

The Freedmen McMillian Family

Walter Mc Millan

Henry W. Mc Millan and his wife, Bessie Brown McMillian, lived in rural Hickory in the early 1930's with a son, Claude. Horace Mc Millan, a boarder and possibly the brother of Henry Mc Millan, was living with the family as well as Bessie's father, Islam H. Brown.

Otha McMillian was born in 1905 in Mississippi and lived in the Freedmen Settlement with his parents, three sisters and one brother. In 1930, Otha was listed living in the Settlement with his wife, Eunice Pruitt McMillian and two of his children: sons, Lern and Sam and a step daughter, eight year old Loraine Johnson. Also living with Otha were several siblings, three sisters: eighteen year old Ella McMillian, seventeen year old Lucile McMillian, fourteen year old Desiree and a brother, thirteen year old Thomas McMillian. *(More on Loraine Johnson in the in The Johnson Petree Story)*

The Mitchell Family

The Freedmen Mitchell Family

Joe and Maude Mitchell lived in the Stout Hill area of rural Hickory and ran a small farm and harvested timber, plus worked in the area saw mills. Their sons as of this printing were Jim and Oscar Mitchell. Jim married Sophie Dyes, the daughter of Louise Babe Salter Dyes and Henry Dyes. The other son, Oscar Mitchell, married Bernice Chapman. Bernice was born on in August 10, 1930 to Wesley and Erma Chapman in Garlandville, Mississippi. At a young age she worked with her parents in a logging camp where she met Oscar Mitchell. After her marriage on February 22, 1950 to Oscar Mitchell she relocated with her husband to the Good Hope Colored Community. Some years later they purchased timber land from Robert Pruitt. Oscar and Bernice had three children: James and Bernard Mitchell and a daughter, Sadie Wash Coleman. Oscar died in July 1986 and is buried in the Good Hope Church Cemetery. Bernice continued to live in the Settlement as a faithful Good Hope Church member until her death. She served as church clerk for many years. Bernice is in the photo on the cover of the book, she is the women on the left with a dear friend, Clatie Bell Edison and fellow Church member. *(United States Census 1920 database with images, wife: Maude, Children: Jim, Geneva, Oskar, Caroline Mitchell in household of Joe W Mitchell, Beat 4, Newton, Mississippi, United States; citing sheet 4B, NARA microfilm publication T625 (Washington D.C. National Archives and Records Administration, n.d.); FHL microfilm 1,820,888.)*

The Norman Family

The Slaveholding Norman Family

Willis Roy Norman, the central figure in the Norman families of Newton County, was a native of Wilkes County, Georgia, who arrived in Newton, County about 1842, in company with his brother, Jesse Norman. A second brother, William Norman, soon joined them. The 1860 Slave Census shows more planters who owned several thousand acres of land and many enslaved workers. William Norman held forty three enslaved laborers and had eighteen slave houses. His brother, Jesse Norman, held fourteen people enslaved and owned two slave houses.

The Freedmen Norman Family

Henry Norman (*See the Freeport Illinois section*)

Celia Norman married Rufus Morris. As of this printing only one child was born to the couple: a male child who died at birth on October 5, 1924 in Hickory and is buried at Good Hope Church Cemetery. Informant: Chaney Brown of Hickory.

Allen Norman was born enslaved in Virginia to John and Ester Norman in 1855. In the 1900 census Allen attested that he had been married to Lucinda, the women listed as his wife, for twenty two years. In the 1880 census Lucinda and Allen had the following children: Mack, E M, Walter, Mary M and Rehovah.

Walter Norman was born in 1883 in Newton County to Lucinda and Allen. He was the grandson of John Norman and the son of Walter Norman and the brother of Rehovah Norman. Rehovah Norman married Harrison Salter, the son of Cason and Cherry Salter. Walter died on April 2, 1943 and was buried in Shiloh Cemetery. Informant: Rehovah Norman Salter (*More on Rehovah Salter. See The Salter of Good Hope Colored Community*)

George Norman married Sarah Kidd. They had a daughter, Lula Norman. She was born in Newton County. She died on August 12, 1915 and is buried in Greenwood Cemetery. Informant: Jim Gillespie, Hickory. Cause of death: tuberculosis.

The Overstreet Family

The Overstreet slaveholders

The Overstreet slaveholders came into Mississippi first from North Carolina and lastly from Georgia in about 1840. The 1850 Slave Schedule of Newton County, Mississippi shows T R Overstreet was a slaveholder born in North Carolina.

The Freedmen Overstreet Family

Armerjean Overstreet known as AJ Overstreet was born in 1889 to Annie Overstreet in Newton County, Mississippi. In 1917, he was living in Lauderdale County where he registered in the World War I draft. In the 1930 census AJ Overstreet was a widower living in Newton County Beat 5 with several family members: Ann Overstreet his mother, a daughter eight year old Iree, a son seven year old Sherman and four year old Daretha Overstreet.

The Pruitt Family

The Freedmen Pruitt Family

Hatch Pruitt and his wife, Clarisse Pruitt, were part of the Pruitt family who were farmers in Newton County. Hatch and Lucy had several children. One son, Robert, was a farmer in the Good Hope area and a member of Good Hope Colored Baptist Church

Robert Pruitt was born in 1890 in Newton County, Mississippi. He and his wife, Maude, lived in an area of the Good Hope Settlement called Stout Hill. The Pruitts had several children: Cleo, Ollie, Ella and Hazel. Maude and Robert were members of Good Hope Church and were a significant part of the Good Hope Community.

Phil Pruitt and Cason Salter were neighboring farmers in the Colored Settlement of Good Hope. In due course Phil Pruitt married Alice Salter, Cason Salter's daughter. Over the years Phil and Alice had a large number of children: Emma, Ruth, Sarah, Ella, Lula, Lela, Cason II, Mattie, Moses, Aaron, Eunice and Susie. Cason II and Ruth died of tuberculosis; Cason in 1919, when he was twenty four years old and Ruth at twenty one years old. Both are buried at Good Hope Church Cemetery. Phil Pruitt died soon after. Alice was listed in the 1920 census as a widowed farmer living in rural Hickory in the Good Hope Colored Settlement.

Alice died on July 14, 1926 and was buried near her husband. *(See The Salter of Good Hope Colored Community)*Emma Pruitt married Walter Chapman and they had several children over the years: Dan, Ezekiel, Levi, Mandy, John, Charlie and Raleigh. Emma died in 1917 in Newton County, Mississippi. Sue Pruitt married John L Johnson, a grandson of Filmore Johnson and they had four children: Mary Ruth, Johnnie Ruth, Rosie Lee, and Amie Lee. Moses Pruitt was born in the Good Hope Colored Settlement to Alice and Phil Pruitt. He married Sophia Brown and had several children: Fred, Oscar, Kenny, Varnell, Okenell, Brooke Wilbur, Dub, Mary and Sonny. Aaron Pruitt also married into the Johnson family. He married Fannie, the daughter of Eliza Johnson Tullos and the granddaughter of Filmore Johnson. They had six children: Alonzo, Lenard, Grace, Thomas, Willie Mae and James T. Aaron and Fannie had contracted tuberculosis and died within a short time of each other. Eunice Pruitt married R McMillian and had two children, Loraine and Gilbert.

Wesley Pruitt was born in 1857, into slavery. At age seven, in 1863, he and millions of enslaved people were freed. As an adult Wesley worked in the city of Newton on Public Works and married Nancy Hitt. Nancy was born in 1858 to Richard Hitt and Angelina Powell of Newton, Mississippi. Wesley and Nancy had a daughter, Rose Pruitt. Rose died on November 4, 1919. Nancy died of apoplexy at age sixty five on November 12, 1923 and is buried in Newton County. Informant: Albert Curry Wesley Pruitt died on July 31, 1917

The Riley Family

The Freedmen Riley Family

William Riley and his wife, Nancy, were early settlers to the Good Hope area. William was born in 1875, and his wife, Nancy, was born in the same year. They, like others in the Colored Settlement, were farmers. By 1893, they had one child, Tommie. Also during this period Willie's younger brother, Matt Riley, was living with his brother and sister-in-law and working as a farm hand. In 1920, Willie and Nancy continued working the same farm. Also working on the farm with Willie and Nancy during this period was their son, Lemon and his wife, Annie B and their two daughters, Ella and Nancy.

The Russell Family

The Freedmen Russell Family

Mack Russell a farmer working on his own account was living in 1930 in Good Hope Colored Settlement. He was living with Mack and his wife, Lucania, and two children; John L Russell, Idell and Clarence born in 1930.

The Stephens Family

The Freedmen Stephens Family

Daniel Stephens was born into slavery in Alabama. At the end of the Reconstruction Period he lived in Clark County near Enterprise, Mississippi. He was married to Lea Hardy. Daniel and Lea had four daughters and three sons: Lizzie (Pinky) was born in 1868 Solomon the oldest son was born in 1872, James in 1874, Eliza in 1876, and Alafair in 1877, and Carly was born in 1878. While growing up in rural Hickory the children helped with work on the farm. Years later Eliza met and married John Brown. *(See John Brown)*

Pinky/Pinkie Stephens While growing up Pinkie lived with her parents, Daniel and Leah Stephens, in several places in Newton and other nearby counties. Possibly her parents were sharecropping and lived and worked for a while on different places. Pinkie her parents and her siblings: Solomon, James, Carly, and Alafair Stephens. They were listed in the 1870 census living in Northwest Beat, Jasper County, Garlandville, Mississippi and in 1880 in Clark County. (*Pinkie Stephens is believed to be the mother of Lilia Toles Johnson, the wife of Daniel Johnson II. See more of Pinkie Stephens with Oliver Toles the father of Lilia Toles*)

The living conditions for sharecroppers were harsh. Most lived in unpainted two to three room shacks near the fields with up to fifteen people living in one house. Their poor diets consisted primarily of cornmeal, salt pork, sorghum, and dry peas. Vegetable gardens were discouraged or prohibited by the landowner to force tenants to concentrate on growing the cash crop. Children worked in the fields with their parents. If they did go to school, it was usually for about six weeks a year. Homes were heated by wood or coal stoves with no indoor plumbing or electricity and usually no screens for the windows. Men wore denim overalls that they purchased, but shirts, dresses, sheets, and diapers were often home-made from feed and flour sacks. (*Encyclopedia of Southern Culture, Charles Reagan Wilson and William Ferris, Coeditors*)

Eliza Stephens, Pinkie's younger sister was born on December 12, 1876 in the Newton County, Mississippi to Daniel and Leah Stephens. Her obituary stated that she was born before Rutherford B. Hayes was President of the United States. Years later she met and married John Brown at an early age. The couple relocated to Joliet, Illinois with their children: a son, Willie Brown and a daughter, Lizzie Brown. Their children grew up in Joliet, married and had children of their own. Eliza and John Brown had two grandsons, Willie Jr. and Goodlow and four great grandchildren. Eliza died on October 4, 1984 at age one hundred and five. Eliza lived over a century on this earth. Eliza Stephens Brown lived a lot of history, her obituary states, "She lived through the tumultuous era of reconstruction when safeguards were removed that could have re- enslaved newly freed men, women and children. She lived through the birth of the Ku Klux Klan, the lynching of innocent people all over the South. She lived through the birth of the Jim Crow Laws designed to re- enslave the Freedmen. She also lived through the hard times of racism and through World War I. Eliza may have heard the words of Frederick Douglass demanding freedom. She may have heard the words of W.E. B Du Bois and Booker T. Washington. She lived through the Great Depression and World War II. She would have read about the Brown vs the Board of Education, not realizing that one of her young descendants, Rubin Salter II, would be one of the attorneys for the NAACP. She was part of the Civil Rights Movement with Dr. Martin Luther King and was able to vote for the first time in the South." (*Eliza Stephens Brown obituary shows her grandchildren living in Buffalo New York. (Information taken from the Obituary of Eliza Stephens Brown) (See John Brown)Researched documents did not uncover any additional information pertaining to Daniel and Leah Stephens children: Solomon Stephens, James Stephens Cely Stephens and Alafair Stephens as of this printing.)*

Tanksley Family

The Freedmen Tanksley Family

Isaac Tanksley married Viola Brown and had a child, Inez. Inez died at age six in 1925, during the influenza epidemic and was buried at Good Hope Church Colored Cemetery.

The Thompson Family

Possible Slaveholders

Duncan Thompson reported eighteen enslaved people in Newton County in 1840.

The Freedmen Thompson Family

Luke Thompson was born in 1802 in Virginia. He married Lena Levy see 1870 census living in Township 5 Range 11, Newton, Mississippi with his wife, Lena Thompson and Mary Thompson; an unidentified relative.

Berry Thompson was born in South Carolina enslaved in 1809. In 1870, when he was sixty one years old, Berry was farming in Newton County in the developing Settlement of Good Hope, Newton County, Mississippi. Living with Berry was his wife, Caroline Thompson, age sixty one and several others possibly the grown children of Berry and Caroline: Julia Thompson age thirty five, Panetta Thompson age thirty, Alexander Thompson age twenty, Martin Thompson nineteen and nine year old Amos Thompson.

Philip Thompson was born into slavery in Mississippi. After he was emancipated he moved away from the Thompson slaveholders as soon as he was able to start his own farm. Philip was able to obtain land in rural Hickory, Mississippi. By 1884, he was married and had started a family. In 1884, a son, Walter, was born.

Walter Thompson married Dora (maiden name not known) and worked a farm in the Good Hope Settlement. As of 1920, Walter and Dora had the following children: Johnnie Thompson, Jessie Thompson and Tereatha Thompson.

Panetta Thompson was born in 1844 in South Carolina. The 1920 United States Federal Census shows Panetta Thompson a seventy six year old widow living in Newton County with her son, Martin Thompson, born in 1864, in Alabama and a Martin Patterson, age 14, possibly a grandson.

David Thompson The father of Charles Thompson

Charles Thompson and his wife, Ann, lived in the Good Hope Community in the early 1880's. The Thompson's had three children during that period. In the census the first child listed was Mary six years old, Eudora was three and the baby Frank was six months old. Charles's father, David Thompson, was living with the family along with a young girl, thirteen year old Emily Hardy.

Edward Thompson was born enslaved in South Carolina. In later years he would be removed to Mississippi by his slave masters. There he met and married Caroline [maiden name not known]. Edward and Caroline may have had several children. One known son was William Thompson.

William Thompson was born on February 28, 1867 in Mississippi. William worked with his father on a small farm in Newton County. Later he worked a farm of his own near the town of Hickory. In 1919, at the age of fifty seven William died. On his death records the place of burial was not stated. Informant: John Thompson

Hester Thompson was born in 1855, enslaved in Mississippi. The 1910 census shows Hester Thompson, a widow farming in Newton County with Loula Whitehead, Clara Eddy and J B Stell.

Jack Thompson married Eliza Tillman, the daughter of Reed Tillman and Emma Klein Tillman. In 1918 when the couple had been married only eight years Eliza died after being exposed to measles, leaving Jack with five children: the eldest daughter, Lillie Mae, was born 1906 and a son, Herman, was born in 1907.

Odessa was born in 1909. Ossie was four years old when his mother died. In 1920 Jack Thompson and his family lived in Beat 5 of Newton County on a farm adjacent to the Frank Petree farm. Three year old Evia and one year old Sylvester, the youngest of the Thompson children, were being cared for by Jack's sister, Anna Arrington. Also living with the large family was Anna's four year old daughter, Susie Arrington.

In 1930 Jack remarried and relocated with some of his children to Police Jury Ward 8, Concordia, Louisiana, where he met his second wife, Eldaria [maiden name not known] Thompson. Eldaria was born 1895 and was twenty years old when she married Jack. (*Source Citation Year: 1910, 1920; Census Place: Township 5 Range 17, Newton, Mississippi; Roll: T624_753; Page: 19A; Enumeration District: 0095; FHL microfilm: 1374766 Source Citation plus Year: 1930; Census Place: Police Jury Ward 8, Concordia, Louisiana; Roll: 789; Page: 8A; Enumeration District: 0011*)

The Tillman Family

The Freedmen Tillman Family

Emma Tillman was born in August of 1865 in Sumter County, Alabama. She was the wife of Reed Tillman and a resident of Hickory, Mississippi. On January 22, 1918 their daughter, Liza Thompson, died in Wickware and is buried in Good Hope Cemetery. One year later Emma Tillman died when she was fifty four years old on September 7, 1919.

The Toles Family

The Freedmen Toles Family

Miner Toles was born in 1848, into slavery in Virginia. He had an enslaved marriage with an enslaved girl, Mary, born in Alabama. As of this printing research did not uncover any records proving who held Miner and Mary and their children enslaved during that period. However, by the 1880 census the family was living in Beat 4 in Newton County on rented land with four children: Oliver age twelve, Joana age eight, Olivia and Octavia twins age five, plus a fourteen year old, Clay Toles not identified.

Oliver Toles was born in 1868 in Newton County, Mississippi. The census records shows Oliver had a previous marriage. Personal documents such as Bible records show it was to Pinkie Stephens. A child, Lila Toles, was born to that union in January 1887. On December 14, 1899, Oliver Toles married Elizabeth/ Lizzie Amis/Ammos. Lizzie was born in 1864 to George Amis/ Ammos and Sallie Vernon. The 1900 census shows Oliver Toles living with his family in Newton County in the village of Conehatta. In 1910, Oliver Toles continued to live in Conehatta with his wife, Lizzie Toles, and eighteen year old Leona Wethers, listed as a stepdaughter. Lilia Toles married Daniel Johnson in 1904, and would not have been living in her father's household during this period. She was possibly married at age seventeen and her first child, France, was born in 1904. *(Marriage Records from 1907 -1911 were destroyed by fire in 1911in Newton County)*

In 1920, Oliver Toles, his wife, Lizzie and their daughter, Leona Wethers and grandson, Essie J. Toles, continued to work a farm in Conehatta. Their grandson, Essie Toles, died in 1919. His death records show his mother was Leona [no last name given and no father stated].

From 1930, until their death Oliver C. Toles and wife, Lizzie/ Elizabeth Toles, were lifelong residents in the village of Conehatta. Both Oliver and his wife, Elizabeth Amis Toles, are buried in the Conehatta Cemetery. *(1920 census records shows Lizzie Amis Toles was the mother of three children) (Oral tradition holds that Lillie Toles Johnson was born to Oliver Toles and Pinky Stephens). (See Pinkie Stephens)*

The Tullos Family

The Freedmen Tullos Family

Elisha Preston Tullos the son of Eliza Johnson and Stephen A Tullos married Esther Gaddis in Hickory, Mississippi in 1927.They had two sons, Gaddis Steven and James Curtis. Elisha's early life was spent as a farmer in the Good Hope Settlement. In 1936, he relocated with his family to Chicago and acquired a job with the Pennsylvania Railroad where he worked until he retired in 1972. Esther had died two years earlier. Over the years he longed for the chance to get back to doing what he loved best; farming and working the land he loved. Then soon after his retirement he bought a small farm in St Anne, Illinois, where he grew his fruits and vegetables until his death in 1988.

Stephen A Tullos was born in 1874 in Newton County, Mississippi and was a lifelong resident of the Good Hope Colored Settlement. The 1900 census shows Stephen A Tullos was married to his first wife, Alice Salter Tullos. Alice was the daughter of Frank and Dora Garner Salter. The Tullos' lived on the farmland adjacent to the James Gaddis farm. Reverend Stephen A. Tullos was also the pastor of the newly built Good Hope Church. He was said to have been a teacher and was called "Fessa Tills" by some community members. A family elder, Broomsy Salter said, "before the church and the school was built Reverend Tullos went into the homes of settlement members evening to teach, especially those boys who were not able to attend school during normal hours because of farm chores." Alice Salter Tullos died in 1905, giving birth to a child who was his stepdaughter and he named her Ruby Maddox. (*The Salter of Good Hope Colored Community*)

Ruby Maddox Tullos was raised by her grandmother, Dora Garner Salter. Connie, the granddaughter of Ruby Tullos Harris, wrote, "I am a member of the Salter family through my grandmother Ruby. Ruby was a niece of Isaac, Anna and Willie Salter. Alice Salter Tullos, the daughter of Frank and Dora Garner Salter died in childbirth and Ruby was raised by her grandmother, Dora Salter. My grandmother Ruby married Stephen Abraham Tullos, a Minster and had three children: Abraham, Mary Alice and a son who died at a young age. Mary [Alice] is my mother and she had three children: two sons, Tullos and Lee and myself [Connie]. Her brother Abraham had ten children and lived on a farm in Mobile, Alabama until his death. Most of his children are living in Mobile on the property he owned at the time of his death." *(Connie had one child, Christopher, and they at the time of this writing lived in San Francisco. Her brother Tullos has two children ,Tullos Jr. who is 35 years old and Michelle 37 they all live in New Jersey. Michelle has one child, a girl named Ashley, age 6. Her brother Lee has one child age 18, and her name is Lindsey. Lindsey lives in Cleveland. My brother Lee lives in Pittsburg, California (See The Salter of Good Hope Colored Community)*Reverend Stephen A. Tullos died in 1890. Ruby died in 1980, and both are buried in the Good Hope Colored Settlement Cemetery.

The Wall Family

The Slaveholding Family

Thomas Wall held as few as two enslaved workers in Newton County in 1860.

The Freedmen Wall Family

Frank Wall was born in 1897, and married Julia and lived near Hickory in the Beat 5 area of Newton County. Julia was born in 1909, and their son John F. Wall was born in 1920.

General Wall I a Mulatto was born in 1884 in Mississippi. He married Nerva [unknown last name] in 1904. In the 1910 census General and Neva Wall were living in Township 5 Range 17 in Newton, County, Mississippi with five children: Robert, General II age four, Mattie age two and Pinkie Wall age one. (*General Wall II is said to be the half-sister of Lilia Toles.*) (*See Who was Lilia Toles? What is her Story?*)

The Wash Family

The Freedmen Wash Family

Henrietta Wash was born in Newton County, the daughter of Rowan Garner and Sallie Norman in September 1882. She was a resident of rural Hickory until she died in 1918, at age thirty two and was buried at Shiloh. Informant: Rowan Norman. Cause of death: tuberculosis

The Watts Family

The Freedmen Watts Family

Early Watts was born in 1888 in Newton County, Mississippi. In 1908, he married Ida [maiden name not known] and settled on a farm in the Good Hope Community near the Jack Thompson homestead. In 1920, the Watts had several children: Master was born in 1909, Frank was born in 1910, and Effie was born in 1912.

The Walker Family

Slaveholding Walker Family

From 1840 until 1860, planters such as James Walker, Benjamin Walker, Hiram Walker, and Henry Walker held a large number of enslaved workers in Newton County.

The Freedmen Walker Family

Nelson Walker was born into slavery in Tennessee. Along the way he met Angel [maiden name not known] who was born into slavery in Alabama. The couple had several children: one known daughter, Angelina, who became the first wife of Frank Petry. Angelina Petry was born into slavery She married Frank Petry at an early age and they had several children. Angelina died on April 7, 1921, and was buried at the old Colored Good Hope Cemetery on Fellowship Road. (*More about Angie in Book Two The Johnson Petry/Petree Story)*

Clemon Walker was born in Newton County near the end of slavery. He married Lucinda Tullos and had a number of children. As of this printing only two daughters have been identified: Mae Bell Walker and Clemmie Lee Walker. Mae Bell met and married her first husband, L. B. Johnson, at a young age. After the death of her first husband, she married Worthy Lee Loving. After the death of her second husband, she relocated to East Saint Louis, Illinois in 1968. Clemmie Lee was educated in the Newton County public school however, she never married. Clemmie died in early 1900's.

The Williams Family

The Freedmen Williams Family

Frank Williams was born in 1869 in Ohio. He migrated to Newton County in the early 1900s. In 1910, Frank was married to Addie Salter, daughter of Frank and Dora Salter. He purchased farm land in the Good Hope area in about 1920, and over a ten year period the couple had four children: Arthur, J.Q, Seymour and Albert. Addie Salter Williams died in 1920, and in that same year, on April 25, 1920, fifty year old Frank Williams married twenty three year old Mary Ella Pruitt, daughter of Simon Pruitt of Jasper County, Mississippi. *(See more JQ, Seymore and Albert Arthur The Salter of Good Hope Colored Community Up North to Freeport, Illinois and to Washington DC in 1940 James Williams Black male, born and died August 8, 1916, Park's Mill, and buried at Good Hope. Parents: Frank Williams and Adie Salter. Addie Salter Williams, Black married female and resident of Hickory. Born June 17, 1894, Newton County, and age 35-1-2. Died July 19, 1919 and buried in Good Hope Cemetery. Parents: Frank Salter (born Newton County) and Dora Garner (born Newton County). Cause of death: nephritis)*

The Wright Family

The Freedmen Wright Family

Alfred Wright married Willie Youngblood Salter, a widow living in Good Hope Settlement in the 1930's. Six of Reverend Alfred and Willie Wright's children were living at home in 1940: Vista, Jeannette, Ora C, Edna, Bonnie, and Vincent. After 1940, more children were born: Ben and Willie. *(See more on Charlie Salter in the Salter Family of The Good Hope Colored Settlement)*

An article of The Freeport Journal-Standard Newspaper stated, "Mrs. Willie Wright,with her children; Edna, Bonnie, and other relatives; the Youngbloods, the Edisons, the Salters, the Normans, the Kidds, the Johnsons, the Haydens, the Pruitts and others in the Freeport Community felt the real pain of the Vietnam War when Sgt. Willie A. Wright was killed in action in South Vietnam on November 6, 1967. Some of the pain a few weeks later, turned into a feeling of patriotic pride when he was awarded a Silver Star posthumously. The headline in the Freeport Journal-Standard said, Freeport Mother [Willie Wright] Given Silver Star. The newspaper reported that the nation's third highest award for gallantry in action was award posthumously Wednesday night to Army Sgt. Willie A. Wright of Freeport, Illinois, Born in 1939 in Good Hope, Mississippi. Sgt. Willie Wright, 29, was killed in action in South Vietnam on November 6, 1967. He was assigned to Company B 4th 173rd Airborne Brigade.

His mother, Willie Youngblood Wright of East Crocker Street, a native of Good Hope Mississippi now living in Freeport, Illinois received the award citation in ceremonies conducted at the VFW Post H 678. Members of the Freeport Army Reserve Unit, headed by Col. Warren T. Rafferty, formed a special honor guard for the ceremonies. Mrs. Wright, who is confined to a wheelchair, pressed the medal to her lips after receiving it from Col. Phillips. A citation accompanying the award was read, detailing Sgt. Wright's actions which led to his death and the Silver Star. Sgt. Wright was cited for unhesitatingly and with complete disregard for his personal safety pulling wounded comrades from under enemy fire. He was killed, the citation said, when he returned, under fire, to pull a second wounded soldier to safety. Sgt. Wright was leading a squad of men on a search-and-destroy mission assigned to take a South Vietnam hilltop when he and his men came under heavy fire. He had been wounded five times in previous action, although none of the wounds were serious."

The Youngblood Family

The Freedmen Youngblood Family

George Youngblood I was born in in 1844 in Mississippi, enslaved. Years later after he was freed he was able to rent a small plot of land and was living in the Chunkyville area with his wife, Sylvia and his children: Martha, Edwin, Daniel, Spann L. Francis. The family was listed in the census as Mulattos. George Youngblood I died before 1930. The 1930 census shows eighty year old Sylvia Youngblood a widow living with her son, George Youngblood II and daughter-in- law, Ida Dyes Youngblood and eight of their children in rural Newton County.

Daniel Youngblood married Adeline Youngblood. He died in 1934, in East St Louis, Illinois.

Frances Youngblood married Emmanuel Salter and had three children. After Emmanuel died, Francis married Liston Lee, the son of Harriett and Seborne Lee I. (*More on Emmanuel and Francis Youngblood Salter see The Salter of Good Hope Colored Settlement*) George Youngblood II married Ida Dyes, the daughter of Matthew and Lucinda Dyes and had several children: Thomas, West, Warren, Lucinda, Daniel, Francis, Nannie Mae, George III, Virginia, Otha, Ida II, Connie, Matthew, Pete, Ida Jean, Ruby, and Connie.

CHAPTER TWELVE

Good Hope Colored Settlement

The Community Expanded

The Early 1910 -1920

In the fifty years following the Emancipation Proclamation the Good Hope farmer had achieved a remarkable effort. They got their own land! Many other Freedmen and many poor Whites were trapped in the terrible sharecropping system. In the ten years between 1910 and 1920, the Colored Settlement had developed to some extent and by 1920 the Settlement was fully developed. It is said by family elders that the Colored Settlement farmers had a long and challenging struggle to obtain their own land and maintain ownership. Many had worked long years as tenant farmers with a limited and often total lack of opportunity to achieve land ownership. Yet land ownership did happen and the community rapidly expanded in the early years. The population of documented settlers rose from about one hundred to four hundred during that period. They were no longer bound together as a "slave community". The residents of the Good Hope Colored Settlement unified themselves as family, farms and community.

By 1930, even more farmers in the community owned land. Several filed land claims on adjacent acreages between the town of Hickory and the Jasper County line to create a large section of contiguous farm and timber land throughout the settlement. (*such as the Johnson Salter and other families in the community*) The Federal Government had a program to sell land, plows and tools cheaply and many took the offer. Land ownership increased. By the beginning of 1940, most farmers in Good Hope Colored Settlement had acquired full ownership of their small farms. These new land owners soon realized, with both tenant farming and with land ownership farming, that supporting a family was challenging. Nonetheless, many agreed that land ownership farming fared much better than sharecropping.

An elder, Broomsy Salter, remembered his father, Isaac Salter, saying "Starting a farm took some money and money was hard to come by." Some remembered, "The first land owners to the Good Hope Settlement had suffered many inconveniences and endured many hardships. Things such as grist mills and saw mills were unknown in the area. Later the Settlement would boast of having a grist mill for grinding corn and a cane mill for making syrup. In an interview with eighty year old Opal Johnson Ford, the granddaughter of Filmore Johnson, she said, "Supplies such as cloth, shoes, nails and other rations were brought in from New Orleans, by Grandpa Filmore, a ten days journey away." Slowly the area began to resemble a thriving rural community. Most families owned a wagon, a plow and two good mules. Little shanties gave way to substantial small houses.

Behind the houses were smoke houses used for curing and storing meat. Also there were chickens in the yards for eggs and eating, hogs for butchering, cows for milking and a large truck patch that provided vegetables for eating, canning and preserving. Fruit and pecan trees and wild berries were plentiful. The majority of farms were family run and provided subsistence and a small income through the sale or trading of any surplus goods. The families often shared livestock, tools and labor as well as worked, played and prayed together. They had long established networks of support among themselves. These networks, consisting of blood relatives and beyond, it most often took the form of an extended family. Family helped family and neighbor helped neighbor. Within such a framework, the settlement increased despite all odds.

CHAPTER THIRTEEN

Timber and Sawmills Impacted

The Good Hope Colored Community

After World War I cotton prices began to drop. To decrease their dependence on cotton Mississippi farmers, both Colored and White, turned to timber. During this period timber created one of the most important crop productions. The sawmills and lumber camps that multiplied in the areas near the Good Hope Settlement created, for the local population, ample opportunities for employment. To help sustain their families many left the farm and went to work for the lumber companies and sawmills in the area. Few natural resources impacted the lives of Mississippians to the degree which timber did. In particular, the southeastern and south central regions of the state received the label "piney woods" because the dominant features of the region consisted of longleaf, shortleaf, loblolly and slash pines. Their use of timber, in particular the pine, influenced the economic, cultural and environmental development of the entire region. *(Researched **By Reagan Grimsley**)(Timber Related Source Materials about Mississippi's Piney Woods: An Archival Survey of the McCain Library and Archives at the University of Southern Mississippi)(Some information in this chapter was taken from work researched **By Reagan Grimsley**)*

In 1910 and 1920, sawmills operated by: George W Griffin, J R Buckwalter Lumber Company, Jim Massie, Martin Carson and the Hogue Lumber Company were all operating in Newton County. In the 1930's, 1940's, and into the 1950's, Eugene White owned and operated sawmills in the near vicinity of the Good Hope Colored Settlement. One sawmill operated by Eugene White was located in Northeast Jasper County and in 1940's he operated sawmills in Chunky. Several descendants still living in Good Hope Community remember working with their parents at the mills. Others recalled hauling timber to the mills in the area. When the men and women who had grown up working on the farm took jobs in the lumber industry some became loggers, truck drivers, sawmill and planning mill workers, and cooks.

CHAPTER FOURTEEN

Good Hope Settlement and The Great Depression

The Great Depression changed the lives of all farmers in Newton County, both Colored and "Whites". The elders said some farmers fared better than the town folks. Many farm families raised most of their food: eggs and milk, butter and beef from their own cows and vegetables from their gardens. This was all true. However, other problems were arising when labor forces on the farms were decreasing. Many young men and women left the family farms in the Colored Settlement in search of any job they could get. As a result of the labor shortage some crops were not planted and revenue from that crop was lost and land taxes were not paid. In the midst of all these factors the farming community of Good Hope made it through the hardships they had suffered. "Tough times aint nothin' new for Colored folk in Good Hope," said eighty year old Opal Johnson Ford. (Granddaughter of Filmore Johnson)

The Good Hope Settlement The Later Years

By the late 1930's and early 1940's Good Hope Colored Settlement emerged as a prosperous farming settlement. These families have been living quiet, comfortable lives for more than three generations as proud hard workers. They owned their homes and the land. Families in the community were bound together by blood and by history and physically by close proximity; they shared the same needs, desires, histories and the same life stories. Only a few written stories regarding their lives from this times period were left behind. To get a better view of their lives and an understanding regarding the relationships within the settlement it can best be made first by ascertaining the times, places and proximities in which they lived. For this purpose the 1940 census records and information from the few remaining settlement members were one of the best means in constructing and rebuilding the agrarian Settlement of Good Hope, Mississippi in Newton County.

How did the 1940 Mississippi Census help? The 1940 census was taken by census takers going door to door and collecting information in specified districts. To insure that no person was omitted from the enumeration and was counted at the beginning of the census day, on April 1, 1940, in rural districts, every farmhouse, shanty, barn, and out building or other places in which a person might live were visited by the enumerator or census takers in successive residential order.

The census records also helped in confirming and revealing neighboring farmers in the Good Hope Settlement; as well as the values of their homes, farms or timberlands and other properties. Plus, it allowed glimpses into the personal lives of the residents such as: did they own or rent, married or single, their occupations and the numbers of children living in the household. (*Enumeration district boundaries have changed over the years. So it is entirely plausible that even if an ancestor appears in the same enumeration district in consecutive censuses, he or she may be in a different district for 1940.*)

An example: Joyce Johnson was born on September 10, 1939 in Newton County, Beat 5, District 12, in Good Hope, Mississippi. Joyce Johnson was six months old when the census taker [enumerator] came to her father's house on that April day in 1940. Archie and his wife, Edna Hayden Johnson, reported to the enumerator that he owned forty acres of mostly timberland which was gifted from his father, Daniel Johnson II. They reported five children living in their household: Alline, Emma, and twins Daniel and Doris, plus six month old Joyce Johnson. *Joyce Salter Johnson*

The listing below is of families whose places of residence after April 1, 1930, and on April 1, 194,0 were in the section of Beat 5, District 12 known as the Good Hope Colored Settlement. According to the 1940 census and family historians and family elders The Good Hope Freedmen Settlement's dwelling places are listed here in successive order whenever possible, beginning with the first homestead visited by the enumerator [census taker]. (*Some family dwelling may be listed as adjacent to, or near, or across from, the next farm or dwelling nearby or down the road no exact distance is noted.*)

CHAPTER FIFTEEN

The Colored Settlement of Good Hope

The Red Dirt Road

The red dirt road *[Good Hope Church Road]* running through the settlement, heading north from the Jasper County line to Hickory, was made by the settlers' wagons for the purpose of trading in the town of Hickory for goods and sundries not grown on the farm. Many Good Hope Church members lived just outside of the Good Hope Community near Hickory in an area known as Stout Hill. Four known families were: the Mitchells, the Robert Pruitt family, Joe and Mattie Gipson and their children: George, Mattie Maud, Mildred, Myrtle, Minnie Ruth, Elona, Grace, Fred, Floyd and Austrila. Living near the Gipsons' were Frank Petry II and his second wife, Louise "Babe" Salter Petry and Louise's children from her first marriage: Sophia and Henry Dyess.

The red dirt road through Good Hope began at what is now Highway 503 and it runs its way through the community which commences a few miles from the Claud and Sylvia Dawkins farmstead and continued toward the Jasper County line. Joe and Mattie Brown owned a rather large piece of land a few miles off the road valued at three hundred and fifty dollars; it became known as the "Brown Section". The Brown's had several children. In 1940, only Walter, Bertha and Maggie Rea were still living with their parents, helping on the farm and attending school during that period. Willie Brown, the grandson of Frank Petry II and the son of Minerva Petry Brown, and his wife, Willie Ann Ware Brown, lived near the Overstreet family. Armerjean Overstreet had a smallholding off the road valued at fifty dollars.

Down the road a ways was the homestead of Claud and Sylvia Dawkins. The 1940 census list Claud Dawkins as owner of the farm with land valued at one hundred twenty five dollars. Living in the home at that time were the Dawkins children: Christina and Jarine, a grandson John McCarty and a boarder Cliff Bates. Claud Dawkins was able to purchase his land in the late 1920's and worked his farm with two of his sons: Spotter, Costeller and a grandson John McCarty. By 1940, Costeller Dawkins had left his father farm to marry Ottolee (Nanny) Brown, the daughter of neighboring farmers Willie and Mattie Brown. Otalee (Nanny) had lived in the Good Hope Settlement all her life.

She attended the settlement school and Good Hope Settlement Church. Otalee worked on her father's farm until she married Costeller. Costeller, his wife and son, "Charles", lived in a little rented house and worked a small farm adjacent to his parents.

Off to the right of the red dirt road was the farmstead of John and Rilla Cook Hamilton. Rilla Cook was the daughter of Eliza Petry and Cornelius Cook and the granddaughter of Frank Petry I. The Hamilton's had lived for years in the settlement with their two daughters: Eliza and Emma. The family were members of the Good Hope Missionary Baptist Church and when John Hamilton died [or some say he was killed.] He was buried in the Good Hope Church Cemetery. After John's death, Rilla and her daughter removed to Meridian, Mississippi.

Clifton Edison said, "I remember sometime after 1940, shortly before I left for the service, Mose and Sophie and all their children moved on "Hamp's" [John Hamilton] and "Cuz" Rilla's old place. In 1940, most of the Pruitt children: Oscar, Bo, Fred, Vernell, Okanell and Broker Lee were attending school or working with their parents on the farm."

The wagon road continued through the settlement physically and emotionally connecting farmsteads and families along the way. It continued on down from the Pruitt farm about one half mile toward a large clearing on the left surrounded by large pines and oak trees. And in the heart of it all, in a large clearing was Good Hope Missionary Baptist Church. The settlement's first and only church in the community. The road leading into the clearing was made there by the residents who drove their wagons to church on Sunday mornings and Wednesday evening services, and by settlement members who lived past the church and the cemetery. The church was the institution of worship, social gatherings and sometimes the courts that often defined acceptable standards. It was a place where problems were discussed. In addition to church meetings held there, many came together for other ceremonial events such as graduations, weddings, births and deaths. The church was a great influence in the lives of the community members both young and old.

The settlement church with its bell tower was part of the fabric of their lives. In days gone by the ringing or tolling of the church bell was meant to let the community know that an ailing community member had just died or about some other emergency. (*The tower is no longer there however, the bell is there mounted on two posts in the church yard.*)

The bell tolled for Milton Hayden in 1929 when he had a heart attack in his corn field. Broomsy Salter tells the story regarding his "Uncle Milt" as he was known. "Papa had bought the Walker place and it was over past Uncle Milt and Aunt Anna's place. Me, Papa and Ruben were in the wagon and had just passed Uncle Milt and his boys, Daniel and Paul, working in field. And before long we heard the bell. You see back then when something happen they tolled the church bell. Papa told Rubin to cut the mules loose and ride up to the church and see what happened. When he got there he said Uncle Milt had died. Well we couldn't believe it we had just passed him in the field."

The bell was tolled later for his son, Reverend Daniel Hayden. In 2001, several of Reverend Hayden's nieces and nephews, the children of his sister Edna and her husband Archie Johnson, now living throughout the country were back home for the homegoing [funeral service] for their uncle Daniel Hayden, who the nieces and nephews called "Uncle Duck". The services were held at Morning Star Baptist Church in Newton, Mississippi where Reverend Hayden was Pastor Emeritus. Uncle Duck however was born and raised in the Good Hope Settlement and was a baptized member of the Good Hope Missionary Baptist Church. One nephew, "Jimmy", felt it was fitting that we should go the short distance down to Good Hope Church and toll the church bell for "Uncle Duck" and we all went down the red dirt road to the church and he rang the bell and it tolled for Uncle Daniel, three times.

Across the road, past the church, was the Good Hope Settlement Schoolhouse: a grey weathered worn clapboard covered building and a nearby playground. Located to the immediate West of the building, was a well and a spring below the hill. The school contained two rooms and a porch across the front. At the center of the building was a potbellied stove and the older boys were required to cut and split wood for the winter months. Separate outhouses on opposite ends of the property were situated for use by the boys and the girls.

Varnell Pruitt Chapman, the oldest daughter of Moses and Sophie Brown Pruitt, talked about her school days at Good Hope School. Varnell said she attended Good Hope Colored Community School in 1938 at age six. She remembered her school days in a personal way. She remembered the wonderful times she had in the little community school and the lifelong friends made there. "Some of the students," she said, "in my class came to school at different times in the morning because of chores at home but we all got out of school at the same time." She continued, "and those of us who took the same route, walked home together, often playing games or teasing one another on the way." (*Varnell, was age seventy nine, during this interview and she clearly remembered that in 1938 at age 6, her first teacher was Exie Johnson*)

Across the road, and down a ways from the church is the cemetery. Good Hope Church Cemetery lies on about three acres of land. Oral history indicates that the cemetery may have been used as a burial ground as early as 1880, and the bodies of the deceased are thought to have been brought from as far away as Newton and Hickory for burial. The earliest marked burial is dated 1898, and lies on the ridge east of the church. A cedar sprig was planted to commemorate the burial. The first burials are believed to have been made on this ridge. (*A survey of the cemetery in 2008 indicates at least 500 burials, many of which are unmarked.*)

The wagon road proceeded past the church and the schoolhouse and continued on through the cemetery and up to the property of Filmore Johnson. This section of the road though the cemetery was known by some of Filmore's great grandchildren as "the Filmore wagon road." In the 1930's, Filmore and his wife, Bettie, and their children lived in a small farmhouse and was thought to have used the short cut though the cemetery to attend church services on Sundays. *[The road through the cemetery was closed in 2007.] (See Filmore Johnson) (Muss and Velma Gooden first owned the land known as " the Filmore land" behind the cemetery until the late 1920s)*

Joyce Salter Johnson: "When I was about nine or ten years old, often on Sundays, in between Sunday school and church we: my girl cousins, sisters and sometime brothers, would walk down the wagon road through the cemetery on what we called the "Filmore wagon road." On those Sundays, if we had the time, we would walk through the cemetery down the road to the little a-frame Filmore house. On one such occasion on our way back through the cemetery my older sister, Emma, we called her "Tut," would walk over to the grave of the ancestor that had recently passed on and call out their name in a low mournful voice. This Sunday the fresh mound was the grave of Cousin John L Johnson. She leaned over and moaned in a deep voice calling "Cousin John L". As she expected we would run screaming through the cemetery up the bank to the church. On this occasion when my sister Tut called for the departed ancestor a pig rooting for nuts loudly grunted a response "Hgh!" She ran and we ran and that was the last of her calling out for the ancestors in the cemetery. We would always make it back just in time to hear the song that brought the congregation back from saying hello to friends and relatives to reverent order and just in time to hear Uncle Ike [Salter] lead the same song that Good Hope Missionary Baptist Church sang at the beginning of each church service until this day. He would begin and the congregation would follow, "Amazing Grace, how sweet the sound", a call and response verse by verse, often adding new verses as the sprit led him.

Back down the wagon road past the cemetery the elders claim in the early days Anthony and Lillie Beason had lived on a small farm near the Muss Godden place. The Beason's son, Leroy, married Ella Mae Davis and by 1940 Leroy and Ella Mae were living in a small house on or near his father's farm. Family members said that both the Beason and the Gooden family had relocated to Jasper County. Reverend Steven A. Tullos had bought the land and was living there with his wife, Ruby, and their children. The next two farms over were operated by Robert and Preston Johnson. Living near Preston was James and Mary Frances Cole. Robert I and Annie Lee Johnson had land valued at two hundred and fifty dollars off the road a ways. Their children: Rebecca and Frances Johnson and a grandson, James Potts, were still living at home, attending school and helping on the farm.

The red dirt road winds its way back past the cemetery, the school house and the church as it heads out beyond the clearing and down toward the Jasper County line. Further down, on the side of the little red dirt road, was the small homestead where John L Johnson and his wife, Suzie, and their children: Mary Ruth, Rosie Lee and Amy Lee lived.

Beyond the John L Johnson place, on the same side of the road, is the Gaddis farm. On the right side of the road, going toward the Wright Family farm, is the Ed and Lela Johnson Edison family farm which is located several yards from the main road. The 1940 census lists the Edison farmstead value at four hundred dollars. Down the road and past a clump of pine and other trees was the large Gaddis farm operated by James and Jennette Gaddis. Beyond the Gaddis property across the road is an area of the Good Hope Settlement that consists of a closely bonded group of family land owners, mostly Salters and Johnsons beginning with the farmland Charlie Salter and his wife, Willie Youngblood Salter, purchased in the early 1920s. Charlie's land was adjacent to one section of Anna Salter Hayden, his sister's farmland at the bottom of the hill across the creek. The farms did not produce a lot of money but it allowed the families to enjoy a "fair- to- middlin' kind of livin'," Anna Salter Hayden said.

Charlie Salter died in 1924 of tuberculosis during the tuberculosis outbreak in Newton County. Charlie's only daughter, Legirtha, died shortly after her father's death during the contagion in the county. In the 1930's, Willie Salter married Reverend Alfred D. Wright. Six of Willie and Reverend Alfred Wright's children were living at home in 1940: Vista, Jennette, Ora C, Edna, Bonnie, Vincent and Willie Wright. *(See more on Charlie Salter in the Salter Family of The Good Hope Colored Settlement)*

Milton and Susie Anna Salter Hayden operated several acres of land in the Good Hope Settlement. Their land was adjacent on one side to pasture land owned by Anna's brother, Charlie Salter, and a brother-in law, Frank Williams. The modest acreage held by the Hayden's did not lend much too planting crops such as cotton and sugar cane or timber as did some properties in the area. Their fields across the road from the Williams' farm produced enough corn for the family and feed for the animals. However, closer to the house was a large clearing for a truck farm. Anna referred to it as her "Truck Patch" where she grew vegetables of all kinds and melons of various types, sweet and white potatoes, greens, sweet corn and peas and a large variety of beans. Past the grist mill on the left and down the lane was the farmhouse. One left side of the farmhouse was lined with pecan trees and on the other side of the house was a fruit orchard with many types of domestic fruit such as figs, persimmons, peaches, pears and apples.

Down the lane in front of the house were wild plums, berry bushes, hickory nut trees and the smaller Carya Glabar ("scaly bobs") nuts trees. In an area near a small stream were wild grapes and Muscadine grapes grew. In back of the house down the hill (known by the grandchildren as the "red hill") was the Indian field and farther down was a creek for fishing.

Milton Hayden was known as an adventurous, enterprising young man and gave in to the call of his brother-in-law, Broomsy Norman, to follow the railroad up North for work during the winter months. Not giving up the farm altogether, he relocated to Freeport, Illinois where he was able to get a job with the Illinois Central Railroad working in the round houses cleaning engines. He was able to send as much as fifty dollars per month back home to the farm. With some of the money he sent home a substantial farmhouse was built to replace the weather worn shotgun farmhouse built by the early settlers to the property. Milton regularly returned to the settlement whenever possible. In 1929 on a return trip to Good Hope Milton died and was buried in the Good Hope Church Cemetery under a small tree. In 2009 the tree which had grown several hundred feet was destroyed by Hurricane Katrina's winds. *(Milton and Susie Anna Hayden- grandparents of the author)*

The next farmstead across the road was operated by Frank Williams and his second wife, Mary Ella William. The Williams' farm was surrounded by farmland held by his brother-in-law Charlie Salter, to the north and a brother, Will Salter, to the south. It is said by an elder that Frank Salter the elder had purchased the land from the Horns in the Good Hope Colored Settlement in 1928. As the road comes to a fork and passes the Salter/ Hayden farm, it turns left and up a slight hill to the Will Salter homestead. His acreages extended to the land owned by his brother, Isaac Salter, and down the hill where Daniel Johnson II held a large track of timber and farm land near the Jasper County line. Past the fork in the road near the Hayden farm and past the mail boxes going south, the next farm on the red dirt road was operated by Isaac and Mary Johnson Salter. The children living and working on the farm in the 1930's were four of their five sons: Clayborn, Broomsy, Lonnie, Robert and a daughter, Addie. An elder son, Rubin Salter I, had married and operated a small farm a short distance down the road with his wife, Mittie Oliver, until the family relocated up North to Freeport, Illinois. (*More on Rubin -Up North to Freeport chapter*)

Years later Isaac and Mary Johnson Salter and some of their children continued to live on the family farm. In 1940 living on the farm with Isaac and Mary were two nephews, Alonzo Pruitt and JT Pruitt, two of the six children born to Aaron and Fannie Johnson Pruitt. Aaron Pruitt, the son of Phil Pruitt and Alice Salter, married Fannie, the daughter of Eliza Johnson. Aaron and Fannie contracted tuberculosis and died within a short time of each other. *Three of the children were raised by Isaac and Mary Johnson Salter; Alonzo, Grace and JT Pruitt and three others were raised by Daniel Johnson II; Lenard, Thomas, Willie Mae Pruitt.*

A short distance down the road, past the Will Salter farmhouse and other out buildings, were pastures on one side of the road and fields for several miles on the other side. After several miles of Will Salter's fields and pastures the landscape turned to a forest like valley and up the hill from the valley is small field on the left and is the beginning of the piney woods behind the little A- famed house sitting off the road home of Archie and Edna Hayden Johnson [in 1940] and five of their ten children. This was the beginning of property of Daniel Johnson II that he parceled out in forty acre plots and was rented by his sons for farming and timber harvesting. Down at the foot of the hill about a mile apart were two little a-frame houses. Several of Daniel's children lived in the houses before they relocated elsewhere. First to move was France and Exie who relocated to Hickory, General and Eloise moved up to Freeport, Illinois with other relatives and lastly Opal and her husband, Rufus Ed Ford, and several of their children lived in the house for a short time.

At the end of the road going toward the Jasper County line was the farmhouse of Reverend Daniel Johnson and his second wife, Mahala Allen. She was a young woman from nearby Paulding, Mississippi. The Good Hope Settlement Community and its red dirt road ended here just a few feet north of the Jasper County line. From this research most of what had once been a red dirt road is now all over grown with trees, vines and wild flowers. However, if you look closely enough you may see deep impression made by the wagon wheels many years ago.

Good Hope Community

And World War II 1939 To 1945

In Newton County and throughout the state of Mississippi sharecroppers and land owners worried that the War would create a shortage of low wage Negro workers. Most farm workers in the area of rural Hickory in the community of the Good Hope Settlement owned their farms. And their sons, who were old enough to go off to war, were working on their fathers' farms. Yet this did not stop them from joining up. More than one half the Negro farmers in the community registered for the draft included in this group were Clifton, Chester and Ardell Edison, Cleo and Otha Johnson, Rubin Salter, Ira Salter and Broomsy Salter. James Paul Gaddis (JP as he was known) joined the Navy during World War II and achieved the rank of Chief Petty Officer.

CHAPTER SIXTEEN

The Complex History Of Frank Petry – Petree I

His children during and after the time of enslavement

All my African-American ancestors since 1700 until 1863 were enslaved. Therefore the questions are: who held them enslaved and where? What was life in Freedom like for them? I descended from two sets of enslaved 2nd great-grandparents: my paternal ancestors, the Johnson/Petry/Petree Levy and maternal ancestors, the Salter /Garner/Hayden. For more than 20 years, I have been collecting pieces of information concerning my paternal ancestors, the Johnson/Petry/ Levy families, while they were enslaved and after Emancipation Proclamation. Deep research was done regarding the part they played in the origin of the Good Hope Freedmen Settlement. "It is like a puzzle. The pieces are slowly coming together." **Joyce Salter Johnson**

After the end of slavery nearly all heads of household who settled in the Good Hope Freedmen Settlement took for their family the surnames of their last slaveholders. In the early census records many surname spellings were altered for various reasons. Of the many reasons some are more apparent than others. The spelling skills of the record keepers were often weak and spelling errors were common. Plus record keepers and almost certainly former slaveholding families choose to distinguish names between "White and Black" individuals by changing the spelling in surnames such as: Kirby/Kerby/Curby, Johnson/Johnston, Gipson/Gibson, Petry/ Petree /Petrie, Cook/Cooke, Salter/Saulter and scores of others. It was this aspect of the system of slavery which created many questions for family researchers. Some blood relatives emerged from slavery with different surnames than that of their parents, brothers and sisters and other family members. Consequently in most cases the family member was lost forever. From this terrible time in America's history, the Johnson/Petry/Kirby family emerged. One family and three surnames spelled several different ways Petre Petry/Petree and Petrey. For this purpose we will utilize the spellings: Petry/Petree, Kirby and Johnson used more often in the 1920's, 30's, and 40's.

The Legend of Filmore Johnson - A Story handed down by Tradition

Family members tell the story this way. "When he was freed, ten or eleven years old Filmore Johnson went out looking for his family." Where he was at that time and where he went in search of his family is not in the telling. Over the years much research was conducted regarding Filmore Johnson. As a result of the recent findings the family and the family historians selected to look more closely at the Filmore Petry/ Johnson legends and are insisting on a less romantic portrayal of these events. The legends of Filmore Johnson are remarkable and inspiring. The story of the Johnson/Petry family history and the development of Good Hope Freedmen Settlement are indeed both complicated and memorable and are part history and part family lore. Still history must respect the facts. Even if the story it tells is more complex and less inspiring. **Joyce Salter Johnson**

When looking at the legend more carefully it tells the story somewhat differently than family lore suggests. Family legends however are not to be ignored. In the case, of the Johnson /Petree/Petry family lore and legends were an undeniable aid in finding links which connected the family when records were not available. Still without verified sources, such as wills, deeds, tax records and personal inventories of the slaveholding families, there is no way of knowing the validity of the stories and legends told. (*The 1870 Federal Census placed ten year old Filmore Johnson living with Daniel Johnson I, an older brother in Beat 5 Section 12 in Newton County, Mississippi in an area that would become Good Hope Settlement.*)

In an attempt to understand Filmore Johnson/ Petree/Petry's life we must start with the beginning of his life. Who were his parents? Was he enslaved? And did he have siblings? What the elders were very sure of however was the fact that Filmore had other family members. The names of his siblings were often mentioned by the family elders such as: Daniel I, Uncle Big Preston Johnson I, "Cousin Rilla" and "Uncle Frank Petry II" and a sister, name is not mentioned. Filmore Johnson's death certificate, census records and family legends together maintain Filmore Johnson was born enslaved in 1854, to Mary Kirby/Curby and Frank Petry/Petree I.

Frank Petry/Petree

The Father of Filmore Johnson

Historical Information

The research information found regarding Frank Petry/Petree I the Father of Filmore is both modest and ambiguous it shows he was born into slavery in 1812 in Virginia or North Carolina. He was enslaved by both the Petry and the Strickland family and possibly the Johnson or the Kirby Family of Newton, County in Mississippi. Frank Petry/ Petree died in 1919 in Hollys Spring, Mississippi when he was one hundred six years old.

Due to the circumstances surrounding enslavement and his advanced age, the names and ages and places of his birth and the birth of his mother and fathers were hard for him to recall. For example: Frank had listed in the 1880 census both he and his parents were born in Virginia and in the 1900 census ninety eight year old Frank Petree/Petry I listed his parents were born in North Carolina. When he was emancipated Frank Petree/ Petry I was living in Marshall County, Mississippi on the Strickland plantation. Much of his background and his parentage history is silent. Almost all details pertaining to the early life of Frank from his birth in Virginia and his arrival in Mississippi remain a mystery.

The Slaveholding Family

Lemuel Weeks Petrie/Petry

Possible Slaveholders

The slaveholding Petrie/Petry family owned several plantations in Mississippi and held over one hundred fifty enslaved workers. Some were procured for farming interests and others were purchased to provide labor necessary for laying tracks for the Jackson and Brandon Railroad. Others were obtained for building bridges that the Petrie family had contracted to construct.

The Slaveholding Petrie family's youngest son, Lemuel Weeks Petrie, was the last heir to the vast Petrie estate. He had married Rosa Farrar of Virginia and settled on a plantation about five miles east of Jackson in Hinds County. Conceivably Frank was among the one hundred plus enslaved workers that were listed in Lemuel Petrie's estate. When Lemuel Petrie died Frank may have been part of the group of enslaved men, women and children who were sold to settle his estate. Researched information shows by 1853 Frank was held enslaved by the Strickland family of Newton, Jasper and Marshall Counties in Mississippi.

If the enslaved Frank came to Mississippi with the Lemuel Weeks Petrie/Petry family he would had lived most of his young life enslaved first in Virginia and later years in Hinds and Rankin Counties in Mississippi. His adulthood is also obscure and can only be partly deciphered. Yet speculations and researched information leans toward Frank arriving in Mississippi with the wealthy Petrie/Petry family as early as 1842. The next window of time into the life of Frank was in 1849, after that in 1852. Vital records show in 1849 a son, Frank Petrie/Petry II, was born Newton County, Mississippi and in 1852 a son, Filmore Johnson, was born to Mary Kirby in Mississippi. Both sons were born enslaved in Newton County. (*Mary Kirby/Curby was listed(as mother) on the death certificate of Filmore Johnson.) (The 1920 census shows a Mary Johnson living with her son, Frank Petry II in Newton County, Mississippi) (Mary spelled "Curby" was carved on her headstone in the "White" Good Hope Church Cemetery near Fellowship Road in the section posted "Colored Cemetery" near several Johnson and Petry/Petree grave sites.)*

However, to date research has failed to recover any information establishing Frank Petry I and Mary Curby / Kirby Johnson on the same plantation during the times of slavery or any time after the period of enslavement. One possible answer may be due to the proximity of the two plantations. The Johnson-Gibson plantation in Newton County where Mary and her children were thought to be held enslaved and the Strickland Plantations in Jasper and Newton Counties where Frank Petry I was held enslaved may have been within walking distance. Mary and Frank perhaps had what was known as an "abroad marriage". This arrangement, where the husband lived on one plantation and the wife on another, was common among the enslaved and the slaveholder. (*"abroad marriage" Some enslaved people lived in nuclear families with a mother, father and children. In these cases each family member belonged to the same owner. Others lived in near-nuclear families in which the father had a different owner than the mother and children. The father might live several miles away on a distant plantation and walk, usually on Wednesday nights and Saturday evenings to see his family as his obligation and masters allowed.)*

Or perhaps Frank I was first held enslaved by the Petrie Family and some years later he was sold to the Johnson family of Newton County and lastly to William Strickland of Jasper, Newton and Marshall Counties in Mississippi. Records only revealed Frank I was removed with the Strickland family to Hollys Spring, Mississippi and was separated from his former family in Newton County through the many years of slavery. While enslaved on the Strickland plantation, Frank entered a second "enslaved marriage" with Mahala, a women living on the Strickland plantation. Their only child, Eliza, was born in 1853. After 1853, history did not reveal any information regarding Frank until after 1861.

Frank Petry / Petree I

Hollys Springs, Mississippi

The Slaveholder: William Strickland

In 1861, the War Between the States was brewing. As the War progressed, William Strickland the slaveholder enlisted in the Confederate army as a first sergeant in Company D, Ninth Regiment, Mississippi: Infantry. He took Frank I along with him. Taking a "slave" to war was not an anomaly; enslaved men on both sides served in the War. They mostly served in assistance roles. In the North, for example, they served as nurses, cooks, teamsters, blacksmiths, drummers and flag barriers. Enslaved men also served in the Confederate Army, although most served as "slave labor forces". They were brought along by their masters to tend to the master's needs in camp. In some cases, these servants were entrusted with a master's personal affects. If his master was killed he was to return his body to his family, if possible.

However, the enslaved Frank was brought along because he had valuable skills as a blacksmith. His capabilities as a blacksmith were in short supply. Blacksmiths were needed for the War effort for various kinds of ironwork from cooking utensils to weapons of war. The United States Confederate Soldiers Compiled Service Records shows the enslaved Frank spent most of the Civil War years, from 1861 until 1863, serving in some capacity in the Confederate Army with his master, William Strickland of Marshall County, Mississippi.

Frank Petry/Petree

In Marshall County, Mississippi 1865

On January 1, 1865, at the end of the period of enslavement, Marshall County, Mississippi freed seventeen thousand men, women and children. Many Freedmen stayed on and worked as sharecroppers and tenant farmers. Some relocated to counties in Louisiana and many went up North. Some went to other counties in Mississippi. Scores went off looking for family members from a previous cohabitation; some came back, and others did not.

The Civil War was over. Frank had served three years in the War with his master. But when he returned to his living quarters on the plantation he was a free man. Frank found work as a blacksmith and lived for a time in Hollys Springs with his common-law wife, Mahala and their eleven year-old daughter, Eliza. When Frank was required to have a surname he chose "Petry/Petree" the surname of his former slaveholders. In 1869, Frank Petry I and Mahala were legally married and were living on a small farm on the Strickland Plantation in Lamar, Mississippi with seventeen year-old Eliza. In 1880, fifty year old Frank I and his wife, Mahala, had relocated to a smaller farm near Hudsonville in Marshall, County. There he worked as a blacksmith possibly for the Mississippi Central Railroad that ran through Hudsonville. In 1880, Eliza was no longer living in the household with her parents. On March 21, 1872, Eliza Petree married Claiborne Cook, a farmer from nearby Benton County, Mississippi.

The mysteries surrounding Frank Petry I continued throughout the latter years of his life. Mary Kirby, the mother of his sons, had died in Newton County in 1896, and sometime after1900 Mahala, his second wife of thirty years, died in Marshall County. During the ten years between the census of 1900 and 1910, Frank I returned to Newton County. The 1910 census shows him in rural Hickory, Mississippi in the Good Hope Colored Settlement living or visiting his son Frank Petry II and other family members. (*The Newton County Census lists ninety eight year old Frank Petry I (index as Peters) living in the household with his son, Frank Petry II. (index as Peters)*

When he returned to Hollys Spring the aging Frank gave up farming and moved in with his grandson, Thomas Cook, on the Strickland Plantation, where he lived until the late 1900's. In 1919, "*The South*", the Hollys Springs, Mississippi newspaper reported, "Frank Petree died on Tuesday, June 3, 1919."

The report continues, "Frank Petree, colored, was 106 years old last March 6. He lived with his grandson Tom Cook on the William M. Strickland plantation in Marshall County, Mississippi."

Did Frank Petry/ Petree I visit his former wife and children in Newton County after he was emancipated before 1910? The ancestors were silent and there was no reply to the questions from historical records. Did he know who and where they were held enslaved? Did he travel back to the Strickland Plantation in Jasper and Newton Counties with the slaveholders? Many of these questions have no answers. In all probability Frank was aware of the location of his children and must have visited as often as he was allowed.

When Frank Petry/Petree was free to do so he chose Petry/Petree, the surname of his former slaveholders, in an attempt to keep in touch with his former family. Considering the relative ease of travel by the late 1900's on the Illinois Central Railroad line from Hollys Springs, Mississippi to Newton, Mississippi it is possible that after and during the time of enslavement many trips were made back and forth by Frank and his family between Newton County and Hollys Springs. During the ten years between the census Eliza Petree Cook had traveled to Good Hope in rural Newton County. She may have made several trips to visit her grandchildren or she may have traveled with her aging father to Newton County. However, on one such trip in 1914, Eliza Petree Cook died and was buried in the Colored Cemetery of the original Good Hope Church on Fellowship Road. After Eliza's funeral Claiborne Cook, her husband, and possibly also her father, Frank Petree I, returned to Marshall County. Claiborne Cook lived on his farm with his daughter, Rosa, until he died. Frank Petree I lived with his grandsons, Thomas and Cleveland Cook, until he died in 1919, at age one hundred six. He is buried in the Hudsonville, Marshall County, Mississippi in the Hudsonville Cemetery.

The children of

Eliza Petree and Claiborne Cook

Eliza Petree, the daughter of Frank I and Mahala Petree, married Claiborne Cook, a Mulatto man, who had been held enslaved on the Cook Plantation in Benton County, Mississippi. With the help of the new Reconstruction Laws, and possibly the Cook slaveholders, Claiborne Cook and his new bride were able to find a small plots of land to farm in Benton County, Mississippi.

Eliza and Claiborne had been married two years when their first child, Rilla, was born. Several years later in 1879, in the midst of the Yellow Fever Epidemic in Marshall and area counties in Mississippi, a second child, John L Cook was born. In 1880, the Cooks continued to live in Benton, Mississippi with their two children: Rilla age six and John L age three months. Family lore dictates and some research shows that sometime after his fourth month John L Cook died, possibly a victim of the Yellow Fever. (*The yellow fever epidemic was catastrophic for the town of Hollys Springs. Between late August and mid-October 1878, the bustling town of 3,500 people dwindled to 800 residents. About 1,400 sick people actually died during the malaria epidemic. The remainder fled out of fear of the disease.*)

The Cook family and all the children may have been stricken with the fever though it appears that only baby John L Cook died. After the epidemic the Cooks stayed on in Benton, Mississippi and worked the small farm for several years. More children were born to the Cooks. Thomas Cook was born in 1883, and Cleveland Cook, a fourth child, was born in 1896. In 1914, Eliza Petree Cook died while visiting family in the Good Hope Settlement and was buried in the Colored Cemetery of the original Good Hope Church on Fellowship Road. After Eliza's funeral Claiborne Cook, her husband and also possibly her father, Frank Petree I, returned to Marshall County. Their son, Cleveland Cook, never married and settled in Hollys Springs, Mississippi. In 1917, he enlisted in the military and served in the Army until 1918. When Cleveland was mustered out of the Army he returned to Hollys Springs and lived on the farm with his widowed brother, Thomas, his new wife, Joise and his grandfather, Frank Petrey / Petree I. Thomas Cook had married a young woman named Joise while his brother Cleveland was in the military and they lived in Marshall County, Mississippi on a farm he rented from the Strickland family. Thomas and his family lived there for several decades until the death of his grandfather, Frank Petry/Petree I. After ten years of marriage, Thomas and Joise were childless. So in 1920, the couple adopted ten-year-old Rosebud/Rosa. In the late 1920's, Joise Cook died in her home with her husband, Thomas and twenty year old daughter Rosebud by her bedside.

Information regarding Eliza and Claiborne Cook's first child Rilla Cook is a bit elusive. However, family lore proclaims Rilla Cook moved to Newton, County in Mississippi. In 1910, she married John Hamilton of rural Hickory, Mississippi. John and Rilla had two daughters, Emma and Eliza and worked on a farm in the Good Hope Settlement. John Hamilton was killed on December 8, 1941, and was buried in the Good Hope Church Cemetery. After John's death, Rilla left the Good Hope Settlement and relocated with her daughters to Meridian, Mississippi.

The Other Story Regarding Frank Petry/ Petree's Children

The Mary Johnson/Kirby family may have originated in Goodman, Harris County, Georgia and it points toward Mary, her sons: Daniel, Preston and [possible William] all being held enslaved by Cicero Johnson first in Georgia and for a short time in Alabama and later in Newton County, Mississippi. Evidence seems to suggest Fillmore's brothers came from Georgia to Alabama and into Mississippi with Cicero Johnson. On two separate occasions in the census Filmore states that his father was born in Georgia. Researchers and some family elders believe that Mary the mother of Filmore was a mixed blood of African and possibly lower Creek or Choctaw Indian. (*More on Mary Kirby*)

The Johnson Slaveholders

Cicero Johnson/ Henry Gibson

Cicero Johnson was a slaveholder who may have held Filmore Johnson and his family enslaved in Newton County, Mississippi. He was the son of Samuel Johnson and Frances Corney Johnson. Samuel and Frances were married on December 3, 1829 in Putnam County, Georgia. They had three children. Their son, Cicero, was born in 1831 in Georgia. His father Samuel Johnson died when Cicero was only sixteen years old. Soon after his father's death his mother remarried John Wright a large plantation owner in Georgia. The 1850 census shows seventeen year old Cicero Johnson was living in Georgia with his mother, Frances, and step-father, John Wright. That same year he was betrothed to young Susan Gibson, the daughter of Henry Gibson. Henry Gibson was a wealthy plantation owner in Harris County, Georgia who held large amounts of land and held forty three people enslaved. On his eighteenth birthday Cicero Johnson inherited a portion of his father's estate. On December 5, 1850, he and Susan were married at her family home. Seven years later in 1857, Henry Gibson had migrated to Alabama along with his daughter, Susan, and son-in-law, Cicero Johnson. (*Henry Gibson lived in Valley Plains, Georgia in 1850. Age: 51 a daughter was born in Alabama in 1857. In 1860 lived in Hickory, Mississippi*)

Henry Gibson and Cicero Johnson settled for a period with their families in Alabama. After 1860, the family migrated into Mississippi along with their enslaved workers and settled in Newton County, in rural Hickory, Mississippi near the Jasper County border.

The slaveholding Johnson and Gibson families were founding members of the "White" Good Hope Baptist Church on Fellowship Road. Mary and her sons and several other enslaved men, women and children lived and worked on the Johnson/ Gibson plantations in rural Hickory. For many years the Johnson, Kirby/ Curby, Petry/Petree and Gibson enslaved families were members of the "Masters" Good Hope Baptist Church on Fellowship Road. After Emancipation Proclamation the families continued to interact with the slaveholders through work and in some fashion through church associations.

When it became necessary to have a surname some of the Johnson/Gibson Freedmen took for themselves the Johnson surnames. After 1870, Henry Gibson the former slaveholder, his son-in-law Cicero Johnson and the Freedmen Daniel Johnson I, his wife Fanny and his young brother Filmore were all neighboring farmers. These families continued to interact through church associations for many years.

Henry Gibson, his daughter Susan and husband Cicero Johnson are buried, in the "White" cemetery at the original Good Hope Church site. Richmond Gibson and others, who were held enslaved by the Gibson/Johnson slaveholders, are now buried about twenty feet nearby in the cemetery posted "Colored" along with Mary Kirby (spelled) Curby the mother of Filmore Johnson and many others. Filmore Johnson married Elizabeth Levy Suttles after he was free to do. (*See more on Filmore and Elizabeth Johnson in chapter eleven*)

Classifying Familial Kinship

Frank Petry /Petree Family

It is difficult to classify familial kinship, many slaveholders did not maintain records outlining enslaved family groups, although in many instances only a mother was listed with her children. In such cases, the identification of the enslaved father on a large plantation may be difficult. Sometimes the father lived on a neighboring plantation. Husbands and wives often resided on separate farms or plantations and were owned by different individuals.

On large plantations one man in three was held enslaved in a different place than his wife and could visit his family only at his master's discretion. On smaller holdings divided ownership was even more common. It was this aspect of the system of slavery which created many questions. Choosing surnames after freedom came often revealed the unquestionable disconnections for families.

Some newly freed people took the names of the slaveholder who originally held them enslaved in hope of family members finding them later. A number of enslaved fathers, whenever possible, took the surname of the slaveholder who held them when they were "Sold Off" for that same reason.

Descendants of Frank Petry/ Petree I

1. Generation One

Frank Petry/ Petree I

Generation 1: *Frank Petry/ Petree I* was born about 1812. Frank may have been held enslaved by Lemuel Weeks Petrie in Hinds County, Mississippi and later enslaved to William Strickland in Newton County, Mississippi. Frank died at the age of 106 in 1919 in Hollys Springs, Mississippi. Frank has had "a slave marriage" with Mary Kirby/ Curby in Newton, Jasper, or Hinds counties in Mississippi. Mary was born about 1815 in Georgia. She died on April 23, 1896 in Newton County Mississippi. She was buried in the original Good Hope Church Cemetery on Fellowship Road Cemetery in an area marked (Colored Cemetery).

The Descendants of Frank Petry/ Petree I

2. Generation Two

Frank Petry/Petree I and Mary Kirby Johnson had;

Generation 2: *Daniel Johnson I* (1. *Frank Petry/ Petree I*) was born about 1824 in Georgia. Daniel had an enslaved marriage with Frances an enslaved woman on the plantation. Frances was born in 1830 in South Carolina and was enslaved in Georgia. Daniel Johnson I and Frances lived in the Good Hope Colored Settlement as early as 1868 possible on rented land. In 1870 Daniel and Frances lived in the Good Hope Settlement. When and how Daniel died is not known. Daniel death remains a mystery. (*See Daniel Johnson I and "the Dyes Incident"*

Daniel and Frances Johnson had:

Generation 3:*Bria or Bamah Johnson* (2.*Daniel Johnson I*) (*1. Frank Petry/ Petree I*)

Generation 2: *William Johnson* (1.*Frank Petry/Petree I*) was born in 1842 in Georgia. William married Lucy Dyes and they had four children. Living in the household with William and Lucy were other relatives a Niece eighteen year old Sophia Dyes and Nephew twenty years old Henry Dyes.

William and Lucy Dyes Johnson had:

Generation 3: *Robert Johnson* (2.William Johnson)(1.Frank Petry/Petree I)
Generation 3:*Mulley Johnson*(2. William Johnson) (1.Frank Petry/Petree I)
Generation 3:*Walter Johnson* (2. William Johnson)(1.Frank Petry/Petree I)
Generation 3:*Frank Johnson* (2. William Johnson) (1.Frank Petry/Petree I)

Generation 2: *Preston Johnson I* (1.Frank Petry/Petree I) was the third son born to Mary Kerby/ Curby and Frank Petry/Petree. **Preston** married his first wife Elizabeth while enslaved. Elizabeth was born in South Carolina in 1849. They worked a farm in the Good Hope Settlement for many years. Elizabeth died in 1910 and is buried in the Good Hope Church Cemetery. Preston second wife was Harriett Johnson. The couple was lifelong members of Good Hope Settlement.

Preston and Elizabeth Johnson had no known children

Generation 2: *Amanda Johnson* (1.*Frank Petry/Petree I*) was born about 1847 in Georgia. Amanda was living with Richmond Gibson family in 1870 in the Good Hope Settlement in New County, Mississippi. The 1870 census list twenty three year old Amanda as a single parent with her eight year old daughter. Amanda is thought to be the daughter of Mary Curry/ Johnson.

Amanda Johnson had:

Generation 3:*Sarah Johnson* (2: *Amanda Johnson)* (1.*Frank Petry/Petree I*)

The Descendants of Frank Petry II

Generation 2: *Frank Petry /Petree II* (1.*Frank Petree/Petry I*) was born in 1844 in Mississippi. He died after 1940 in Newton County, Mississippi Frank Petree II married Angelina Walker

Frank II and Angelina Walker Petree/Petry had:

Generation 3: *Mamora Petry* (2.*Frank Petree/Petry II) (1. Frank Petree/Petry I* was born in 1870 in Newton County Mississippi

Generation 3: *James Madison Peatry* (2.*Frank Petree/Petry II) (1. Frank Petree/Petry I*) was born in 1873. James married Hattie Howes. In 1930 James and his family relocated to Chicago,Illinois. At age sixty four James died on March 10, 1940. His Burial date was March 16, 1940. Burial Place: Glenwood, Ill. Cemetery Name: Mt. Glenwood. [James spelled his surname "Peatry"]

James Madison Peatry I and Hattie Peatry had:

Generation 4: Gertrude Peatry(3.*James Madison Peatry I) (2.Frank Petree/Petry II) (1. Frank Petree/Petry I)* Gertrude married Willie Lee Gibson son of George W. Gibson and Jennie Jackson.

Gertrude Peatry and Willie Lee Gibson had

Generation: 5 need more information

Generation 4: *Horace Peatry* (3.*James Madison Peatry I) (2.Frank Petree/Petry II) (1. Frank Petree/Petry I)* was born on December 30, 1898 in Newton County. Mississippi. His WW I draft registration was in Chicago, Illinois.

Generation 4: *Filmore Peatry* (3.*James Madison Peatry I) (2.Frank Petree/Petry II) (1. Frank Petree/Petry I)* was born on April 6, 1900 in Newton County, Mississippi. He married Sally maiden name not known. His WW I draft registration was in Chicago, Illinois. Filmore Peatry died on February 19, 1975 in Chicago, Cook County, Illinois.

Filmore and Sally Peatry had:

Generation 5 more information

Generation 4: *Annie Petree* (3.*James Madison Peatry I) (2.Frank Petree/Petry II) (1. Frank Petree/Petry I)* was born about 1902 in Newton County. Mississippi.

Generation 4: *Emma Peatry* (3.*James Madison Peatry I) (2.Frank Petree/Petry II) (1. Frank Petree/Petry I)* was born on August 23, 1906 in Newton County. Mississippi. She died on March 16, 1978 in Chicago, Illinois.

Generation 4: *Johnnie Petree* (3.*James Madison Peatry I) (2.Frank Petree/Petry II) (1. Frank Petree/Petry I) SHE* was born in 1909 in Newton County. Mississippi.

Generation 4: *Clifton Petry* (3.*James Madison Peatry I) (2.Frank Petree/Petry II) (1. Frank Petree/Petry I*

Generation 3: *Minerva Petree/Petry* (2.*Frank Petree/Petry II)* (1. Frank Petry/Petree I) was born in 1874 in Newton County. Mississippi. She married Jerry Brown her first husband on December 24, 1888.

Minerva Petree/Petry and Jerry Brown had:

Generation **4:** ***Birdie Brown*** (**3.***Minerva Petree/Petry*) (**2.***Frank Petree/Petry II*) (**1.** *Frank Petree/Petry I*) was born Oct 1890 in the Good Hope Settlement in Newton County. Mississippi. Birdie married Robert Carroll.

Birdie Brown and Robert Carroll had:

Generation: 5 need more information

Generation4: ***Willie Brown*** (**3.***Minerva Petree/Petry*) (**2.***Frank Petree/Petry II*) (**1.** *Frank Petree/Petry I*) was born in Jan 1892 in Newton County, Mississippi

Generation 4: ***Thomas W. Brown*** (**3.***Minerva Petree/Petry*) (**2.***Frank Petry II*) (**1.** *Frank Petry I*) was born in 1893 in Newton County, Mississippi.

More on **Generation 3:** *Minerva Petree/Petry Brown*
When Jerry Brown died Minerva married a Mr. Carter [as of this printing his given name is not known]

Minerva Petree/Petry and Mr. Carter had

Generation 4: ***Henrietta Carter:*** (**3.***Minerva Petree/Petry*) (**2.***Frank Petree/Petry II*) (**1.** *Frank Petree/Petry I*) was born in 1900 in Newton County, Mississippi.

Generation 4: ***Anabel Carter*** (**3.***MinervaPetree/Petry*) (**2.***Frank Petry II*) (**1.** *Frank Petry I*) was born in 1902 in Newton County, Mississippi.

More on **Generation 3:** *Minerva Petree/Petry Brown Carter*
Minerva Petree/Petry married a widower George Gibson. George's wife Jennie had died at a very early age leaving him with ten children to raise. From 1910 until 1940 Minerva and George were farmers in the Good Hope Settlement and were faithful members of the Good Hope Colored Baptist Church.
Minerva Petree/Petry and George Gibson raised

Generation 4: Martha Gibson
Generation 4: Ed Gibson
Generation 4: Willie Gibson
Generation 4: Pearl Gibson
Generation 4: Nathan Gibson
Generation 4: Ina Gibson
Generation 4: Joe Gibson
Generation 4: Luther Gibson
Generation 4: Otto Gibson
Generation 4: R. Gibson

Generation 5: Grandson James L Brown
Generation 5: Grandson Roy L Evans

More on **Generation 3:** *(Minerva Petree/Petry Brown Carter Gibson)*
Minerva died on June 15, 1941 in Newton County. Mississippi. She was buried in Good Hope Church Cemetery on Good Hope Road

Generation 3: ***Maggie Missouri Petry/ Petree*** (2. *Frank Petree/Petry II*) (*1. Frank Petree/Petry* I) was born in May of 1875. Maggie married W. J (Joe) Brown and had fourteen children over the years.

Maggie Missouri Petree and W. J (Joe) Brown had

Generation 4: ***Frank Brown*** (3.*Maggie Missouri Petry/* ***Petree***) (2. *Frank Petree/Petry II*) (1. *Frank Petree/Petry* I) was born in 1893
Generation 4: ***Edgar Brown*** (3.*Maggie Missouri Petry/* ***Petree***) (2. *Frank Petree/Petry II*) (1. *Frank Petree/Petry* I) was born in 1893.
Generation 4: ***Lucius Brown*** (3.*Maggie Missouri Petry/* ***Petree***) (2. *Frank Petree/Petry II*) (1. *Frank Petree/Petry* I) was born in 1894 and died in infancy

Generation 4: ***Olivia Brown*** (3.*Maggie Missouri Petry/* ***Petree***) (2. *Frank Petree/Petry II*) (1. *Frank Petree/Petry* I) was born in 1897. At the age of fifteen Olivia married Willie Gibson. Willie and Olivia had one child, a daughter, Dorries. When Olivia was nineteen years old she contracted tuberculosis and died in 1919.

Generation 4: *Lonnie Brown (3.Maggie Missouri Petry/ Petree)* (2. Frank Petree/Petry II) (1. Frank Petree/Petry I) was born in 1899.

Generation 4: *Sophie Brown(3.Maggie Missouri Petry/ Petree)* (2. Frank Petree/Petry II) (1. Frank Petree/Petry I) was born in 1904 and married Moses Pruitt. Moses Pruitt was born in the Good Hope Colored Settlement to Alice Salter and Phil Pruitt

Sophie Brown and Moses Pruitt and had

Generation 5: Oscar P Pruitt
Generation 5 Fred Pruitt
Generation 5 Ormee Pruitt
Generation 5 Kenny Pruitt
Generation 5 Varnell Pruitt
Generation 5 Okenell Pruitt
Generation 5 Brooker Lee
Generation 5 Wilbert Pruitt
Generation 5 Sonny Pruitt
Generation 5 Mary Alice Pruitt

Generation 3: *Thomas Jefferson. Peatry* (2.Frank Petree/Petry II)(1.Frank Petree/Petry I) was born in1876 and married Lilla [maiden name not known] Thomas Peatry and Lillia lived at 474 East 41st Street in Chicago, Illinois and worked at International Harvester

Thomas Jefferson and Lillie Petree had

Generation 4: *Eldon Edward Petree:* (3Thomas Jefferson Peatry) (2.Frank Petree/Petry II)(1.Frank Petree/Petry I) was born in 1896 in Good Hope in Newton County, Mississippi. He died on December 4, 1971 in Chicago, Illinois. He registered during WW II in Chicago, Illinois. Eldon live for a while in 1930's in Freeport, Illinois with relatives.

Generation 4: *Olice Petree*: (3Thomas Jefferson Peatry) (2.Frank Petree/Petry II)(1.Frank Petree/Petry I was born in March 1899 in Good Hope Newton Co. Mississippi. He died on October 13, 1989 in Cook Co. Illinois.

Generation 4: *Willie M. Petree*: (3Thomas Jefferson Peatry) (2.Frank Petree/Petry II)(1.Frank Petree/Petry I) was born about 1901 in Good Hope Newton County. Mississippi.

Generation 4: *Arthur Petree:* (3Thomas Jefferson Peatry) (2.Frank Petree/Petry II)(1.Frank Petree/Petry I) was born about 1903 in Good Hope Newton County. Mississippi.

Generation 4: *Burnice Peatry:* (3Thomas Jefferson Peatry) (2.Frank Petree/Petry II)(1.Frank Petree/Petry I) was born on April 15, 1905 in Good Hope Newton County. Mississippi. Burnice married Bessie Butler. Bessie was born on January 21, 1911. She died on August 21, 2010 in Burbank, Los Angeles, California. He died on August 24, 1981 in Chicago, Cook County, Illinois.

Generation 5 needs more information

Generation 4: *Grady Petry:* (3Thomas Jefferson Peatry) (2.Frank Petree/Petry II)(1.Frank Petree/Petry I) was born on February 22, 1907 in Good Hope, Newton County, Mississippi. He died on Jun 30, 1992 in Chicago, Cook County, Illinois. Grady Petry married Florence Mitchell on June 15, 1933 in Chicago, Cook County, Illinois. Grady later married Ann Reed on June 30, 1953 in Chicago, Illinois.

Grady Petry married Florence Mitchell had

Generation 5: need more information

*More on **Generation 3: Grady Petry***

Grady Petry married Ann Reed and had
Generation 5: Ann Peatry

Generation 4: Lawyer Peatry: (3*Thomas Jefferson Peatry*) (2.*Frank Petree/Petry II*)(1.*Frank Petree/Petry I*) was born in Good Hope Newton County, Mississippi in 1910. He died on December 30, 1973 in Chicago, Cook County, Illinois

Generation 4: Angeline Petry (3*Thomas Jefferson Peatry*) (2.*Frank Petree/Petry II*)(1.*Frank Petree/Petry I*) died at a very early age and is buried in the old Good Hope Church Cemetery posted "Colored Cemetery"

See more on Frank Petree II
Lucie Jones *was listed in 1940 as head of household living in Beat 5 of Newton County, Mississippi with one child; fifteen year old Roy Jones and her grandparents one hundred and three year old Frank Petry Jr. and eighty three year old wife Louise Salter Petry.*

CHAPTER SEVENTEEN

Slaveholding Kirby Family of Newton County

Mary Johnson/ Kirby/ Curby

The Mother of Filmore Johnson

Mary Kirby, the mother of Filmore Johnson, [spelled Kirby on Filmore's death certificate] is believed to have been held enslaved by John Kirby/Kerby of Newton and Jasper Counties. She is alleged to be the Mary Johnson in the 1870 census in Newton County listed as the mother of Frank Petry II. Plus research reveals the same Mary Kirby Johnson was living in the Good Hope Colored Settlement in rural Hickory, Mississippi in 1880 and is said to be the mother of Daniel Johnson I, Preston Johnson, and a daughter, Amanda Johnson.

Defending the theories regarding Mary Curby/ Kirby was not an easy task. But with research, insights, recollections and perspectives from family elders, several facts were established connecting Mary Kirby/Curby Johnson to the Johnson/Petry/Petree family and the "original" Good Hope Church Community on Fellowship Road. Mary Kirby/Curby was born in 1815 in Georgia and lived in rural Hickory, Mississippi in the Good Hope Colored Settlement with her sons. Mary died on April 23, 1896. She is buried in the old Good Hope Church Cemetery near the Good Hope Baptist Church on Fellowship Road posted "Colored Cemetery". Her head stone read "Mary Curby Died April 23, 1896."

The Descendants of Filmore Johnson

Generation 2: *Filmore Johnson*: (*1.Frank Petry/Petree I.*) was born on March 15, 1858 in Mississippi. Filmore Johnson married Elizabeth Levy in 1877 and had thirteen children. Elizabeth was the daughter of Simon and Julia Levy. Filmore died on December 13, 1945 in Newton Co. Mississippi. He was buried in the Good Hope Church Colored Settlement Cemetery.

Filmore and Elizabeth (Bettie) Johnson had :

Generation 3: *Fannie E Johnson* (2.

Filmore Johnson) (*1.Frank Petry/Petree I*) was born in August 1874 in Newton County. Mississippi in the Good Hope Colored Settlement. Fannie married Seaborne Lee II son of Seaborne Lee I and Harriett Lee. They had one child during their marriage. Fannie died in Chicago and was buried in the Good Hope Church Cemetery in the Good Hope Colored Settlement

Fannie Johnson and Seaborne Lee I had one child:

Generation 4: *Daniel Lee (3.Fannie Johnson)* **(2.** *Filmore Johnson)(1.Frank Petry/Petree I)*was born in 1900 in Newton County, Mississippi in the Good Hope Colored Settlement. While living in the Good Hope community Daniel Lee married Missouri Christine Allen and moved up to Chicago in 1919. Missouri was born on April 12, 1901 in Mississippi. She died on July 4, 1995 in Chicago, Cook County, Illinois. He died on September 26, 1989 in Chicago, Cook County, Illinois.

Daniel Lee and Missouri Christine Allen had one child:

Generation5: *Felix Raymond Lee* **(4.** *Daniel Lee)(3.Fannie Johnson Lee)* **(2.** *Filmore Johnson)(1.Frank Petry/Petree I)* Felix Raymond Lee was born on April 4, 1918, in Hickory, Mississippi. Moved up to Chicago with his parents in 1919 Had five children. Felix Died in Chicago, Illinois

Felix Raymond Lee had

Generation 6: Elnora Lee
Generation 6: Lillian Lee
Generation 6 : Rachel Lee
Generation 6 : Arnold Lee

Generation 3: *Daniel Johnson II:* **(2.** *Filmore Johnson) (1. Frank Petrey/Petree I)* was born in Newton County Good Hope Colored Settlement near Hickory, Daniel Johnson II continue Mississippi on February 24, 1880. When Daniel was about twenty-five years old he met Lillie Toles the love of his life. Lila was a delicate young woman not quite seventeen. Soon after they were married Daniel wrote in his Bible "Daniel Johnson II married Lilia Toles on November 27, 1904. In the early 1900s Daniel II purchase 287 acres of land in rural Newton County Daniel Johnson II became a member of Good Hope Colored Church on October 11, 1919; Lillie died in 1933. Daniel Johnson II died on November 11, 1956 and is buried in Good Hope Church Colored

Cemetery.

Daniel Johnson II and Lillie Toles Johnson had

Generation 4: *France Johnson (3.Daniel Johnson II)* **(2.** *Filmore Johnson) (1. Frank Petrey/Petree I)* was born in 1905/ 1907 in Good Hope Colored Settlement he married Exie Carroll the daughter of Albert and Callie Tate. Albert Carroll was the son of George and Katherine Carroll. **France** and Exie lived in the Hickory area until France died on September 10, 1946 She later relocated to Chicago, Illinois with her children.

France and Exie Carroll Johnson had

Generation 5: Marshall Johnson
Generation 5: Bettie Johnson
Generation 5: Daisy Johnson
Generation 5: Lillie Johnson
Generation 5: Timothy Johnson

Generation 4: *Robert Johnson(3.Daniel Johnson II)* **(2.** *Filmore Johnson) (1. Frank Petrey/Petree I)* born in1906

Generation 4: Robert Johnson II was born in 1908 in the Good Hope Community he worked as a young man as a farm hand and in the timber industry. He later removed up to Freeport and Rockford, Illinois and worked in the foundries in the cities. In Rockford he met and married Lilian and lived in Rockford for a number of years. When he returned to Mississippi he married his second wife Daisy Chapman. Robert return to the north and lived with several brothers and sisters in Rockford, Freeport, Illinois and Cleveland, Ohio Robert Johnson is buried in the Good Hope Colored Cemetery.

Robert and **Lillian Johnson** had the following children:
Generation 5: Alfred Johnson
Generation 5: Christie Johnson
Generation 5: Tharvel Johnson
Generation 5: David Johnson

Robert and **Daisy Johnson** had the following children:

Generation 5: Albert Johnson II
Generation 5: Carroll Johnson
Generation 5: Walter James Johnson
Generation 5: Isedore Johnson
Generation 5: Oscar Earl Johnson
Generation 5: Raymond Johnson
Generation 5: Emmet Johnson
Generation 5: Linda Johnson

Generation 4: *Charles Johnson* *(3.Daniel Johnson II)* *(2. Filmore Johnson) (1. Frank Petrey/Petree I)* was born in 1905 in The Good Hope in 1920 at age 16 he relocated Freeport, Illinois with a cousin Rubin Salter. While in Freeport he met and married Katharine Mosley in 1932. Charles and Katharine lived in Freeport until retirement when they relocated with their children to Minnesota. Charles died Minnesota in 1992

Charles and Katharine Johnson had

Generation 5: Katharine Mosley
Generation 5: Charles Johnson
Generation 5: Carol Johnson
Generation 5: Delbert Johnson
Generation 5: William Johnson
Generation 5: Harold Johnson
Generation 5: Jerry Johnson

Generation 4: *Blanche Johnson* *(3.Daniel Johnson II)* *(2. Filmore Johnson) (1. Frank Petrey/Petree I)* was born in Good Hope Mississippi in 1910. She like her brothers and sisters during the Great Migration and earlier relocated "Up North" Her dictation was with family who had settled in Freeport and Rockford Illinois. She married Frank Burris and raised a nephew as her own. They later relocated to Cleveland, Ohio where she lived for most of her life. Blanch died on May 23, 2000

Generation 4: Archie Johnson *(3.Daniel Johnson II)* (**2.** Filmore Johnson) (**1.** Frank Petrey/Petree I) was born on 8 Oct 1911 in Good Hope, Mississippi. Archie married

Edna Hayden in 1934 and worked in the timber industry. Edna was the daughter of Milton Hayden and Susie Anna Salter. Edna was born on September 10, 1913 in Good Hope Mississippi near rural Hickory, Mississippi.
Edna was a teacher in the settlement school. In 1950 Archie and Edna relocated up to Freeport, Illinois. Archie worked for a while in foundries in Freeport and Rockford, Illinois and later began his own business scrap metal hauling and disposal business, later known as "Johnson and Sons"
Archie died on November 9, 1995 in Freeport, Illinois and is buried in the Freeport City Cemetery Edna died on February 20, 2001 in Freeport, Illinois.

Archie and **Edna Hayden Johnson** had the following children:
Generation 5: Alline Johnson
Generation 5: Emma Ruth Johnson
Generation 5: Daniel Spencer Johnson III
Generation 5: Doris Johnson
Generation 5: Joyce Marie Johnson
Generation 5: Billy G. Johnson
Generation 5: Edna Earl Johnson
Generation 5: Paulette Lynette Johnson
Generation 5: Robert Louis Johnson
Generation 5: Walter James Johnson

Generation 4: General Johnson *(3.Daniel Johnson III)* (**2.** *Filmore Johnson) (1. Frank Petrey/Petree I)* was born in 1914 in Good Hope Colored Settlement near Hickory, Mississippi. General married **Elouis** Eloise was born about 1921 in Mississippi. In the late 1940's they a relocated to Freeport, Illinois

General and **Elouise** Johnson had:

Generation 5: Charles Johnson
Generation 5: Curtis Johnson
Generation 5: Janette Johnson

Generation 4: *Ruth Johnson* *(3.Daniel Johnson II) (2. Filmore Johnson) (1. Frank Petrey/Petree I)* was born about 1915 in the Good Hope Colored Settlement. She married Anderson Hester and relocated to Freeport,

Illinois with her husband in the early 1930's. Ruth died in 1936 during child birth. Her Death Certificate shows her mother as Lila Toles in entry for Ruth Hester, August 10, 1936; Public Board of Health

Ruth Johnson Hester was born to Daniel and Lila Toles on February 6, 1915 in Hickory, Mississippi in the community of Good Hope in Newton County. Ruth married Anderson Hester when she was about 19 years old. Some years later she relocated up north with her brother Charles to Freeport Illinois. On August 10, 1936 Ruth died shortly afterward giving birth to a son Charles. She was buried on August 14, 1936 Hickory, Mississippi Good Hope Cemetery.

Ruth and Anderson Hester had one child:

Generation 5: Charles Hester Johnson *Ruth Johnson (3.Daniel Johnson II) (2. Filmore Johnson) (1. Frank Petrey/Petree I)* was raised by his uncle Charles Johnson in Freeport. Charles spent most of his adult life in Rockford, Illinois. Charles died in Rockford in 2013 and is buried in Freeport Illinois City Cemetery.

Generation 4: Emma Johnson *(3.Daniel Johnson II) (2. Filmore Johnson) (1. Frank Petrey/Petree I)* was born 1916 in the Good Hope Colored Settlement. Emma married Carter Ford in the early 1940 and they relocated to Cleveland

Emma Johnson and Carter Ford had:

Generation 5: Myrna Carter

Generation 4: *Albert Johnson I (3.Daniel Johnson II) (2. Filmore Johnson) (1. Frank Petrey/Petree I)* was born about 1918 in the Good Hope Settlement he attended the Good hope colored school and moved up to Freeport, Illinois in 1938 In the Freeport he met and married Jessie Lee Burris in 1945.

Albert and Jessie Lee Johnson had:

Generation 5: Charlotte Robinson Johnson
Generation 5: Albert Johnson III
Generation 5: Jennie Johnson
Generation 5: Michelle Johnson
Generation 5: Leon Burris

Generation 4: Otha Johnson I *(3.Daniel Johnson II) (2. Filmore Johnson) (1. Frank Petrey/Petree I)* was born on January 21, 1921 in Good Hope Hickory, Newton County. Mississippi At an early age he joined the Good Hope Baptist Church. In 1939 he relocated to Freeport, Illinois where he met and married Martha Bruce on July 31, 1943. Otha was a member of St. Paul Missionary Baptist Church, in Freeport, Illinois. He worked at Honeywell's Micro Switch (Freeport) for 21 years. While in Freeport, Illinois He also worked at Gunite Foundry in Rockford, Fairbanks Morse and the Illinois Central Railroad. He served in the U.S. Air Force. Otha died on January 18, 2003 in Freeport, Stephenson County. Illinois. He was buried in Chapel Hill Memorial Gardens Freeport.

Otha and **Martha Johnson** had the following children:

Generation 5: Otha Johnson Jr.
Generation 5: Frances Johnson
Generation 5: Karlene Johnson
Generation 5: Twila Johnson
Generation 5: Terrence Johnson
Generation 5: Kevin Johnson
Generation 5: Tracy Johnson

Generation 4: *Opal Johnson (3.Daniel Johnson II) (2. Filmore Johnson) (1. Frank Petrey/Petree I)* was born on 21 Jan 1921 in Good Hope Settlement Mississippi. Opal married Rufus Ed Ford and they worked a small farm in the community until Ed died. Opal and moved up to Newton to be near her children where she lived until she died.

Opal Johnson and **Rufus Ed Ford** had

Generation 5: Oliver James Ford
Generation 5: Ernestine Ford
Generation 5: Sammy Lee Ford

Generation 5: Otha Dave Ford
Generation 5: Oliver James Ford
Generation 5: Ruby Nell Ford
Generation 5: Dorothy Ruth
Generation 5: Linda Fay Ford
Generation 5: Billy Ray Ford
Generation 5: Marion Fay Ford
Generation 5: Edward Ford
Generation 5: Dauphine Ford

Generation 4: *Walter Johnson* (Saul) *(3.Daniel Johnson II)* *(2. Filmore Johnson)* *(1. Frank Petrey/Petree I)* was born about 1923 in Good Hope Newton County. Mississippi. Walter died at age seventeen and never married. Occupation: soldier. He died on January 3, 1941 in Newton County Hospital in Mississippi. He was buried in Good Hope Church Cemetery, Cause of death: pneumonia and influenza.

Walter J. Johnson (1924–1941) Newton, Mississippi **Walter Johnson** was born in Good Hope Colored Community in Newton County to Daniel Johnson and Lillie Toles. Walter attended the little Colored community school and at the age of seventeen he signed up for Military duty. Soon afterward he contracted pneumonia and influenza. Walter died in Newton, Mississippi Hospital on January 3, 1941 and is buried in Good Hope Church Colored Cemetery. (*More about Walter*

Walter J. Johnson never married – no children.

Generation 4: *Tommie L. (T L) Johnson* (*3.Daniel Johnson II)* *(2. Filmore Johnson)* *(1. Frank Petrey/Petree I)* was born about 1925 in Good Hope Settlement Newton County. Mississippi. He relocated to Freeport, Illinois met and married first wife Joyce Lenoir He married his second wife and third wife Christine

Tommie L. (T L) and (1st wife) Joyce Lenoir Johnson had
Generation 5: Tommy Johnson
Generation 5: Alvin Johnson
Generation 5: Ray Johnson

Tommie L. (T L) and (2nd wife) Martha Johnson had
Generation 5: Dawana Johnson
Generation 5: Vickie Johnson
Tommie L. (T L) and (3rd wife) Christine had no children
Generation 3: More on Rev. Daniel Johnson II
Daniel Johnson II married his 2nd wife Mahala Allen Johnson in 1933. Mahala Allen Johnson died on September 15, 1994 in Paulding, Mississippi.

Rev. Daniel Johnson and 2nd wife Mahalia Johnson had

Generation 4: *Filmore Clarence Johnson* *(3.Daniel Johnson II)* (2. Filmore Johnson) (1. Frank Petrey/Petree I) was born October 2, 1946 in Paulding Mississippi. Clarence served in the Air Force attended Alcorn State relocated to Denver Colorado, received engineering degree married Helen Jackson retired to Raleigh, North Carolina died in 2009 buried in Good Hope Cemetery

Filmore Clarence Johnson and Helen Jackson had

Generation 5: Tonya Johnson
Generation 5: Tracee Johnson

Generation 4: *Georgann Johnson* *(3.Daniel Johnson II)* (2. Filmore Johnson) (1. Frank Petrey/Petree I) **married**

Generation 5:Demetria L Bridges
Generation 5:Centralia E Bridges
Generation 5: Thomas Bridges

More on Reverend Daniel S. Johnson's Bible
Reverend Daniel S. Johnson had a Bible that was is in the care of his oldest living son Charles Johnson. After Charles died his children located the Bible. Inside the Bible were little bits of paper with sermon notes and brief biographical information on the family. Charles had left a letter written to the family regarding the Bible and its contents in part the letter directed" that the

Bible and its contents be keep safe and shared by the family". The Bible and the yellow faded time worn notes are very fragile and in need of special care. Harold and other families members agreed that the Bible and its contents be handle as little as possible. Therefore all of; or as much as possible were copies and is printed in this book.

Copies held by Harold Johnson

The Descendants of Dorris Johnson and Annie Johnson

More on Daniel Johnson II; In the early 1900 as a young man, prior to his call to preach, Daniel shared a common law relationship with Fanny Beason and two children was the result of that relationship; a son Dorris Johnson, born in 1901 and a daughter Annie Johnson born in 1902. Daniel gave his children his name and after the relationship was mutually over Daniel continued to maintain the relationship with his children and his grandchildren.

Generation 4: Dorris Johnson (3.Daniel Johnson II) (2. Filmore Johnson) (1. Frank Petrey/Petree I) was born in 1902 to Daniel Johnson II and Fanny Beason. The 1930 census shows Doris was married to Lizzie [maiden name not known]

Dorris Johnson and Lizzie had the following children:

Generation 5: Charles Johnson born in 1924
Generation 5: Carl Johnson was born in 1928
Generation 5: Phronia Johnson born in 1930.

Generation 4: Annie Mae Johnson(3.Daniel Johnson II) (2. Filmore Johnson) (1. Frank Petrey/Petree I) was born in 1903 she later married Mr. Clemon Walker and had 13 children: Annie Johnson Walker obituary printed in 1999 shows 98 year old Annie had at the time of her death;

fifty grandchildren and one hundred and thirteen great grandchildren and fifty one great- great-grandchildren.

Annie Johnson Walker and Clemon Walker had 13 children:

Generation 5: Johnnie Ruth Walker
Generation 5: Clemmie Walker
Generation 5: Earlene Walker
Generation 5: Lula Walker
Generation 5: Mildred Walker
Generation 5: Edna Ruth Walker
Generation 5: Mae Bell Walker
Generation 5: Earnest Walker
Generation 5: Martha Walker
Generation 5: Bonnie Bell Walker
Generation 5: Aaron Walker
Generation 5: Charlie Walker
Generation 5: James Walker
Generation 5: Lonnie Walker

The Descendants Of Filmore and Bettie Johnson continue

Generation 3: Robert Johnson (2.Filmore Johnson) (1.Frank Petrey/Petree I) was born in Newton County he married Annie Lee.

Robert and Annie Lee Johnson had;

Generation 4: John L. Johnson (3.Robert Johnson) (2.Filmore Johnson) (1.Frank Petrey/Petree I) married Susie Pruitt the daughter of Alice Salter and Phil Pruitt John L. and Susie Pruitt Johnson had:

Generation 5: Johnnie Ruth Johnson married John D. Brown
Generation 6: Johnny D. Brown
Generation 6: James D. Brown
Generation 6: Mary Ruth Brown

Generation 5: Mary Ruth Johnson

Generation 5: Rosie Lee Johnson had
Generation 6: Robert Overstreet
Generation 6: Shirley Moore
Generation 6: Mary Moore
Generation 6: Gendolyn Johnson

Generation 6: James Earl Johnson
Generation 6: Johnny Johnson

Generation 5: Amy Lee Johnson and Henry Gaddis had
Generation 6: Lacy Gaddis

Generation 4: Claudius Johnson (3. Robert Johnson) (2.Filmore Johnson) (1.Frank Petrey/Petree I

Claudius Johnson married Hazel had
Generation 5 Jacqueline Wilkins

Generation 4: J.P. Johnson (3. Robert Johnson) (2.Filmore Johnson) (1.Frank Petrey/Petree I
Generation 4: Dave Johnson (3. Robert Johnson) (2.Filmore Johnson) (1.Frank Petrey/Petree

Dave Johnson I married Alice Tate and had
Generation 5: Dave Johnson II
Generation 5: Dan Johnson

Generation 4: Tom E. Johnson (3.Robert Johnson I)(2.Filmore Johnson) (1.Frank Petrey/Petree I)

Tom E. and Bonnie Bogan Johnson had
Generation 5: Charles Johnson
Generation 5: Jerry Johnson
Generation 5: James Johnson
Generation 5 Billy Johnson
Generation 5 Willie Johnson
Generation 5: Larry Johnson
Generation 5: Glen Johnson
Generation 5: Albert Johnson
Generation 5: Robert Johnson

Generation 4: *Eretia Johnson* (3.Robert Johnson I) (2.Filmore Johnson) (1.Frank Petrey/Petree I)

Eretia Johnson Potts and Potts had
Generation 5: James Potts
Generation 4: Rebecca Johnson (3.Robert Johnson I) (2.Filmore Johnson) (1.Frank Petrey/Petree I) married Aaron Mc Glothin I

Rebecca Johnson and Aaron McGlothin had
Generation 5 Aaron McGlothin II
Generation 5: Gloria McNease
Generation 5 :Glyndia McGlothin

Generation 3: *Eliza Johnson* (2.*Filmore Johnson)(1.Frank Petry/Petree I)* was born in Newton County in 1884
Eliza Johnson and Guss Toullos had

Generation 4: *Fannie Johnson (3.Eliza Johnson* (2.*Filmore Johnson) 1.Frank Petry/Petree I)* she married **Aaron Pruitt Aaron and Fannie had contracted tuberculosis and died within a short time of each other.

Aaron and Fannie Johnson Pruitt had
Generation 5: Alonzo Pruitt
Generation 5: Lenard Pruitt
Generation 5: Grace Pruitt
Generation 5 Thomas Pruitt
Generation 5: Willie Mae Pruitt
Generation 5: James T Pruitt

Generation 4: *Elisha Preston Tullos* *(Eliza Johnson)(2.Filmore Johnson)(1.Frank Petry/Petree I)*

Generation 4: *Elisha Preston Tullos* the son of Eliza
Johnson and Gus Tullos married Esther Gaddis in Hickory, Mississippi in1927 and they had two sons. Elisha and Esther early life was spent as a farmer in the Good Hope Settlement. In 1936, he relocated with his family to Chicago and acquired a job with the Pennsylvania Railroad where he worked until he retired in 1972. Esther had died two years earlier.

Elisha Preston Tullos and Esther Gaddis had

Generation 5: Gaddis Steven Tullos
Generation 5: James Curtis Tullos

Generation 3: *Julia Johnson* (2.Filmore Johnson)(1.Frank Petry/Petree I) was born in Newton County in 1886.

Generation 3: *Mary Johnson* (2.Filmore Johnson) (1.Frank Petre/Petree I) was born in Good Hope Colored settlement in Newton County in 1888. Mary married Isaac Salter the son of Frank and Dora Salter. In the early 1900's they lived and operated a farm in the Good Hope Settlement and was a pillar of both the settlement and Good Hope Colored Settlement Church.

Mary and Isaac continues
Mary and Isaac in their later years moved up to Freeport, Illinois to be near their children. Both died in Freeport and both are buried in the Good Hope Church Cemetery.

Isaac and Mary Salter had:

Generation 4: *Rubin Salter I (3.Mary Johnson) (2.Filmore Johnson) (1.Frank Petre/Petree I)* was born in 1909 in Good Hope Colored Settlement.. Rubin moved up to Freeport, Illinoi s at a young age. When he found work he returned to Mississippi and married Mittie Mae Oliver in Enterprise, Mississippi and he and his bride returned to Freeport. The Salters were passionate entrepreneurs, owning Salters Grocery and Luncheon as well as the Salters Bar- B-Que Ranch. Mittie was a strong civil rights activist in the Freeport community. Rubin died in 1990 in Freeport, Illinois.

Rubin and Mittie Oliver Salter had

Generation 5: Rubin Salter II
Generation 5: Larry Salter
Generation 5: Yvonne Salter

Generation 4: *Willie Clayborn Salter (3.Mary Johnson) (2.Filmore Johnson) (1.Frank Petre/Petree I)* was born was born about 1912 in the Good Hope Mississippi. He was also known as "Clayborn." When he was a young man he left Good Hope for work up north to Freeport, Illinois.

Willie Clayborn Salter and **Queen Esther Burris** had

Generation 5: Thomas Calvin Salter was born in 1937.

Later Clayborn met and married Laura Millie Pearson. Clayborn was called to preach and was ordained at Saint Paul Baptist Church in Freeport, Illinois. After several years as pastor at St Paul Church M.B. Church Clayborn was called to preach at New Zion M.B. Church in Rockford, Illinois where he pastored for thirty eight years. He was co-owner with his son Thomas of several businesses. Clayborn died in Rockford in 2005.

Generation 4: Broomsy Salter*(3.Mary Johnson) (2.Filmore Johnson) (1.Frank Petre/Petree I)* was born in 1913, in Good Hope Colored Settlement attended Good Hope School and married Christine McGee in Mississippi. Broomsy enlisted in the Army in 1945, and after the war he relocated with his wife to Freeport, Illinois, Broomsy was a pillar of the Freeport Community until his death on 15 Nov 2009.

Broomsy and Christine Salter had no children:

Generation 4: *Lonnie Salter (3.Mary Johnson) (2.Filmore Johnson) (1.Frank Petre/Petree I)* was born in 1917 in Good Hope Colored Settlement in Newton County, Mississippi. He relocated to Chicago where he was employed by the Burlington Railroad Lonnie Married Edna Shadwick in 1942 Lonnie Died in Chicago, Illinois on December 11, 1990

Lonnie and **Edna Shadwick Salter** had:

Generation 5: Edna Salter
Generation 5: Lonnie Salter

Generation 4:*Addie Lee Salter (3.Mary Johnson) (2.Filmore Johnson) (1.Frank Petre/Petree I)*was born about 1918 in Good Hope Colored Settlement in Newton County. Mississippi. Attended Good Hope School then relocated up to Freeport, Illinois with older brothers. Addie met and married Clifton Thurston.

Addie and Clifton Thurston had one child:

Generation 5: Mary Ruth Thurston

Generation 4: Robert Salter *(3.Mary Johnson) (2.Filmore Johnson) (1.Frank Petre/Petree I)* was born in 1920 in Newton County, Mississippi. Robert married Oshia Bell Strong and relocated up North to Freeport, Illinois with other relatives.

Robert and **Oshia Bell Salter** had the following Children

Generation 5: Maxine Strong
Generation 5: Linda Salter
Generation 5: Brenda Salter

Generation 3: Preston Johnson II *(Filmore Johnson) (Frank Petry/Petree II.)* was born in Good Hope Settlement in Newton County in 1891. Preston Johnson married Classie Dawkins Johnson and had two children. Preston died in in 1897 in Rockford, Illinois at the age of ninety six.

Preston Johnson had

Generation 4: Cleo Johnson

Generation 4: Larraine Johnson

Lorrain Johnson married Douglas Thurmond and had
Generation 5: William Thurmond
Generation 5: Delores Thurmond
Generation 5: Sharon Thurmond

Generation 3: *Minerva Johnson* *(2. Filmore Johnson) (1. Frank Petry/Petree I)* was born in1893 in Good Hope Mississippi. Minerva Johnson married Horace Mc Donald and relocated to California.

Generation 3: *Lela Johnson* *(2.Filmore Johnson) (1.Frank Petry/Petree I)* was born in Newton County in June 1896.

Lela Johnson married Ed Edison. In 1920, Ed and Lela made their home in Jasper County about five miles south of the Colored Settlement of Good Hope Later they purchased farm land in the Settlement where they lived and farmed with their Children. Lela Johnson Edison died in 1995 in Freeport, Illinois.

Lela Johnson and Ed Edison had

Generation 4: *Ardell Edison* *(3. Lela Johnson) (2. Filmore Johnson) (1. Frank Petry/Petree I)* the elder son of Ed and Lela Johnson Edison and his brothers and sisters attended Good Hope Colored School and helped with chores on the farm. Ardell register for the draft during WW II in Newton County, Mississippi. After the war Ardell stayed on in the community and married Clatie Bell Patrick, in 1948.

Ardell and Clatie Bell Patrick Edison had

Generation 5: Frances Delores Edison
Generation 5: Bruce Edison
Generation 5: Lela Edison
Generation 5: Sandra Ellen Edison
Generation 5: Eric Edison
Generation 5: Fredrick Edison

Generation 4: *Percy Edison* *(3. Lela Johnson) (2.Filmore Johnson) (1.Frank Petry/Petree I)* died at a young age.

Generation 4: *Maudie Edison* *(3. Lela Johnson) (2.Filmore Johnson) (1.Frank Petry/Petree I)* was born in Good Hope Mississippi in 1921 She attended the Good Hope and other schools. Later she would be hired as one of the teachers in the little two room school in the Good Hope Community. In 1940 she relocated to Freeport, Illinois where she met and married Roger Massey. Maudie Died in 2005 in Freeport, Illinois

Maudie and Roger Massey had no children:

Generation 4: *Chester Edison* (3.*Lela Johnson*) (2.*Filmore Johnson*) (1.*Frank Petry/Petree I*)

Chester married Vergie had no children

Generation 4: *Clifton Edison*(3.*Lela Johnson*) (2.*Filmore Johnson*) (1.*Frank Petry/Petree I*)

Clifton and Rena Mae Morris Edison had

Generation 5: Renee Edison
Generation 5: Stanley Edison
Generation 5: Edward Edison
Generation 5: Ray Edison

Generation 4: Francis *Earlene Edison Broomfield* (3.*Lela Johnson*) (2.*Filmore Johnson*) (1.*Frank Petry/Petree I*) Earlene was proprietor of a restaurant and was famous in all of Mississippi for her wonderful food.

Earlene and Hardy. Doby had

Generation 5: Melvin Ship
Generation 5: Arthur Doby
Generation 5 Davey Doby

Generation 4: ***Johnnie Edison I (3. Lela Johnson) (2. Filmore Johnson) (1. Frank Petry/Petree I)*** was born in the Good Hope Settlement worked with his father attended the settlement school Married Nannie Mae Youngblood and removed up to Freeport, Illinois. Johnnie died in 1990. Nannie continues to live in Freeport.

Johnnie and Nannie Youngblood Edison had

Generation 5: Johnnie Edison II
Generation 5: Gerry Edison

Generation 4: ***Oliver James (OJ) Edison I (3.*Lela Johnson*) (2.*Filmore Johnson*) (1.*Frank Petry/Petree I*)*** was born in Good Hope Mississippi he migrated to Freeport; Illinois met and married Maxine Cain. The couple had five children. Years later Oliver James was called to preach and pastored a

church in Des Moines, Iowa. When he retired he returned to the Good Hope settlement where he severs as the associate Minister at the Good Hope Baptist Church. His wife Maxine died and is buried in the Good Hope cemetery. Reverend Edison continues to live in the Good Hope Community area.

Oliver J. (OJ) and Maxine Cain Edison had

Generation 5: Carla Edison
Generation 5: Keith Edison
Generation 5: Olivia (Libby) Edison
Generation 5: James(Jimmy) Edison
Generation 5: Darrell Edison

Generation 3: ***Sallie Johnson* (2.*Filmore Johnson*) (1.*Frank Petry/Petree I*)** was born in Good Hope Colored Settlement The youngest of three siblings she lived in the community with her parents until 1815. In 1851, she married Frank Salter II the son of Cason and Cherry Salter. Frank was born on March 10, 1892 in Good Hope Mississippi he died in Chicago, Illinois. Sallie died in 1991 at the age of ninety-nine.

Generation 4: *George Buster Salter* (3.*Sallie Johnson*) (2.*Filmore Johnson*) (1.*Frank Petry/Petree I*) was born in Good Hope Mississippi in 1916, to Sally and Frank Salter II. George moved with his family to Chicago in 1927, where he attended school. He was in the Navy in 1942. George and his wife, Louise Lucille Stroter, met in high school and they were married in 1941. George Salter died in Chicago in 1999. Louise died in Chicago.

George and Louise Stroter Salter had

Generation 5: Brenda Salter
Generation 5: Henrietta Salter

Generation 4: *Louis Salter I.* (3.*Sallie Johnson*) (2.*Filmore Johnson*) (1.*Frank Petry/Petree I*) was born in Good Hope Settlement near Hickory, Mississippi. He died on August 18, 2002 in Chicago,

Illinois. Louis married Doris Ann White. Doris was born on July 23, 1921. She died on 26 Jan 1989 in Chicago, Illinois

Louis married Doris Ann White and had

Generation 5: Louis Salter II
 Generation 5: Ronald Salter
Generation 5: Andrew Salter
Generation 5: Melvin Salter

Generation 4: *Eula Mae Salter* (3.*Sallie Johnson*) (2.*Filmore Johnson*) (1.*Frank Petry/Petree I*)   was born in Good Hope Mississippi she and her family moved up to Chicago in 1942 she met and married Derrius Jones. Eula worked for twenty six years for the Burlington Northern Railways. Eula died in Chicago in 1989.

Eula Mae Salter and Derrius Jones had:

Generation 5: Charlotte Jones
Generation 5: Sherry Jones
Generation 5: Barbara Jones

Generation 2: More on Filmore Johnson
Filmore Johnson and Pearl's mother had
Generation 3: *Pearl Johnson (1.Frank Petry/Petree I)*
Pearl Johnson married ? and they the following children
Generation 4:
Generation

CHAPTER EIGHTEEN

The Father of Elizabeth Levy Johnson

Simeon [also known as Simon] Levy is the father of Elizabeth (Bettie) Levy Johnson. (*See 1870 United States Census*) Simeon was born enslaved in 1842, on the Sarah Moses Levy plantation in Kershaw County, South Carolina. Simeon was born one of eight known children to his enslaved mother, Nancy. After Sarah Moses Levy's death, per her will, Simeon and his seven brothers and sisters, his mother and her husband, Kennedy, all became the property of Sarah's son, Chapman Levy, and were relocated to Mississippi and held enslaved by several Levy descendants until he was freed in 1863.

Information regarding the Levy Slaveholders of South Carolina

Levy, a Jewish family name, this name is usually delivered from the ancient Spanish fortress of EL Castro, which was called "the town of the Jews" by Jewish medieval chroniclers in the Iberian Peninsula. The first Jewish families arriving in Spain during the times of the Roman Empire had Greek, Latin and Hebrew names. In the early eighth century, when Spain was conquered by the Arabs and came under Islamic rule, it became the shelter for many more Jewish people where they enjoyed religious freedom and were greatly involved in the government and administration. After the tenth century, when Spain was reconquered by the Christians, these same Arabic and Hebrew names were still being used by the Spanish Jews or Sephardic Jews. It was not until the sixteenth century inquisition that Jewish people changed names, when they were forcibly converted and baptized and took Spanish-Christian names, becoming the "New Christians" or "Marranos" of Spain. Yet the same conservatism and love of tradition can be seen among the Marranos, who retained their Spanish-Christian names when much later they were able to re-convert to Judaism, just as those who fled the country tended to keep their Spanish names wherever they moved to. This trend among Sephardic Jews to retain their family names intact has enabled family historians to trace closely their histories. Especially interesting is the fact that large proportion of Spanish names is transported from place names. **Courtesy of the Jewish Heritage Collection of the College of Charleston Library, Charleston, South Carolina**

The city of Camden is the only city in South Carolina besides Georgetown where the Jewish people settled in numbers prior to 1800. An early sign of Jewish people in the Camden District where found in the Columbia, South Carolina record is the birth of Chapman Levy. Chapman Levy I was born on July 4, 1787 in Camden, South Carolina to Samuel and Sarah Moses Levy.

He had one sister, Eliza Levy. Eliza Levy married Dr. Edward Anderson I and they had two children: a son, Chapman Levy Anderson II and a daughter, Lucy Anderson. On December 25, 1818 Chapman Levy I married Flora Levy I and they had a son, Chapman Edward Levy III and a daughter, Flora Eliza Levy II.

Chapman Levy I studied law and was admitted to the Bar in Columbia, South Carolina. In the late 1820's, he formed a law partnership with his lifelong friend, William McWillie. He also ran a brickyard in Columbia that used enslaved labor. In 1820, Levy held thirty one enslaved workers, twenty one of whom were employed at his brickyard near the Columbia Canal. These numbers, while low compared to plantation slave holdings, made him the largest Jewish slaveholder in South Carolina.

In 1816, an insurrection was plotted by enslaved men in Camden, South Carolina. Several were held enslaved by Chapman Levy. Some were executed as leaders and most held as witness. Tom, the brother of Simon 2nd great grandfather to the author stated that he had met March at the brickyard and, "He asked me if I would join him to fight this country—that the black people who did not join they would be killed. The second trial of July 4 ended in a "Not Guilty" verdict for Tom who had produced no defense witnesses against the State's two witnesses. I said "I would not join. He said then they would kill me." Another man, March, the property of Chapman Levy, was found to be the leader and was hanged before the trials began. When the trials were over Levy petitioned the State for the value of his lost property and was granted $142.43 in compensation. Following the insurrection Levy sold the brickyard. *(See story of 1816 Insurrection Plotted by Enslaved Men in Camden, South Carolina) (See uprising by enslaved worker at the Brickyard in 1816)* ***(Stephen, Adam and Chapman Levy's boyhood playmate known as "Ole Kennedy", was held as a witness in the insurrection trials.)***

Prior to emancipation, many Negroes in America attempted to server the bonds of slavery by both overt and covert means. Some overt actions are well known: for example, the bloody rebellion of Nat Turner and the earlier attempted revolts of Gabriel Prosser in Virginia and Denmark Vesey in South Carolina. In the latter conspiracy, discovered in Charleston in 1822, procedures for trail and punishment were based upon a precedent set six years earlier in the quelling of a less well-known insurrection plot in Camden, South Carolina by people held enslaved by Chapman Levy and other in Camden, South Carolina.

In the early 1800's, Camden had long known the insecurity of warfare and conflict. Indian attacks had threatened the areas through the mid-1700's. During the Revolution, fourteen military engagements had been fought within a radius of thirty miles of the town. In 1780, Lord Cornwallis had occupied Camden, fortifying it with a log wall and five earthen forts as British headquarters for the Southern campaign. Local men who refused to pledge loyalty to the king were imprisoned in chains. Treachery, betrayal, and murder were not uncommon during these times as neighbors and relatives were forced to choose between partisan and loyalist cases.

The Fourth of July of 1816, however, seemed to be a holiday worthy of an especially joyful celebration. The previous year a treaty had ended the War of 1812; the British were now completely vanquished. Peace, prosperity, and security seemed assured. Yet, victories for freedom were empty for more than one-half the area's populace—those held in slavery. During the Revolution, the British had offered the lure of freedom to Negroes who would desert patriot masters and serve the Royal cause. Existing Revolutionary accounts from Camden indicate that both loyalist and patriot masters consumed a great deal of time pursuing runaways and otherwise controlling "their slaves." Although enemy-incited, wide-scale slave rebellions never materialized, the possibility of danger from blacks remained a concern in the early 1800's, as the Negro populations continued to increase.

A Quaker prophet passing through South Carolina between 1800 and 1804 warned that, unless slaves were freed, the recent horrors of the rebellion in the island republic of Santo Domingo could become a reality here. Fulfillment of the prophecy must have seemed underway in 1816, when a number of enslaved men in Camden actively embarked on a plot for armed rebellion. They planned to seize arms from an unguarded powder magazine in the town, striking on the Fourth of July when they expected "whites" to be in a carefree and inebriated state, celebrating the anniversary of political freedom. The captured arms would be turned on the white populace—and the slaves would be free.

One of their own race betrayed the plan, however, Scipio, a slave of Colonel James Chesnut, in mid-June went to his master's room to warn him and his family, then living near the powder magazine, of the dangers to them. Colonel Chesnut, according to contemporaries, was held in high regard by his slaves, among whom he was active in Christian ministry.

Instructing Scipio to attend the meetings of the rebel slaves to obtain further information, Colonel Chesnut, an aide-de-camp to Gov. David R. Williams, alerted the governor. Williams in turn gave Chesnut instructions which were to be kept secret from all but the town council. From that point on, leading citizens of the town, with advice of Governor Williams, moved to quell the rebellion by secretly gathering evidence.

Details of the proposed conspiracy, as reported by Camden attorney Francis Dellesseline, show the ambitious nature of the uprising: July 2nd to investigate "information given to the council of an intended insurrection of the slaves in the neighborhood. The council consisted of R. W. Carter, John Reed, Wyatt Stark, Dr. William Langley (then editor of the Camden **Gazette**), and the Intendant, Abram Blanding. The notes of the meeting have been identified as being in Blanding's hand.

Of the slaves questioned, seven denied knowing anything at all about a conspiracy; four of these—March, Ned, Cameron, and Jack—were also later hanged as ringleaders. Two other slaves who were also later hanged—Isaac and Spottswood—admitted knowledge of the plot but denied taking part themselves. Information gathered at this meeting was obviously not considered final proof of guilt or innocence. Judging from the notes, no witnesses at the preliminary but two Negroes accused [Tom, the brother of Simon 2nd great grandfather to the author] who was tried and freed. There were also other slaves who were accused by witnesses but not brought to trial.

The two who were most frequently implicated in pre-trial testimony were March and Isaac. Each was accused by three witnesses. Tom stated that he had met March at the brickyard and, "He asked me if I would join him to fight this country—that the black people who did not join they would be killed. I said I would not join. He said then they would kill me." Another slave testified that at the brickyard March, asking him to help fight and get guns, said he was going to get "a heap more" people to fight. The witness then said that March had often stopped blacks to talk with them.

Though twice questioned at the hearing, Isaac maintained his own innocence but implicated March, stating that twice March had asked him to join him in the plot to take the magazine. Isaac admitted, "I have said . . . that I thought it would be a good scheme if they could get through with it, but that Negroes were so deceitful that it would not do. [Others] said the same."

The lengthiest testimony against Isaac was given by Spottswood, also later condemned. Spottswood stated, "About a month ago . . . Isaac said he had a notion so get a parcel of men and go and fight the white people." Isaac asked Spottswood to join but the latter claimed he did not say whether he would or not, adding "Isaac. . .said if I told he would have me killed." Isaac allegedly directed Spottswood to speak to as many blacks as he could and recruit them to the cause.

Spottswood was accused of being involved in the plot by an elderly witness who stated, "He said they (the blacks) were going to rise and take the country. I said they had better not. He said he was one that was to rise. That they did not want old people to take any part in it." Spottswood admitted telling the other slave about the gathering of insurrectionists, but said, " I don't recollect whether I agreed to join or not."

As a result of evidence gathered at the meeting of the town council, trials were set immediately for several slaves. The trials were conducted by a court composed as provided by law, consisting of two Justices of the Peace, Thomas Salmond and John Kershaw, and five freeholders: Benjamin Bineham, Joseph Brevard, Burwell Boykin, Thomas Whitaker, and Benjamin Carter. The official records of the dispositions of the cases still exist, but lamentably there are no transcripts of testimony given. If the court records are bound (as they appear to be) in the order in which the trials were held, then the first tried was March, on July 3.

 The charge stated against him, as against all the other prisoners, was "attempting to raise an insurrection amongst the slaves [of South Carolina}." All pleaded "Not Guilty." Two other trials on July 3 examined Cameron and Jack. The State produced three witnesses against March, and called March as one of the five witnesses against Cameron. Three slaves testified against Jack. Each of the three cases was adjourned until July 4—ironically the day which had been set for the uprising—when each defendant was given a chance to produce witnesses on his behalf. None being presented, March, Cameron, and Jack were each declared "Guilty" and July 5 they were sentenced to hang that afternoon from four to five before the town goal.

Four trials were begun July 4, the first that of Isaac. Among the fur prosecution witnesses were March, Spottswood, and Scipio—the informant. Although Isaac presented one slave as a defense witness, he was adjudged "Guilty" and on the fifth sentenced to hang that afternoon.

The second trial of July 4, ended in a "Not Guilty" verdict for Tom who had produced no defense witnesses against the State's two witnesses. In the third case of the day, the Court tried Spottswood, calling three witnesses, including Isaac and Scipio. Having presented no witnesses in his behalf, Spottswood was declared "Guilty" and on the fifth was sentenced to hang with the others.

The final trial on July 4, ended with a curious punishment, the reasons for which are not included in the court record. Scipio was the only witness in the case against Stephen who presented one slave to testify in his defense. Stephen was declared "Guilty" and, on the fifth, the Court ordered that Stephen[great grandfather to the Levy of Freeport, Illinois "have the sentence of death passed on him at the same time that his fellows are condemned—and that his pardon of his said sentence be announced to him—after all the ceremonies of execution have been made."

One trial was held on July 5, that of Ned. For an unexplained reason, the Court convened with John Kershaw and John Reide as justices and only four of the other original members, "Thomas Salmond one of the justices and Joseph Brevard Esq. Having withdrawn." The trial was obviously held before the afternoon hangings for Isaac appeared as a State witness. Four days later on July 9, Ned presented two witnesses in his defense but was declared "Guilty" and sentenced to be hanged on Friday, July 12. The final one of the six conspirators to be executed, Ned was the only one to die alone.

Two trials were held on July 8, the first against "Big Negro Frank." The State called nine witnesses, among them six whites. Big Frank was declared "Guilty" and sentenced to solitary confinement. The Court ordered, however, that his clergyman be allowed to visit him. In the second trial of the day, the State called a free mulatto woman to testify in the case against Rantey, but the Court decreed him "Not Guilty" and subsequently freed him.

On July 9, the Court freed five slaves, George, Andrew, another George, Joe and Deck. On Friday, July 12, [Abram brother of Simon Levy] and Catoe were tried together and both were freed. The business of the Court was finally completed five days later on July 17, with the re-opening of the case of Big Frank, who had been sentenced to solitary confinement. Two blacks and three whites were examined on the part of the State and the witness. As a result, Big Frank was sentenced to one year in irons in solitary confinement. However, the Court said that his master could release him at any time he would agree to remove Frank from the United States

Sarah Moses Levy - The Slaveholder

The Story of Nancy and Old Kennedy

The Parents Of Simon Levy

The Kershaw County, South Carolina Deeds of Records, has wills, references and accounts of Samuel, Sarah and Chapman Levy's land interests, chattel and personal possessions. Records reveals Samuel Levy begin purchasing enslaved Africans as early as 1796. Before his death in 1779, he held two people enslaved.

144

In 1810, Sarah Moses Levy lists twelve enslaved workers. The 1842 will of Sarah Levy recorded in South Carolina lists Nancy and her children: Abram, Thomas, George, Mary, Nancy, David, Kennedy Jr., and Simon. Old Kennedy was listed as her husband. Also those held enslaved in the will of Sarah Levy were listed in the will of Chapman Levy of 1849. *(There are several documents and records listing names of the men, women and children the Levy families held enslaved. The earliest was in a book entitled "Mary Chestnut's Civil War" (the memoires of Mary Boykins Chestnut.) The author was a friend and neighbor of the Levy family in Camden, South Carolina. In the book she described in detail "The 1816 Slave Uprising of Camden South Carolina", where many of the men who participated in the insurrection were held enslaved by Chapman Levy.) (See Facts and Legends regarding Julia and Simon Levy after 1870) (See more Filmore and Bettie Johnson)(The Jews of South Carolina, written by Barnett Abraham Elzas Abraham and published by Lippincott in 1905)*

In the 1800 census Sarah Moses Levy [the mother of Chapman Levy and the widow of Samuel Levy] was listed as head of household living in Camden, South Carolina with two children: a son, Chapman Levy and a daughter, Eliza Levy, plus four people she held enslaved. In 1801, she purchased twelve year old Nancy from a neighbor Stephen Boykin and in 1812 she purchased a young man, Kennedy, from Abram Blanding also a neighboring planter. Nancy and Kennedy were held enslaved by Sarah Moses Levy for more than twenty nine years. Over the twenty nine years Nancy, Kennedy and Sarah's son, Chapman Levy, lived in the big house in close proximity and worked and perhaps played together. As a result Nancy, Kennedy and the young master Chapman, had formed a unique relationship. Do to the personal nature of work done in "the Big House" and the constant proximity with the slaveholders. This was not an uncommon element of slavery. In this case the special connections were thought to be by blood kinship. Whatever the reason, the relationship between Kennedy, Nancy and Chapman Levy continued throughout the years.

Chapman Levy married Flora Levy and had two children Flora Eliza and Chapman Edward Levy II. The first wife of Chapman Levy I died in 1823; he married his late wife's sister, Rosina. His second wife died childless in 1826. He never married again but was said to have fathered children with women he held enslaved.

145

Years later Nancy and Kennedy were able to marry and over the years Nancy had eight children. [It is not proven that Kennedy was father to all of Nancy's children.] Like all enslaved couples, Kennedy and Nancy needed permission from their mistress to marry. From all indications, Sarah Moses Levy gave them her consent, and perhaps her blessing. During the time of slavery, the enslaved marriages had no legal protection.

Sarah Moses Levy could at her discretion break up the marriage and separate the family as she desired. Instead of being separated the family of Kennedy and Nancy continued to live as man and wife while enslaved for more than twenty five years. When Sarah Moses Levy died Old Kennedy as he was called and Nancy must have been saddened by her death yet the possibility of separation was a chronic threat for them. Like others, when the "masters" died their world would change.

Fear lessened for Nancy and Kennedy after hearing the results of Sarah's will: It read, in part "my Negro woman Nancy: her husband Ole Kennedy and children Abram, Tom, George, Kennedy II and Simeon, purchased by me, for my son Chapman Levy, it is my directions, desire and earnest request that Ole Kennedy shall be kept with his wife and each treated with kindness and all reasonable indulgence and if my son Chapman Levy shall desire to purchase him to add to his happiness it is my directions that he shall have him at the price of three hundred and fifty dollars and that the money which shall be paid for him shall be invested and added to the estate of my grandchildren." (*Directions from the will of Sarah Moses Levy*) Chapman Levy paid the three hundred and fifty dollars for Old Kennedy and did not separate the family as stated in the will of his mother

By 1834, Chapman Levy relocated to Mississippi where he was engaged in law, politics and as a land speculator. In 1835, Levy was listed as a resident of Noxubee County, Mississippi where he owned several hundred acres of land and paid taxes on eleven enslaved men, women and children.

Levy was a man of high profile and influence in his home state for 30 years before relocating to Mississippi. At the Nullification Convention of 1832, Levy argued vigorously against the right of a state to disobey a federal law.

His legal work drew him to the western territories from which the Indians were being expelled. Once Chapman was in Mississippi almost immediately he was urged to run for Congress and five years later was nominated for governor on the Democratic ticket, but he declined to run. Some research reports Levy declined to run because of his mother's illness. In early 1840's, Chapman Levy returned to South Carolina to care for his mother. *(Source: Letter to Joel Poinsett)*

When Chapman Levy died in 1849, at age 62. He was buried in Kirkwood Cemetery among families with names such as: Anderson, Hemingway, and former Governor Willie McWillie. According to available resources, this friendship continued after the two men migrated to Madison County, Mississippi. When Chapman Levy died, his holdings Old Kennedy, Nancy and her children Adam, Abram, Tom, George, Kennedy II and Simeon were held together enslaved over the years by several Levy family descendants in Mississippi

The Levy Slaveholders

In Mississippi

Sarah Moses Levy died in 1842, and in her will she left her holding to her grandchildren and their descendants. At the same time a codicil to Sarah Moses Levy's will gave her son, Chapman Levy, the right to purchase, from her estate, her personal household servants. These were Chapman's enslaved childhood playmates: Nancy, Ole Kennedy and their children. The codicil states "they not be separated." Chapman Levy purchased the household servants and their children and he returned to Mississippi. Per his mother's wishes they were not separated during his life time. On November 19, 1849, seven years past the death of his mother, Chapman Levy died and was buried at St. Philip's Church Cemetery near the McWillie Plantation in Kirkwood, Madison County, Mississippi. It is assumed Nancy and Old Kennedy died soon afterward. Per the intent of Sarah Levy's will the enslaved family of Nancy and Old Kennedy were not separated while held as the property of Chapman Levy (*See Levy descendant chart*)

The Descendants of Samuel and Sarah Moses Levy

Generation 2: Chapman Levy: married Flora Levy I

Chapman Levy and Flora Levy I had

Generation 3: Chapman Edward Levy III
Generation 3 Flora Eliza Levy II married Thomas S. Anderson I
Thomas S. Anderson and Flora Eliza Levy II had

Generation 4: Chapman Levy Anderson II

Generation 4: Thomas Anderson II
Generation 4: Edward Anderson II
Generation 4: Flora Anderson III

Generation 2: Eliza Levy: (1: Samuel and Sarah Levy) Eliza Levy married Dr. Edward Anderson I

Eliza Levy and Dr. Edward Anderson I had

Generation 3: Chapman Levy Anderson II (died in 1848 in Mississippi) childless
Generation 3: Lucy Anderson married **Adam McWillie** (son of Governor William McWillie of Mississippi)

CHAPTER NINETEEN

The Enslaved Children of Nancy and Old Kennedy

Slaveholding Levy/Anderson Family of Mississippi

After the Emancipation Proclamation, most of the Levy Freedmen who were held enslaved by the Chapman Levy descendants were documented working under Freedmen contracts to Chapman Levy's grandson, Edward H. Anderson II and other Levy descendants in Madison County, Mississippi. However, the emancipated children of Nancy Levy: Linna Levy Thompson, Mary Levy, Nancy Levy, Adam Levy, Tom Levy, George Levy, David Levy and Simeon Levy were not listed in that group and were listed in the 1870 census living in rural Hickory in Newton, County Mississippi. Why was Simon and his siblings, Nancy's freed children, living in Newton County Mississippi?

Chapman Levy's Daughter, Flora Eliza and her husband, Thomas S. Anderson I

Chapman Levy's daughter, Flora Eliza and her husband, Thomas S. Anderson I left South Carolina in 1845, and relocated to Madison County, Mississippi. When Chapman Levy the slaveholder died, Flora Eliza Levy Anderson was named heir to her father's estate and her husband, Thomas S. Anderson I was made executor of the estate. In 1851, six years after their move to Mississippi Flora Eliza Anderson died. Flora's sons, Edward Anderson II, Chapman Levy Anderson II and Thomas Anderson II, became the heirs to her father's estate which included Nancy's children. In 1853, Flora's widowed husband, Thomas S. Anderson I, married Ellen Mary Davis, the daughter of Mary Ellen Davis and a niece of Joseph and President Jefferson Davis.

The 1860 census shows Thomas S. Anderson I with his second wife, Ellen Mary Davis, plus his minor sons by his late wife, Flora Eliza Levy: fifteen year old Edward Anderson II, fourteen year old Chapman Levy Anderson II and ten year old Thomas Anderson II, had all relocated to Hinds County where they lived on a prosperous plantation in Raymond, Mississippi.

Thomas S. Anderson I brought with him the men, women and children they held enslaved, including Simeon and his siblings who were to be held in trust for his minor sons, the grandchildren of Chapman Levy.

One year later, Thomas Salmond Anderson I died of pneumonia at his residence in Jackson, Mississippi. If Sarah Levy's will was followed to the letter when Thomas Salmond Anderson I died the enslaved Simeon and his siblings were held on the Anderson plantation in Raymond, Mississippi in Hinds County in trust for Chapman Levy grandsons by their stepmother, the widow Ellen Mary Davis Anderson.

Shortly after the death of her husband, Ellen Mary left the plantation in Raymond to live in their residence in Jackson with eleven enslaved workers. [Possibly Simeon and his siblings] Ellen Mary Davis Anderson continued to maintain her residency in Jackson during the War.

The Christmas following the death of her husband, President Jefferson Davis reportedly, in the midst of the War, returned to Jackson to have Christmas dinner with his niece in her home in Jackson. (*Thomas Salmond Anderson had passed away 10 months earlier. Jackson News newspapers listed the visit of President Jefferson Davis*)

The questions remain: What happened to young Simeon and his brothers and sisters? Did he and his siblings and others upon hearing the rumors of President Abraham Lincoln's emancipation orders run off to the Union camps rather than allow themselves to be recaptured by the Confederate Army and face an uncertain fate? The raging Civil War, the Battle at Raymond, Mississippi on May 12, 1863 and the Battle at Jackson on May 14, 1863 added to the many reasons for them to flee. With the progression of the Union Army's advances into southern territory in the final months of the Civil War hundreds of thousands of enslaved men, women and children were freed. Perhaps Simeon and his siblings were moved to the Anderson plantation in Newton County, Mississippi anticipating Sherman's march through Jackson and Raymond, Mississippi.

When Sherman's army came through Mississippi, the home of Ellen Mary Davis Anderson was burned during the sieges at Jackson. When the War was over Mrs. Davis Anderson was able to relocate to Florida. However, due to the great loyalty she held for her uncle, President Jefferson Davis and the Confederacy, she refused to take an Oath of Allegiance to the U.S. Government. (*See the Times Democrat, Monday, February 12, 1912 and the Jackson News, February 12, 1912)(Kennedy II may have stayed on with Ellen M Davis Anderson. He was found living in Florida in the 1870 census*)

A story told to me by my elder cousin Rubin Salter II that was told to him by our great grandmother Elizabeth Levy daughter of Simon/Simeon Levy.

In my excitement of finding our grandma Bettie's enslaved family and their slaveholders, I told the very complicated story to every family member who would listen. Most listened politely, but when I told eighty three year old Rubin II the story this summer at a family reunion his eyes lit up, and he began to tell me this story. Rubin had the rest of the story. He had heard from grandma Bettie what happened to Simon and his siblings during and after Sherman's March through Jackson and Raymond and during the time when Ellen Mary Davis Anderson's house was sieged. Grandma Bettie (Elizabeth Levy), the daughter of Simon Levy tells the end of the story this way.

"Some of this I know for sure came from the memories of our great grandmother at the age of six." Rubin said. It is a little story, a short story. She begins the story this way every time she tells the story... "the soldiers, the Yankees, they were running through Missie's house taking things and Missie is crying and I ran after them and grabbed Missie's skirt tail. I told them to leave my Missie alone, she said over and over again. Leave my Missie alone! she cried... and they did and Missie got away!" But Ruben II said in years later she had another ending to the story as she reflected on the horrors of slavery. She said, "If I'd a knowed then what I knowed now I would have said, 'You can take the heifer'."

Can we assume that her mother Julia Levy was with her at this time?

CHAPTER TWENTY

The Emancipated Family Of Simeon Levy in Newton County

The surname Levy is rare for people of African descent because it is a Jewish surname which is easy to tie back to Chapman Levy, a prominent Jewish lawyer. In his will, he named all his slaves and many ended up working post slavery for his descendants in Mississippi. (Anthony Sanders)

During the final days of the War many enslaved workers freed themselves by running away. After the War many stayed on and worked often on the same plantations under what became known as "labor contracts." The labor contracts, which the Freedmen's Bureau assisted in drawing up, consisted of agreements between freedmen laborers and planters stating terms of employment, such as pay, housing and medical care. From the time between 1866 and 1870, nearly all Levy Freedmen were listed under contract on the Edward H Anderson II plantation in Attala County, Mississippi except Simon Levy and his sibling.

Simon Levy and several of his siblings were listed in the 1870, 1880, and 1900 census living and working on neighboring farms near and in the Good Hope Freedmen Settlement in rural Hickory, Mississippi in Newton County and did not appear on these contracts. It is believed that an overseer for Dr. Edward H Anderson I of Madison County, Mississippi may have replicated that same role for the Andersons in Newton County. It cannot be said for certain, however, there were prominent Anderson families who had enslaved workers in Newton County during that period.

James Anderson was born in South Carolina. He came to Newton County from South Carolina about 1855, and was listed in the 1860 census living in Newton County with wife, Althea, and daughter, Eliza Anderson. Martha W Anderson was born in 1826. She married William Norman in 1843 in Lauderdale County, in Mississippi. By 1850, Martha Anderson and William Norman were living in Newton County in Mississippi.(*Citing "United States Census, 1860", database with images, Family Search 30 December 2015, J Anderson, 1860.*)

The Sibling of Simon Levy

Living in Newton County, Mississippi

Federal records including the census help to shed some light on family roles within the newly freed family households. However, the 1870 census does not indicate relationships of family members such as brothers and sisters. Fortunately some of the siblings of Simon Levy were identified and affirmed in Sarah Levy's will. It states; "my Negro Nancy and her children Abram, Tom, George, Kennedy Jr. and Simeon purchased by me, for my son Chapman Levy". After relocating to Mississippi more children were born to Nancy and Old Kennedy and some may have died and some moved on to other areas. However, several brothers and sisters not listed in the will of Sarah Levy were validated in Chapman Levy's will.

The Siblings of Simon Levy in Newton County

Adam Levy: was born in South Carolina, his birth and death date is unknown. He was listed as the son of Nancy in the 1848 will of Sarah Levy and was, purchased after Sarah Levy death by Chapman Levy. Adam was a witness in the "Slave Insurrection Trial of 1816" organized by men held enslaved by Chapman Levy in Camden, South Carolina.

Linna Levy Thompson: was born in South Carolina and listed as a slave and daughter of Nancy in the 1848 will of Sarah Levy. Linna was purchased by Chapman Levy after the death of Sarah Levy. The 1870 census shows Linna Levy Thompson a widow living with the following children; Hester Thompson born 1850, Laura Ann Thompson born 1864, Charles Thompson born 1865, Edward Marshall Thompson born 1869 and Mary E. Thompson born 1873.

Nancy Levy was born in 1835 in South Carolina and was listed as "a slave" and daughter of Nancy in the will of Sarah Levy. Nancy was purchased by Chapman Levy from the estate of Sarah Levy.

Mary Levy Thompson was born in 1840 in South Carolina and was listed in the will of Sarah Levy as "slave" and daughter of Nancy after Sarah Levy died Mary was held enslaved by Chapman Levy. Mary had two children Laura and Charlie Levy.

Thomas Levy was born in 1842 in South Carolina and listed as "a slave" and son of Nancy in Sarah Levy's will. Thomas was purchased by Chapman Levy from his mother's estate. In 1870 thirty year old Thomas Levy was living in Newton County Mississippi in the household of Calvin and Eliza Thompson and their one year old daughter Mary Jane Thompson.

George Levy. Listed as a "slave" and son of Nancy in will of Sarah Levy, later held by purchaser Chapman Levy was born in 1842 in South Carolina.

Simeon Levy- was born about 1844 in South Carolina. Simon is listed as a "slave" and son of Nancy in the will of Sarah Levy. (He died about 1875 in Newton Co. Mississippi.) *(2nd great grandfather of the author Joyce Salter Johnson)*

Kennedy Levy Jr. was born about 1846 in South Carolina. **Kennedy** married **Annie Williamson** May16, 1872 in Jacksonville, Duval County. Florida. Annie was born about 1847 in Florida. They had the following child:

George Levy was born on September 23, 1876 in Jacksonville, Duval County, Florida. He died in 1955 in Jacksonville, Duval County, Florida.

Rebecca Levy was born about 1878 in Florida
Alfred Levy was born in May 1880 in Florida

John Levy was born on 15 Oct 1882 in Jacksonville, Duval Co. Florida. He died on 29 May 1934 in Jacksonville, Duval Co. Florida. He was buried in Greenwood.

David Levy: Birth/death date unknown. Held enslaved by Chapman Levy. *(David was born to Nancy after the death of Sarah Levy and was not listed in her will)*

Beginning in 1866 and by 1900, the Levy siblings were living in Newton County along with other relatives. The 1870 census shows twenty eight year old Thomas Levy living in Newton County Township 5, Range 12 near the Good Hope Colored Settlement. Mary Levy married Edward Thompson and settled in the county and had two children: Laura and Charlie. Living in the household with the Thompson family was Mary's sister, Nancy Levy and her son, Charlie Levy.

In 1880, twenty six year old Charles Levy was living with his wife, twenty three years old Nancy Levy and their son, Roam Levy. Twenty four year old Missouri Levy and her children: Nancy Ann Levy, Josephine Levy and two year old Mollie Levy, were living in Newton County with Henry Ware and his wife, Mollie and four children: Frank J Ware and Mc Willie Ware and two daughters, Ida June and Henrietta Ware. The 1900 census shows Oscar Levy living in Beat 4 in Newton, Mississippi with his sister, nineteen year old Betty Levy Norman, his brother-in-law, twenty six year old Clarence Norman and their daughter, Nancy Norman and a cousin, Annie Scott.

CHAPTER TWENTY ONE

The Father of Elizabeth Levy Johnson

1870 Newton County, Mississippi Census
Household   RoleGender   Age
Simeon Levy father   M   26
Julia Levy   mother F   24
Elizabeth Levy child   F   7

Simeon [also known as Simon] Levy is the father of Elizabeth [Bettie] Levy (*See 1870 United State Census*). He was born enslaved in 1842, on the Sarah Moses Levy plantation in Kershaw County, South Carolina. Simeon was born one of eight known children to his enslaved mother, Nancy. After Sarah Moses Levy's death, per her will, Simeon and his seven brothers and sisters, his mother and her husband, Kennedy all became the property of Sarah's son, Chapman Levy and were relocated to Mississippi and held enslaved by several Levy descendants until they were freed. Simeon was listed on the 1867 Tax Rolls of Newton County, Mississippi as a free man. In 1870, twenty seven year old Simeon Levy was listed living in Newton County with his wife, twenty four year old Julia Levy [no maiden name known] and seven year old daughter, Elizabeth Levy. Simon and Julia worked as tenant farmers on the Jones plantation near the Good Hope Freedmen Settlement.

After many years researching information regarding Simon and Julia Levy nothing has been revealed concerning Simon or Julia Levy after 1870. Family legends advocates: Simon Levy and his wife were apparently killed during some altercation; as the story goes "he was caught and killed." Years later the story was told by Bettie to her children and grandchildren. Bettie said she was around twelve years old when it all happened and she ran to the creek to hide. In the telling the story ends there. Family members have different views and theories as to disappearances of Julia and Simon Levy (*See Family Lore and legend Regarding Simon and Julia Levy*)

An elder once said, "What's been written ain't necessary so –then or now. We hear the stories of old uncle so and so who had to leave the area and was never heard of again or that he had to leave because he had Klan trouble – or something like his name used to be but he changed it to such and such –because Klan trouble." Despite conclusive evidence of atrocities committed against the Freedmen in the community on the part of the Klan such as the case were: a group of Klansmen murdered a Freedmen and his daughter and blamed the killing on the dead father. They were never caught or prosecuted. However, years later the story was repeated by family many times through the generations in many different ways and most believed it to be true. One theory is that such oral stories fabricated by the Klan ran rapidly through all families such as the Simon and Julia Levy story. **Citing this Record** "United States Census 1870," database with images, *FamilySearch*(https://familysearch.org/ October 2014), Bettie Levy, father Simeon Levy, mother Julia Levy Newton County, Mississippi, United States; citing p. 60, family 50, NARA microfilm publication M593 (Washington D.C.: National Archives and Records Administration.

Julia Levy

Mother of Elisabeth Levy

1870 Newton County, Mississippi Census

Household	Role	Gender	Age
Simeon Levy	father	M	26
Julia Levy	mother	F	24
Elizabeth Levy	child	F	7

Family lore dictates Julia Levy lived a very short life and may have died a very tragic death. As the legend suggests (See Facts and Legends regarding Julia and Simon Levy after 1870)

Family lore dictates Julia Levy lived a very short life and may have died a very tragic death. The information concerning the early life of Julia Levy and the years after 1870 is a mystery. Who were Julia parents? What was her maiden name? Were the Suttles family of Newton County her slaveholders? Was she a descendant of the Choctaw Indians? Many questions remain unanswered. As of this printing Julia Levy is known only in historical documents. After many years of researching still little is known; plus little was known by the family elders. (*See Facts and Legends regarding Julia and Simon Levy after 1870*).

Some known facts concerning Julia Levy. In 1842, Julia was born enslaved in Alabama. She is listed in the 1870 Newton County, Mississippi Census as the wife of Simeon Levy and as the mother of Elizabeth Bettie Levy. Julia Levy [spelled Julie Leavy] is listed as the mother of Elizabeth Bettie Levy Johnson on her death certificate, dated December 23, 1952. A granddaughter Earline Edison Broomfield in her book <u>Davey's Half – Way Home Café</u> tells the story this way: "My grandmother Bettie Johnson said she was an only child. She never knew her father. She remembered when she was six years old, standing on a block along with her mother, being sold to a man named "Sutton". She grew up as Betty Sutton." Earlene is the daughter of Lela Johnson Edison. (*Suttles [spelled Sutton] was listed by family members as mother's maiden name in the obituary of her daughter Lela Johnson Edison*)

CHAPTER TWENTY TWO

The Suttles Family Slaveholders

A Suttles Family Researcher Wrote:

Isaac Suttles I was born in Virginia. He was very young when his family settled in Wilkes County, Georgia in 1786. When Isaac was about twenty three years old, he went out on his own and settled in Elbert County in Georgia. There he married Sarah Meredith, the widow of James Meredith. It was there that Isaac began his long career as a Baptist preacher. Over little more than a decade, Isaac gradually acquired and operated a significant plantation and held many workers enslaved. Eventually Isaac sold out and moved to Clarke County, Georgia where he oversaw the management of the plantation of his wife's late husband. In 1817, he brought his family to the newly opened lands of Cahawba County, Alabama Territory and created a settlement known as Suttlesville. At more than seventy years of age, Isaac accompanied some of his married children to Lauderdale County, Mississippi where he died in 1842.

Isaac Suttles II was born in 1856 in Georgia to Isaac Suttles I and Elizabeth Childs Suttles. Isaac Suttles II married Lurana Caddell who is said to be a descendant of the Choctaw Indians. Isaac Suttles II and Lurana Caddell had a daughter, Elizabeth Ann Suttles, born in Bibb County, Alabama on June 14, 1836. Elizabeth Ann married Maherschel Hashebez, surnamed White, a Baptist minister in Lauderdale County, Mississippi. The couple had three daughters. Family story has it that Elizabeth Ann Suttles White wrote a letter to her daughter, Eliza White, it said the following," I was born in an Indian camp in Alabama and was married in an Indian camp in Lauderdale, Mississippi."

On April 8, 1982 a granddaughter wrote: "Grandpa and Grandma Mahuschel Hashebez White and Elizabeth Ann Suttles were living in Mississippi when the rumor of war started with Grandma's family in an Indian (Choctaw) Camp. The government had given the Choctaws all the land northwest of the Mississippi. I think Grandma's folks died on the trail of tears. Grandpa took Grandma and their four daughters into Texas and settled around Greybill, Texas. They had only been there about a year when Grandpa got his draft papers from Mississippi.

He had built a small log cabin and cleared enough land to farm a small crop. They had some cows and chickens. When Grandpa left the Civil War had started on April 12, 1861 and lasted to 1865. When Grandpa came home he brought one of his buddies with him, named Andrew. At that time all the Indians were on the war path. They robbed and burned down all the white people homes during the Civil War. They came to Grandma's and they had stolen all her stock but an old grey mare. Grandma hid the four little girls in flour barrels. Grandma would tie the mare to the corner of the cabin. They checked the mare out and some in the group told the head Indian, Grandma was an Indian and they didn't take the mare. Grandma would never say she was Indian (that's why Mama and her sisters didn't get headrights, when the government settled off with the Indians). She always said she was Black Dutch.

With this information and more research a case could be made with little uncertainty that Elizabeth Ann Suttles White was of the Choctaw Tribe. However does that mean that Julia Levy was held enslaved by the Suttles of Alabama and Newton and Lauderdale Counties in Mississippi? And can we assume that to be the case in view of the fact that in 1880 Elizabeth Bettie Levy's daughter Julia had married Filmore Johnson and she and husband are tenant farming on Elizabeth Suttles plantation, a former "Suttles" slaveholder in Newton County. Mississippi.

CHAPTER TWENTY THREE

Elizabeth Levy Johnson

The Early Years 1863 -1877

1870 Mississippi Newton County, Township 5 Range 13
Simeon Levy 26 black male born in South Carolina
Julia 24 black female born in Alabama
Elizabeth (Bettie) Levy was born in 1863 in Alabama

Groom's Name: Filmore Johnson
Bride's Name: Betty Levy
Marriage Date: November27, 1877
Marriage Place: Newton, Mississippi

Elizabeth [Bettie] Levy was born in 1863 in Alabama. The only known child born to Simeon (Simon) and Julia Levy. Simon was born enslaved in South Carolina and Julia was born enslaved in Alabama. In 1870, when Bettie was seven years old she was living with her mother and father in Newton County Mississippi in the Good Hope Freedmen Settlement. Sometime after 1870 and before 1880 Bettie's parents had vanished from the community and from historical documents. Family members assumed they were killed or it was necessary for their safety to leave the area. Six years of Bettie's life, until her marriage, remains a mystery. How and where she met Filmore Johnson is unknown. The Freedman Bureau Marriage Records shows Elizabeth Levy was nineteen years old on November 27, 1877 when she was legally married to Filmore Johnson. Family oral history claims Bettie and Filmore were married in a ceremony in the woods long before being legally married in 1877. (*See Facts and Legends regarding Julia and Simon Levy after 1870*) Once she was married she relocated with her husband near Hickory, Mississippi. Filmore and Bettie lived in Hickory where she made baked goods and blackberry wine and sold it to Troy Brand the local grocer. (*See interview with the grandson of Troy Brand the grocer.*)

By 1880, Filmore and Bettie had relocated to rural Hickory and settled on farmland in the Good Hope Colored Settlement with two small children: two year old Fannie and a son, four month old Daniel. The couple built a small house below the newly built settlement church. Bettie had a small garden and chickens and she sold their eggs along with her baked goods and blackberry wine. Filmore grew his own tobacco that he used himself. It is said the he traveled to New Orleans for supplies and sold them to the community. (*See more on Filmore and Elizabeth Johnson*) (*See more on Elizabeth Levy Johnson in The Johnson Petree Story*)

Facts pertaining to Elizabeth Levy Johnson: It is written in a Bible that belonged to her son, Reverend Daniel Johnson II, "Bettie Johnson's maiden name was "Levy." In 1919, Bettie wrote her maiden name on the death certificate of her daughter, Eliza Johnson, as "Suttles." In 1990, Suttles [spelled Sutton] was listed by family members as mother's maiden name in the obituary of a daughter Lela Johnson Edison.

Elizabeth Bettie Levy Johnson is documented in census records, marriage records, on her children death certificates and obituaries. The 1870 Newton County, Mississippi Census documents her as Elizabeth Levy born in 1863 to Simon and Julia Levy. The 1870 census shows her father, Simon Levy, born in South Carolina, her mother, Julia Levy, [no maiden name given] born in Alabama.

The State of Mississippi's marriage certificate documents an Elizabeth Levy married to Filmore Johnson in 1877. The Mississippi State Census from 1880 until 1940 documents Bettie Johnson living in Newton County with her husband, Filmore Johnson and their children. Elizabeth Bettie Levy Johnson died in 1952 in Good Hope, Hickory Newton County, Mississippi and is buried in the Good Hope Missionary Baptist Church Cemetery. *(On December 23, 1952 at eleven in the morning, Bettie Johnson died at the home of her daughter, Mary Johnson Salter, in Good Hope, Mississippi in rural Hickory, Mississippi. Mary reported to the coroner with her mother's death information such as name of the deceased and date of birth. Mary mistakenly reported her mother's date of birth as 1880. Elizabeth (Bettie) Levy was born in 1863 in Alabama. Elizabeth Levy Johnson is buried in Good Hope Church Freedmen Cemetery, Good Hope Mississippi)*

Lilia Toles Wife of Daniel Johnson II

Who was Lilia Toles? What is her Story?

During this research Lilia Toles' death and marriage certificates were requested. The request was denied due to incorrect and various dates on her death and marriage records and it was returned stamped "not enough correct information." Lilia Johnson's birth, death and marriage dates given by family members over the years do not correlate with what is on file in historical records.

Recent research discovered in the office of social security dated 1936 shows: " Lilia Tobb Johnson [maiden name Toles spelled Tobb] requested by Daniel Johnson a claim for their minor child Tommie Lee Johnson."

Lilia died young and her youth is a mystery. It is not known why she did not live with her parents. A note found in the Bible belonging to Reverend Daniel Johnson II written by his son, Charles Johnson reads: "Oliver Toles is the father of Lilia Toles. Pinkie Stephens is the mother of Lilia Toles and General Wall is half- brother to Lilia Toles." I will try to unravel this information and hopefully will be able to come to some conclusions and see where General Wall fits into this. After much research I can to this conclusion regarding the information found in Daniel's Bible. (*Some records attest to Oliver Toles being the father of Lilia Toles Johnson and Lizzie Amiss is her mother. However, other family elders declare that her mother is Pinkie Stephens. It is not clear that Pinkie Stephens is the mother of Lilia Toles. Plus researched information shows that Lizzie Amiss, the second wife of Oliver Toles, is not her mother*)

Looking into General Wall I being Lilia Toles Johnson's half- brother: The 1910 census record shows General Wall I a mulatto born in 1884 living in Beat 5 Range 17 in Newton County with his wife Nerva Wall and their four children: Robert Wall age five, General Wall II age four and Mattie Wall age two and Pinkie Wall an infant. General Wall I may have named his infant daughter Pinkie in honor of his mother "Pinkie Stephens?" Lilia Toles Johnson name her son in honor of her brother General Wall I who named his son General II and years later Lilia and Daniel named their son General Johnson III.

Lilia Toles was born about 1889 to Oliver Toles and his unnamed first wife [at this printing possibly Pinkie Stephens]. The family historians maintained Lilia lived with her parents for a short time before she went to live and work for Will and Lillie Gipson. In 1899, when Lilia was very young Oliver Toles married his second wife Lizzie Amis.

The 1900 census shows Oliver and Lizzie Amiss Toles had been married one year. Lizzie was the mother of two children: Lenora eleven and Ruby age nine. Oliver Toles lists the two girls as his stepchildren and he affirms that this was his second marriage. Lilia Toles is not listed living in the household.[Neither former spouse's names were documented in the census.] When Lilia was seventeen years old she married Daniel Johnson II a land owner and a Circuit Preacher in the Good Hope Settlement. Daniel and Lilia had fourteen children over the next twenty three years. Lilia Toles Johnson died on May 25, 1933 and was buried in the Good Hope Missionary Baptist Church Cemetery.

Lilia Toles Mother

Pinkie Stephens was born in 1868 in Mississippi to Daniel and Leah Stephens. In the 1870 census when Pinkie was two years old she was living with her parents in Northwest Jasper Garlandville, Mississippi. In 1880, when she was twelve she was living with her parents in Clark County, Mississippi with five of her siblings: Eliza Stephen born in 1876, Solomon Stephens born in 1872, James Stephens born in 1874, Carly Stephens born in 1877, and Alafair Stephens was born in 1878. Pinkie Stephens was no longer living with her parents after 1880, nor was she found listed living in any household in any census after 1880. By the 1890 census Pinkie Toles would have been twenty two years old living in Jasper County with her husband, Oliver Toles and a baby daughter, one year old Lilia Toles. (*This cannot be proven as the 1890 United States Census was destroyed by fire*) The 1900 census shows Oliver Toles married to Lizzie Amiss living in Newton County.

Lilia's Story From Researched Information

and Family Lore

These stories should not be dismissed. By using family stories to tell the story a less complicated and a more romantic story can emerge.

Daniel Johnson was about twenty five years old when he met sixteen year old Lilia Toles; exactly where I don't know. Some believed because he was a Circuit Preacher he met her in Church. They say Lilia was both physically beautiful and spiritually beautiful as well and Daniel was taken with her from the start. The elders, mostly the elder women, tell the story this way. "It was well known that Reverend Daniel Johnson had a roving eye and he too was mighty 'good lookin'." But as the saying goes "he was smitten with Lilia."

The story picks up again with Daniel "coming a-courtin." Lilia Toles was not an orphan at this point in her life however, she was not living with her parents. Opal Ford Johnson says this regarding her mother. "Mama's mama had died and her father, Oliver Toles, had married again." She said, "When mama was between seven and ten years old Miss Lillie Gipson, 'a White women,' asked mama's daddy if she could come by to help her around the house cause she had five boys they were in need of a lot care. The elder aunts all agreed that Miss Lillie Gipson was a good Christian white lady and it would be good for Lilia to do just that.

Lilia Toles had lived and worked for Miss Lillie for several years when she met Reverend Johnson. When Daniel came "a courtin", so they say, Miss Lillie sat him down for a little talk. She warned him that he was not to "play- a-round" with Lilia and break her heart "like you did to the others before you got saved." Will and Lillie Gipson was very fond of Lilia. Close family members said that by then she was more than a servant to the family [which many others believe she may have been blood related also.] From all indications Daniel convinced Miss Lillie of his intentions. Lilia Toles was sixteen years old when she married Daniel Johnson II in November of 1904. After the wedding Daniel took his bride with him to the Good Hope Freedmen Settlement where he had a house built on several acres of land. . On his wedding day he wrote in his Bible, "Daniel Johnson married Lilia Toles on November 27, 1904."

CHAPTER TWENTY FOUR

Family Lore and Legend OF The Ancestors

Family stories and oral tradition is something every family has and cherishes. Family members grow up hearing the same old stories repeated over and over again. Often it is when genealogy research begins and you try to pin down the information or to substantiate the stories with records; then you realize there might be a difference in what we thought we knew about family history and what is actually true. Should we dismiss all of these family stories we heard from our ancestors? No, because it is believed that many or most family stories have some element of truth to them. For that reason alone these important stories regarding great grandma Bettie and other family members will be considered in this section for future generations. These stories here may be boring to everyone except the family historian. **Joyce Salter Johnson**

In some family stories, the historian would require considerable better evidence to substantiate such a claim because of the implausibility of the whole situation. Lest you think this is too much of a "reach," let us contemplate the following stories. Family legend advocates: Simon Levy and his wife were apparently killed during some altercation; as the story goes "he was caught and killed." Years later the story was told by Bettie to her children and grandchildren. Bettie said she was around twelve years old when it all happened and she ran to the creek to hide. In the telling the story ends there.

Opal Johnson Ford the granddaughter of Elizabeth Bettie Johnson tells another version of the story: My grandma Bettie's mother was killed by her stepdaddy. He was a jealous man, is what we know or what most folk said he was a jealous man…. and he traveled a lot. One day when Grandma Bettie's ma was trying to leave with her mother she said "when I would have been about twelve years old" Bettie and her mother take off running. Bettie escapes and hides in a body of water among the reeds. The mother is killed by the husband. The man was captured how long after that I don't know – and by whom I don't know. How long Grandma Bettie stayed in the water and where she went after that we don't know and how and where she met Filmore is also unknown.

Maybe they met at Good Hope Church. "Grandma Bettie," she said, "is known to have Indian blood, possibly Choctaw."

Another story told in recently by a great grandson Reverend OJ Edison: he claims as he understood it the story went this way. It seems that for whatever the reasons Bettie's father, no names mentioned, and his brothers may have killed a white man and buried him in a cow pen. Sometime later they were found out and as the story goes some men came to the house and killed both he and his wife.

More Family Stories

Grace Pruitt Suggs tells a story regarding the wedding ceremony of her grandparents, Filmore and Bettie Levy Johnson in addition to the legendary tale of ten year old Filmore finding his family after slavery and other stories. Eighty five year old Grace describes the story told to her by her grandmother Bettie this way: "we were married and were listed in the state records just like the White folks." Of the wedding ceremony itself Grace said, "They were down there in the woods with the Indians and there was a lot of food in a big pot.

First the grownups ate from the big pot and then the children ate. Filmore and Bettie were told to get up on a stump, words were spoken. She did not remember what except the words, 'now you are married'." (*The traditional Choctaw Wedding Ceremony is similar to what she remembers of the story. (See: Traditional Choctaw Wedding Ceremony) Family story has it that Elizabeth Ann Suttles White wrote a letter to her daughter, Eliza White it said the following" I was born in an Indian camp in Alabama and was married in an Indian camp in Lauderdale, Mississippi. Bettie must have heard this from her mother regarding Elizabeth Ann Suttles wedding)*

There were thousands of intermarriages between the groups. Indians disappeared into the enslaved population. Freemen have in the same way been absorbed by Indian tribes. As a result, there are many people of African descent, who despite outward appearances, identify as strongly with their native heritage as any other. Yet there is no sage wisdom or advice regarding Indian ancestry. After much research, as of this printing it appears that both Filmore and Bettie have many blood lines. The heart is what is important in this. The elders will tell you and that you will know in your heart…. What else would explain the intense craving to find the ancestors? No one can take your heritage away. We can only be who we are and what we choose to make of ourselves.

CHAPTER TWENTY FIVE

The Hardy Salter Family

Jasper County and Newton County 1870-1900

The Early Years

The 1860 United States Census was the last census showing the enslaved listed by age and gender only in the household of the slaveholding families. In 1866, a census was held in most southern states freed men, women and children were required by law to have a surname. Former enslaved men and women were able to choose any name they desired. In most cases they chose the name of the last slaveholder. In some cases they chose the name of a previous slaveholder. And in other cases they did not choose a name of any former slaveholders. Some wanted to distance themselves from slavery altogether. After Emancipation Proclamation from all indications and research information Hardy chose "Salter" [spelled "Saulter"] as a surname for his family and settled in Mississippi in Jasper County.

The Hardy Salter family once freed appeared not to continue their contact with the Salter /Saulter families, however, Hardy had taken the Salter /Saulter surname. One former slaveholder Augustus Salter [spelled Sartor], was listed in the 1850, 1860, 1870, 1880 United States Census and lived in Jasper County. The 1866 Mississippi State and Territorial Census Collection in Jasper County, Mississippi list Augustus Sartor living on a farm in North East Jasper County. Listed in the 1866 Mississippi State Census living near Augustus is the recently freed Frank Salter, [spelled Saulter] the son of Hardy Salter and twenty-five unnamed members of his household. *(Augusta Sartor relocated to Montrose in Jasper County and is buried in the Montrose Cemetery. Later the Sartor Family descendent migrated to Louisiana. (Per Skip Weber great-great-grandson of Augusta (spelled) Sartor)*

Except for the former enslaved Salter no one with the surname Salter were found living in Jasper or Newton Counties after 1880. There are a variety of speculations that would account for the apparent break with the former slaveholding families. Hardy may have signed a mandatory labor contract and was sent out to work on the Griffin farm.

Or perhaps, as suspected, the Griffins/Horn/ Mc Carty and the Salter/Sartor families may have had family ties either through business or marriage. Also, often after the War several plantation owners left the area leaving their former enslaved workers behind. Recent research shows the Hardy Salter/ Saulter families were listed in the 1870 census living on the Griffin farm in Jasper County and working as farm laborers. Living with Hardy is his wife, Louisa, a son, Alfred Salter and twenty- eight year old Charley Mc Carty and three Mc Carty children, Peter age three and two, daughters ages two and one. *(In the1880 census Frank Salter states his parents Hardy and Louezer (Louisa) were born in Virginia. The 1870 census shows Hardy Saulter/Salter and his wife Luezer (Louisa) born in North Carolina.)*

In 1880, Hardy and his wife, Louisa continued to live on the Griffin farm in Jasper County. The aged couple planted what they could with the help of young Peter Salter. Hardy's second son, Cason Saulter, his wife, Cherry, and their two children lived on the adjacent farm. The Washington Salter family had lived in Jasper County adjacent to the Hardy Salter family from 1870 until sometime after 1880. Research shows the family migrated to Delhi, Louisiana. *(Peter Salter was listed a Peter Mc Carty in the 1870 census)*

Hardy and Louisa Salter died sometime between 1881 and 1890. After the death of Hardy and his wife their descendants set out to accomplish a new kind of freedom. The Salter Freedmen began to build their own community within the rural southern areas, and setting about as best they could, starting their own farms and small businesses. The Salter family wanted nothing more than to be free and enough land to make a living for themselves and their children.

In the 1870 Census Frank Salter [spelled Saulter], was listed as; a farm laborer on rented land, with his wife seventeen year old Dora, a daughter six month old Mary Francis and a brother, Alfred Saulter. By the 1880 census Frank had relocated with his wife and daughter and his brother Alfred and settled in Newton County near the developing Freedmen Settlement south of Hickory, Mississippi. Frank, Dora and Alfred worked as laborers on what appeared to be the Robert Griffin farm adjacent to a farm belonging to Richard K. Horn. Also living with the family was 11 year old Luezer Saulter. As of this printing no information regarding Luezer has been discovered that would help to explain her connections with the family. Family elder could not recall any stories related to her identity. It is possible that she may have been a sister to Frank, Cason and Alfred. Luezer would have been twenty one years old and was not found in the 1880 census she may have died before the next census, or married, and would have been listed with her husband's surname.

After, 1880 Frank, his wife and their fifteen year old daughter Mary Frances had settled in Newton County. Between 1870 and 1880 three more children were born to Frank and Dora: Charity, Louise, and Alice. By1900 Frank and Dora had moved to the Good Hope Freedmen Settlement. Susie Anna had married Milton Hayden, Addie married Frank Williams and Isaac married Mary Johnson, daughter of Filmore Johnson and they all settled in the community of Good Hope. Bob, the twin brother of Isaac, had died by 1910. Charley, Willie, Lucy and Nellie remained in the household. The 1910 census shows the younger children of Frank and Dora and a five year old grandchild, Ruby Maddox, still living in the household. (*See Index of Family Given Name for Ruby Maddox*) (*Ruby is the daughter of Alice Salter*) *Alice was no longer living in the household. In 1893 when she was seventeen Alice married Stephen Tullos and the couple had moved to Meridian, Mississippi by 1910. Alice died sometime before 1920.*

Frank Salter died sometime before 1920. The 1920 census shows Dora, a seventy years old widow had moved back to Jasper County. Dora was living on a small farm with her grandson Dan Salter, her mother Hannah Garner and her sister Massalee Garner. After her mother died Dora moved back to the Good Hope Settlement. One year later eighty-one year old Dora died in her home in Good Hope Settlement.

Cason Salter the second son of Hardy Salter married Cherry Anderson in 1870 and they had thirteen children. Cherry died in 1928. After Cherry's death, Cason relocated to Chicago, Illinois to live with his children. Several of his descendants, Warren, Harrison, George and Frank, left the South during "The Great Migration" and migrated to Chicago. Cason died about 1930 and is buried in Chicago, Illinois.

Alfred Salter/ Salter the youngest son born to Hardy and Louisa Salter was born enslaved in Alabama in 1854. Alfred moved into Newton County in Mississippi in 1880 with his older brother, Frank Salter. Alfred married Mariah his first wife in about 1890. Mariah died around 1898. Ninety six year old Mariah Saulter Wilson, her name sake and granddaughter, tells the story of her hardworking grandmother and as a very young woman, after the birth of her eight children, "she worked right up to her death."

After working in the kitchen most of the day cooking and baking she sat in a chair and died. By the early 1900's Alfred married a second time to Mandy Beason and they had one son, Handy Beason Saulter. Handy Salter was listed in the 1910 census living with his grandparents, Handy and Lillie Beason in Jasper County.

We have no further information on Alfred, Lillie or Handy as of this printing.

The Salters and other newly freed men and women in the county were able to buy land in Newton County, along the Jasper County border in what is now called Good Hope Colored Settlement Community. Landownership, however, did not exempt the Salters and other community members from segregation and discrimination sanctioned by Jim Crow legislation. To minimize their influence, the families of Good Hope ventured beyond their community only when necessary. However, the Salter elders had a very secure knowledge of what they believed and what they were about, despite their early beginnings. They knew their strengths and their set of beliefs. They were hard workers, farmers, teachers, timber men, preachers and small businessmen. Mary Salter Stamps, the daughter of Will Salter, said at the 40th Salter/Saulter Family Reunion in Minneapolis, "We are who we are because of them."

Salter Family Of Good Hope Settlement

Frank Salter was born in 1835 in Georgia (Possibly Washington County GA). After he was freed he relocated with his wife and children to an area in rural Hickory, Mississippi. He married Dora Garner in 1868, when she, was thirteen years old and Frank was twenty three. They had several children. Frank was able to buy several acres of farm land in the settlement. (*More on Frank Salter The Salter of Good Hope Settlement*)

Lillie Salter Colman was the daughter of local farmers, Cason and Cherry (*Johnson Anderson*) Salter. Lillie married Willie Coleman who was a farmer in the Good Hope community (*See Salter family history*) at a very young age. (As of this printing they had no children.)

The elders recalled she was very beautiful and adventurous. She visited her big brother Frank Salter and his wife Sallie Johnson Salter in Chicago as often as she could. In 1919, after returning home from Chicago she contracted tuberculosis and died on December 23, 1919 and she is buried in Good Hope Missionary Baptist Church Cemetery.

Addie Salter the daughter of Frank and Dora salter. Addie married Frank Williams and they had the following children; Arthur, J.Q, Seymour and Albert. Frank purchased farm land in the Good Hope Colored Settlement in about 1920 Addie Salter died in 1920 and is buried in the Good Hope Church Cemetery (*More on Salter The Salter of Good Hope Settlement*)

Mary Francis Salter the daughter of Frank and Dora salter. Mary Francis married a farmer Henry Dyess and they worked a large farm in the Good Hope Colored Settlement. In 1892, a son Thomas Dyess was born. In 1895, Mary Francis died and is buried in the Good Hope Church Cemetery. In 1899, Henry married Louise (Babe) Salter the sister of his late wife.(*More on Salter The Salter of Good Hope Settlement*)

Louise Salter married Henry Dyess after the death of his first wife. The family remained in the Good Hope Settlement and continued farming Henry and Louise had three known children Frank, Sophia and Rebecca Frances. Rebecca Frances was born on August 13, 1914 and died five days later. Living in the home in 1910 was seven year old Lucile Dyess and five year old Henry Dyess Jr. Sophia married Jim Mitchell and they had a daughter Theresa. Theresa married Percy Chapman and had three children. In the early 1950's Theresa and Percy Chapman relocated to Denver, Colorado. Theresa died in 2016 in Denver. In 1920, sixty-three year old Henry died sometime before 1930, and Louise married Frank Petree Jr. they continued to live on the Dyess farm in the Good Hope Settlement until their death. (*More on Salter The Salter of Good Hope Settlement*)

Isaac Salter the son of Frank and Dora Salter married Mary Johnson. Mary was the daughter of Filmore and Bettie Levy Johnson. Mary and Isaac had six children; Rubin, Clayborn, Broomsy, Lonnie, Robert and a daughter Addie Lee. Isaac and Mary were born in Good Hope and were members of Good Hope church. Isaac was one of the trustees that help raise money to build the church. Both Isaac and Mary played vital rolls in the church and in the community. In 19,35 they took to live with them three orphan relatives Alonzo, Grace, and J T July 7, 1886 died in Freeport Illinois on January 1969 (*More on Salter The Salter of Good Hope Settlement*)

Will Salter owned a large piece of land that extended to the land owned by his brother Isaac Salter. Daniel Johnson the son of Filmore had a large track of timber and farm land near the Jasper County line. Will Salter the youngest child of Frank and Dora Salter married Judy Pruitt, Will enlisted in the army and fought in World War I. Will and Judy had six children; Classie, Ruth, Mary, Ivory, Grace and Rebecca. Decades later the land remains in the hands of his descendants. Most of the land purchase by the Salter families. (*More on Salter The Salter of Good Hope Settlement*)

.

CHAPTER TWENTY SIX

Stories From The Good Hope Colored Settlement

Stories and Legends

Oral history and legends run rampant in ancestry compilation. Sometimes memories are pure fabrication, however not to be ignored. Here are some of the stories, facts and legends told over the years. Like any oral stories, the accounts of earlier times are what are remembered from the life of the person telling the story. In these simplified stories and experiences of the men and women of Good Hope, Mississippi, from the beginning is the story of community, plain and simple.

Joyce Salter Johnson how much of what I remembered of my great grandpa Filmore and how much was told to me by my elders I am not sure. The elders and family historians maintain Fillmore Johnson never worked at manual labor after slavery. That he was among the pioneer land owners in Good Hope Colored Settlement. He owned land, a horse and buggy, several suits of clothing and is said to have traveled frequently to New Orleans. The old folks said "he had Indian in him."

Memories of Good Hope Settlement School 2009:

Brooke Lee Pruitt Story: She attended Good Hope School between 1942 until it's closing in 1951. "I remember the little two room school" She said "I remembered that the two class rooms were separated by a slatted wall that hung from the ceiling. The wall was raised every morning as we recited the pledge of allegiance to a flag that hung over the stage in the upper grade class room. "Each class room" she recalled "had two small windows in front and in back." The windows had glass panes but were protected from the sun by what she called "old fashioned pull up shades". The school had no porch, or a very small porch, that she remembered. She did not however recall the table with the water barrel that stood in the school yard.

Brooke continued "and I remembered the names of the teachers. Salome C. (Chapman) Hayden (*Miss Hayden*) as we all call her, was our first teacher in the lower grades, grades one through five. Edna (Hayden) Johnson was the teacher for the students in grades six through eight. The little school closed before Brooke was to be moved to the upper class room. **Brooke Lee. Pruitt** (*Brooke Pruitt is the daughter of Moses and Sophie (Brown) Pruitt)*

Mary Salter Stamps, a former Principle, teacher, and student at Good Hope Community School, was born in 1927, and in 1934 attended first grade at Good Hope School at age six. After 8th grade in 1941, Mary attended high school in Jasper County and graduate from that high school in 1945. She attended two years at Jackson Teacher College. After teachers college she was hired by the Newton County School district as teacher and principle at Good Hope School with a salary of $60.00 per month. Mary remembered the teacher's desks were on a raised platform on each side of the class room there were three or four rows of double desks for the students in each class room. She remembered during this time students were grouped according to their achievement levels and according to their development levels and according to their ability.

Mary said "attending and teaching in a two room school had its advantages such as knowing everyone, and looking out for one another. The disadvantages were the other classes being taught at different times, making it difficult to concentrate on your own studies. However, the students were quiet despite all the different grades levels. And no one was allowed to leave their seat without permission. "Mary taught at Good Hope School from 1946 until 1947, and soon after that she moved to Denver, Colorado and continues to reside there today. (*Mary Salter Stamps is the daughter of Willie Salter and Judie Pruitt Salter)*

Clifton Edison age eighty-three was born in 1926, and in 1931 began attending Good Hope Colored School (as it was called then.) "I started in the first grade and finished the eighth grade." Cliff's response when asked if he remembered his teachers "oh, I remember some of the teachers, mostly by their last names, like Miss Dunlap and Miss Adams," he said. He did however, remember the first names of two very special teachers, Maudie Lee Edison, his sister, and "Frances Chapman because she was very pretty". He said. Cliff remembered a lot about the little two room school house such as the boy's outhouse across the road behind the church. He remembered that the water came from a spring on the school property. He said that the classroom was quiet despite all the different grades in the rooms, and that you didn't get out of your seat without permission.

He also remembered that the student desks, when he attended the school, were rough, wooden slab bench with table that sat two across. Eighty-three year old Cliff smiled and explained "I didn't mind sitting two across, because that gave me a chance to sit by the pretty girls." "The sad thing about that," he recalled, "was most of the girls in the classroom were related to him one way or another."(*The son of Ed Edison and Lela Johnson Edison*)

Broomsy Salter was the oldest alum to tell his story. Ninety-four Broomsy Salter, the grandson of Filmore Johnson remembered that up until age eight he attended school in the church building across the road before the schoolhouse was built. He stated "the year I was nine the school house was brand new, built by the Chapman family, Lemon Chapman and his boys." Cousin Broomsy recalled that his father, Isaac Salter, was one of the church trustees. He sold timbers off the church land to pay for building the school. Papa's duty, also as church trustee, was to oversee the school's finances." Broomsy remembered the early teachers of the school. "There was a Miss Norris," he said, "who lived in Chunky and whose husband brought her 15 miles into Good Hope each day." Rev. Stephen Tullos was the teacher for the upper class room during that year. After that he recalled an Emma McElroy from Lawrence. "Miss McElroy taught there until I graduated. After that I moved to Meridian. And then the service and then I moved to Freeport, Illinois. I was drafted and served in World War II."

An interview with Mariah Saulter - Marie Wilson

She said "my family attended Mt Prospect Church. When I was about 14 or 15 years old your grandpa Reverend Daniel Johnson II was preaching revival service there." "I liked your daddy Peck [Archie Johnson] Reverend Johnson's son and he would walk me home after church service."

"When my daddy saw him walking me home he told me that he could not walk me home again and he said if he should see me walking with that little short fellow again he would give her a good whooping. So the next night I tried to get out of going to church because I had told Peck that he could walk me home. I did not want to tell him that papa would whop me if I did." She said, "I couldn't get out of going to church so I had to tell your daddy that my daddy said he could not walk me home." She said, "Later on when I was old enough, when I saw him again, he was so in love with my cousin, Edna, your mother and she was so pretty…. your mama married him about three or four years later.

So you see, you could have been my daughter if my daddy would have let me walk home with Peck." She laughed and said, "Maybe he knew better 'cause Edna had all of you children." (*Over the years Edna Salter Hayden and Archie Johnson had ten children.*)

"After I finished school I was a teacher in the Rose Hill, Mississippi School. I later met a man from Laurel Mississippi. He soon left to find work in the car industry in Detroit. He sent for me and we were married there." She said her father did not know if he liked that but he accepted it. She said her daddy said, "don't lay a hand on her, if you have to hit her send her home first."

She said, " I went to work in a beauty shop in 1940 working for three dollars an hour." She continued, " times were really hard between 1940 and 1950. In 1949, I pawned my class ring for food. I bought my class ring back from that shop as soon as I got the money. Things went well for us after that period. I bought my house and Janice was born."

I asked about the Saulters which is her side of the family. "Salina's brother, Killie, died in the service." She said, " My older brother, Otto, left home. He was so mean after his wife died he came here to live and said he would never go home again and he didn't. I had to build a room on to the house. He stayed there until he died. That was the same room that my sister Ollie lived in later Now Ollie is gone…Salina is gone too," she said. "We had a sister, Mary, and she died, Sam still lives in California. I am ninety years old and I live here alone in this three bedroom house and have no plans of leaving."

When asked about her parents she said, "My grandmother's name was Mariah. She died when she was very young. I didn't know her very well. I heard she worked hard all day in the fields and came home to cook and one day while she was cooking she sat in a chair in the kitchen and died. I also had a brother, Elbert, but he got in trouble with the law or the KKK, and he changed his name to Happy Jack. I don't remember my granddaddy at all but I remember his brother, Uncle Cason. She remembered how he loved to go with Clayborn in his car when Clayborn was still living in Mississippi.

Interview with Broomsy Salter, son of Isaac Salter and Mary Johnson Salter -1996: When asked did you know Grandpa Filmore's family, his father, mother, brother or sisters? He said, " No, I didn't know them but I heard tell of them. Some, anyway, let's see, his brother, Uncle Big Preston, not the Uncle Preston you know his son, this was his brother. He was a Johnson like Grandpa Filmore after slavery. Then there was another brother, Uncle Frank Petree. (He pronounced it "Peachtree.") He was sold into slavery by the master. I heard tell of a sister and another brother but I never heard their names called."

Earlene Edison Broomfield wrote memories for her son Davey in her book: Davey' Half Way Home

"My mama never had a job except cooking for her family and cooking for what she called the "Tractor" meeting, what is now called the "Revival". "The Revival was held at Good Hope Church. First Sunday in August for as many years, at least before I was born. This day has been a special day. A steer, we called it a young bull was killed for fresh meat. The first sweet potatoes were scratched by papa, so Mama could make her good sweet potato pies. For me those were the good times, because I knew my mother and father loved and protected us and taught us to love one another

Earlene Edison her brothers and sister; Johnnie Chester and Maude all moved up to Freeport, Illinois in her book she wrote. About the Jolly Aide Kool Aide – "mama" she wrote: "traded eggs for it if she did not have a nickel. We would meet the store truck over on the main road and buy a candy bar for a few pennies, which was so hard to come by. Davey let me tell you about the ice. We were so glad to see the ice man coming! Papa or mama would save that dime to give to the iceman for a small block of ice and mama would wrap it up in an old raggedy quilt. We had a hold in the ground filled with sawdust to keep the ice in so it would not melt so fast."

What Earlene Remember about her grandparents: Filmore and Bettie, Johnson "My grandmother" she said was an only child. She grew up as Bettie Sutton [Suttles] she never went to school, but she was smart, wise and intelligent. She made all of her clothes by hand. She made aprons out of flour sacks. She boiled the sack in the soap she made herself until they were snow white. She wore her apron to church starched and iron – she made her starch out of flour and water. She always made two pockets on her apron. All of her grandchildren tried to sit next to her on Sunday school because they knew she had tea cakes in her pockets.

She died when I was fourteen years old." She wrote: "I also remember two of his brothers. He told us that he and his two brothers were sold into slavery to different families. He knew his mother and father and he knew all three of his brothers. When they got old they kept up with one another. My grandfather and all of his brothers could read and write. He was a Johnson. His brothers were raised as Petry and one Uncle Preston was a Johnson. I remember all three Daniel, Preston Johnson, and a brother Frank Petry II.

CHAPTER TWENTY SEVEN

Up North

Community Members Leaving the South

Up North to Freeport, Illinois

Between the turn of the century and 1930, more than one million African American southerners set out on one of America's most important mass movements. These people migrated from the South's countryside to the cities in the North. They hoped to find better jobs, a new sense of citizenship and a new respect for themselves, their families and a chance at a new life. Thousands leaving the South headed for cities such as Detroit, Cleveland, Baltimore, Philadelphia and Chicago. From hundreds of southern cities and small towns, they boarded trains. Some stopped along the way in small railroad towns such as Freeport, Illinois.

The Move to Freeport, Illinois

In an interview with 93 year old Vivret Norman, the great grandson of Hardy Salter, he remembered: "It was the railroad that brought most people up from the South, but that's not the reason my dad, Broomsy Norman, left Lawrence, Mississippi."

He continued, "Papa was never intending to move to Freeport. He had never heard of Freeport. Papa was working in Mississippi near the Good Hope Settlement 'share-cropping' for five dollars a year, trying to feed a large family when most of that went to the company store at the end of the year. Papa decided to find something better "Up North." You see, Papa was a good strong worker and the White folks he worked for didn't want him to leave. But in 1914, he took off running anyway with them close behind. He jumped into a boxcar on the Illinois Central Railroad line and, unbeknownst to him, they locked him in. He had reached Centralia, Illinois, two days later when finally he got someone's attention, and he was able to get out.

"Papa said he hoboed to a small town in Illinois called Haldane. There he was able to get a job with the railroad as a Gandy Dancer, He was such a hard worker, there he was offered a job in Freeport working in what he said was called the "Freeport Yard." "In November of 1915, when I was about six months old, with my mother, Nellie Salter Norman (the daughter of Frank Salter and brothers and sisters, we all moved up to Freeport. We lived at that time at 51 Sherman Avenue." "Later," he continued "Papa was able to get rail passes for relatives to come to Freeport. That first year, your Grandpa Milton Hayden came up."[i]

After years of farming and at the urging of his brother-in-law, in 1916, Milton Hayden left his farm in Good Hope, Mississippi, and came to Freeport. His first employment was at Stover Manufacturing Company and later for the Illinois Central Railroad cleaning the engines at the roundhouse.

In an interview with Edna Hayden Johnson, she recalled her father's [Milton Hayden] exodus to the North. "It was the railroad that brought us up from the South to Freeport," she said. "The Illinois Central offered Black men much more [money] than what they would have made in the South. My daddy worked in the roundhouse, cleaning the engines. The men made very good money, but it was dirty work, a job most folks didn't want to do. "Often," she continued, "the wives and the youngest children were left behind and when the men received their paychecks, they would then send a portion of their salary back home." She said her father would send as much as fifty dollars per month back home to the family. Refusing to abandon the farm he owned altogether, whenever possible, Milton returned to Good Hope. In 1929, on one such trip, Milton died while working his fields.

As a young girl, during the 1920's, Edna spent most of her summers with her father and mother in Freeport along with her sisters, Angie and Josephine and brothers, David, Daniel and Paul. David married Tressie Poe and made his home in Freeport. Angie Hayden, the oldest daughter of Milton, came to Freeport at age 13 and married Marshall Bruce in 1922. The 1923 Freeport Directory lists Marshall Bruce and Angie Hayden Bruce living on Wright Street. Milton Marshall Bruce II was born in 1926. Josephine Hayden married Herman Ligon in 1935, and they lived in Freeport on Sheridan Avenue. In the late 1920's, Edna and Daniel returned to Mississippi. Edna married Archie Johnson in Mississippi and in the fall of 1951, the family moved up to Freeport. Daniel Hayden married Salome Chapman, and they made their home in Good Hope, Mississippi. Paul stayed on and attended school in Freeport.

In 1928, Broomsy Norman died in an accident while cleaning engines at the Wallace Railroad Yards. His death certificate, dated June 17, 1928, showed that Broomsy Norman died in Saint Francis Hospital, the result of shock from loss of blood due to injuries sustained accidentally when he was run over by Illinois Central Railroad Engine No. 448 while cleaning it.

In an interview in 2001, Broomsy Salter reminisced, "In 1926, my brother Rubin and your Uncle Chuck, [Charles Johnson] moved up to Freeport from Good Hope, Mississippi. They lived with the Norman family; we were all family and so we slept where we could." He recalled, "Later, more relatives from Good Hope Settlement came to Freeport.

James Gaddis, Selma Maddox, Moncrief Salter, James Quincy (JQ) and Albert and Arthur Williams all came looking for work. Broomsy continued, "Rubin worked at the Senate Hotel and Chuck and Arthur worked at Stover Manufacturing Company. J.Q. worked at the Glass Company for a short while. He and his brother Arthur left Freeport before 1930 for Washington, D.C. The rest ... James [Gaddis] and Selma worked for the railroad a few years and returned to Mississippi. Moncrief relocated to Rockford, Illinois." "Charles Johnson," he said, "married Katharine Moseley here in Freeport and Rubin went back down South for a short while. He married Mittie Oliver and came back to Freeport."

Thomas Dyess was born 1891 in the Good Hope Settlement the son of Mary Francis Salter Dyess and Henry Dyess. Mary died soon after giving birth. In the 1910 census nineteen year old Tom Dyess was listed as a boarder living on the Thomas and Lillie Petry/ Petree farm in Good Hope Colored Settlement. In 1916, Tom relocated up north to Freeport, Illinois where he lived on Sherman Ave with a relative Josephine Hayden Ligon. In 1917, during World War I he registered for military duty in Stephenson County Illinois. After the War Tom returned to Freeport and worked as laborer on the Illinois Central Railroad. However by 1930, when he was thirty nine years old, Tom returned home to the Good Hope settlement where he lived with his Uncle Henry Dyess and other relatives until his death in 1972. (*See The Salter of Good Hope Settlement*)

William Kidd was born in the Good Hope Settlement in Newton County was invited by his cousin Broomsy Norman to join the growing number of family members in Freeport. In 1925, William arrived in Freeport and by 1930, he moved his wife, Minnie, their five children and one grandchild up to Freeport.

Some Stayed - Some Returned

The Great Depression saw thousands of farmers lose their land. This was a major downfall in the history of the State of Mississippi. Cotton prices plummeted leaving many in poverty. It was during 1930-1960 that the Good Hope Community began to change in character, nearly all of the settlement was abandoned as young people migrated north and to other counties in Mississippi. Many left the farms for towns and cities, cutting their ties to the land on their own accord for as many reasons as there are people.

Many others returned: the Edison brothers, ninety year old Cliff and his brother Oliver James (OJ) are fourth-generation descendants of the Johnson/Petry settlers. Both OJ and Cliff were born in the Good Hope Settlement. Clifton stayed on in Good Hope until he was drafted in 1945; he served his time in WWII. After many years of living in other states, Cliff's love for Good Hope brought him back home, this time to stay. A sister, Earlene Edison, after living in the North for decades, returned home. Reverend OJ Edison returned after many years away and he continues to guard the legacy by keeping a family member in the pulpit of the Good Hope Settlement Missionary Baptist Church.

Epilogue

The Good Hope Colored Settlement proved that African Americans have played a vital role in building this nation. Eager to live and prosper as free people, they established settlements such as The Good Hope Community. Many of these communities were destroyed by racial violence or injustice, while some just died out. However, Good Hope, Mississippi still stands as a reminder to the descendants of their ancestors.

They left Good Hope on their own accord for many reasons. However, the Little Community of Good Hope, Mississippi is very much alive today. The church without its bell tower and the old cemetery still beckon the families back and they return to memories of home. Those descendants…

The Anderson Family . The Bates Family. The Beason Family. The Bogan Family. The Bolton Family. The Brown Family. The Chapman Family. The Cole Family. The Cook Family The Croft Family. The Curry Family. The Davis Family. The Dawkins Family. The Doby Family. The Dyess Family. The Edison Family. The Evans Family. The Ford Family. The Fielder Family. The Gaddis Family. The Garner Family. The Gibbs Family. The Gibson Family. The Gipson Family. The Gooden Family. The Graham Family. The Griffin Family. The Gully Family. The Hall Family. The Hamilton Family. The Hardy Family. The Hayden Family. The Horn Family. The Johnson Family. The Jones Family. The Kirby/ Curby Family. The Kidd Family. The Lee Family. The Levy Family. The Mc Carty . The Mc Millian Family. The Mc Cune Family. The Mitchell Family. The Norman Family. The Odson Family. The Overstreet Family. The Love Family. The Petry/ Petree Family. The Potts Family. The Pruitt Family. The Riley Family. The Russell Family. The Salter/ Saulter Family. The Tullos Family. The Stephen Family. The Suttles Family. The Tanksley Family. The Tankson Family. The Tatum Family. The Thompson Family. The Tillman Family. The Toles Family. The Wall Family. The Wash Family. The Watts Family. The Walker Family. The William Family. The Wright Family. The Youngblood Family

Appendices

Family History Writer Darrel Fielder and former resident wrote*: "Information on the 'Dyess Rebellion of Newton County' can be found in the book <u>History of Newton County</u> by A J Brown, pages 162-169. It also references an article in the Meridian Mercury February 8, 1868. To me, this is a very important event since African Americans took the initiative to fight back against being accused of stealing as a pretext of driving them from their land. The Dyess family actually strategized and organized an initial attack and then a counter attack."* **Darrel Fielder** An article published in the Meridian Mercury on February 1868. *(From the perspective of the reported in 1868)*

"In 1868, the Freedman Bureaus were well established in the state and Military Government toughly engrafted upon it. This new state of things begat idleness among the Negroes. They also became more insolent to white peoples and harder to govern and thus began trouble that ended in very tragic events in the county of Newton.

When a Negro felt himself aggrieved or insulted, he reported it to headquarters, and if it were thought proper the white man was brought upon trial. Negroes would not work, and in many instances resorted to taking things. The most lamentable occurrence took place in (South- Eastern) part of the county in which two men were killed and another wounded, the particulars are as follow.

The two Denis brothers, living about 6 or 8 miles South-East of Hickory missed some hogs and went in search of them among the Negroes living near then, who they suspected of being the thieves and made a close search that they found a portion of the pork buried in the yard of one of the Negroes yard. After an unsuccessful attempt to settle the matter by compromise, one of the Denis brothers went to Hickory and sued a warrant to have the guilty parties arrested.

The precise scene of the shocking deed is about midway, between Hickory Station, Newton County and Garlandville, Jasper County [Good Hope community]. Daniel A. Denis and Edward Denis originally from the state of Georgia but more recently from the state of Alabama, and came to this State about 10 years ago and settled on a plantation and have since been working together. Industrious and honorable men they both severed in the war. Their ages were 54 and 51.

"There is a family of Negroes living near the Denis plantation formerly belonging to the Dyess plantation family. They lived nearby when they were slaves. They are four brothers, perhaps five, believed to have been concerned in the murderous assault. Their names are Prince, Orange, John, Sonny and Joe all are the Dyess Negroes. (*See* Good Hope Colored Settlement Pioneers Stories: *regarding the Dyess family of Good Hope*) They were squatter about nearby.

The Mrs. Denis had missed hogs they suspected the Dyess Negroes having stolen from them. Ed. Denis; with Mr. Tucker went to Prince Dyess's home to search. They found Prince's wife cooking fresh hog meat asked where she got it she said she got it from Uncle Henry Dyess. They went to Uncle Henry about it who said they did not get it from him.

This was Friday: Prince was not at home. Went after dark and he was not at home yet. Went in the morning and still not home. Told the woman she would have to go to Hickory [for questions]. She then showed them the meat buried in a box. They started to leave with her; and met with her husband and Orange [Dyess] his brother; both had doubled barrel shot guns. A conversation ensued Prince confessed that he killed the hog and said the woman should not be held. Then Denis told Prince that he must go [to Hickory] and he would make it as light as possible provided he would leave the County, he said he would but he was hungry and would go after he had something to eat. Denis with Tucker waited until evening and Prince did not come as promised. So they sued for a warrant. The warrant was given to Mr. Gibson special deputy to execute.

A posse of the Denis brothers, Ben Griffin, Jonas Nelson, and Jack K. Horn and Sim Perry after dark went to Prince's [Dyess] house. They did not find him at home failing in their object and not suspecting a conspiracy, lighted a torch, call upon some dogs, and turned it into a possum hunt. They caught one possum returned home.

They were in 100 yards of home, crossing a branch, Ed Denis bearing the torch next to Daniel Denis in advance, others following, when a volley was fried into the party at close range Daniel Denis it is supposed fell dead. Gibson and Griffin and Nelson were more or less severely wounded by the fire. The Negroes rushed from their ambush. Old John Dyess the father of the five sons encountered Ed Denis who seemed to have stood his ground were killed. Edward was heard to exclaim "Prince don't kill me; the voice of Little John Dyess was heard saying kill him.

184

Daniel Denis laid dead shot twice. Ed was apparently run through with a sword. The Black Prince [Dyess a Civil War Veteran] wore a sword by virtue of his service in the War with Old John the old daddy of these young devils. [John Dyess and his sons were Civil War Veterans] The next morning about 20 men from Garlandville[Jasper County] appeared upon the scene. The Negroes too seemed to have improved the time to recruit their forces. Flushed with victory and confident of their numbers they sent a message to the party to come and arrest them. The Party of whites from Garlandville went up to old John house and several were wounded the first was returned and 2 Negroes were shot. It is Negros news that one was killed but doubtful.

Old John was wounded and sent to Hickory where we lose track of him and will not attempt to find him again; Daniel Johnson, *(See Good Hope Colored Settlement Pioneers Stories: regarding Daniel Johnson the son of Frank Petry Sr. and Mary Johnson)* in the Sunday fight has been arrested and committed to Jasper County jail. [*Last known documentation for Daniel Johnson was in the 1880 Census living in Jasper County with his wife Frances*]

Tobe Gentry in the Sat night's massacre has been arrested and put in county jail. Beside old John, Joe and his son, Uncle Henry Dyess's brothers both in Saturday's fight, were caught. A certain restless Negro who is well known in Newton County has on several occasions shown a disposition to incite his people to violence, was out early on Wed morning. It was said here on Wed am Negroes engaged in war on Newton had sent here for reinforcements 'The law was not trouble with any trials of those assassins. The vengeances of the white people were speedy'.

But they did not enjoy the rest as soon as the facts doubtless greatly exaggerated against the whites and mitigate. The Law was not on the part of the Negroes. The Blacks arrested on Murder and lynching were tried before military court some who had but little to with the punishment of Negroes were tried and set free."

Violence in the South continued. In Southeast Mississippi in Newton, County as late as 1890 violence erupted in the small town of Hickory, Mississippi.

Family History Writer Darrel Fielder wrote: *"The incident involving Shep Jones, William Fielder and D. Dawkins. Bear in mind, this was written from the perspective of the majority population. Cousin Ruby Jean, Shep's granddaughter, tells it differently. Shep Jones married Scotia Fielder. Shep and Scotia had a daughter named Mae Ida. Mae Ida is Ruby Jean's mother. The article must be balanced against her personal oral story. Shep escaped (with the help of William Fielder and D. Dawkins) but was never heard from again. Shep was able to escape "oversees" according to Ruby Jean. Mrs. Ann Burks at the Newton County Genealogical and Historical society was very instrumental in locating this article and transcribing it."*

Shep Jones Still at Large

The Newton Record December 15, 1908

"Slayer of A. J. Wall Has Not Been Apprehended"

"Dee Dawkins a friend of Jones meet death at the hands of a mob"

Church and lodge hall burned

"Although for several days following the tragedy there was considerable excitement in the community where A. J. Wall was murdered last week at the hand of the Negro Shep Jones. Things have quieted down somewhat now but so far as known, the Negro is still at large. Some think that he was captured and killed but his cannot be confined. In last week's paper it was reported that blood hounds were taken to the scene of the killing to try to capture the fugitive. When the party [The Klan] from here reached there, about 2 o'clock the dogs were put on the trail and ran about two hours chasing through a field where it was said that Jones was seen to pass and running into a reed brake on the place of J. B. Chapman a few miles south of here where the trail was lost on account of a heavy rain that was falling

No more [words missing]…til the following day when the news came that he had been seen about 4 miles south of Hickory [Good Hope Colored Community] and the dogs were carried there when they struck the trail again. The dogs then traced him to the home of Bill Fielder his father in law but he was not to be found there. According to reports from what is believed to be a reliable source, "the posse" told Fielder that he must tell what had become of Jones.

This he refused to do until he was tortured and put through what the party called the "third degree". When he finally divulged the fact that another Negro named Dee Dawkins had spirited the fugitive away.

Not long after this, Dee Dawkins was seen returning home, riding horse back, and leading another horse, and he was taken in charge. When asked where Jones was, he told the crowd that is none of their business whereupon he was informed that he would either tell or be killed. His reply was told by a citizen who lives down about Garlandville [Jasper County] who did not himself see the affair stated Dawkins said "he would die and go to hell before he would tell" and made a move to draw a pistol when he was filled with bullets. Whether this is the correct version of the affair or not is not known, but it is known that Dee Dawkins was found dead by the road side Saturday morning with four or five bullet holes in him. Just what became of Fielder is not known but he was missing at that time. It was reported at one time that he had been hung but this was never verified.

The country south of here was alive with people for a day or two following the killing in search of the murderer and they became wrought up that some of the mob element stuck a torch to a large Negro church and a lodge hall near Garlandville, Mississippi and burned them to the ground one night. This act was deplored on the part of the good white citizens of Garlandville as it is not believed that the Negroes there had anything to do with the killing.

The funeral of Mr. A. J. Wall took place last Friday in Garlandville. Where the ceremony was carried out by the *Woodmen of the World* of which he was member and a large crowed was out to witness the last obsequies. Deceased was one of the county's best citizens and his death is greatly deplored. He leaves a wife and seven children who have the sympathy of all in their great misfortune." (*Woodmen of the World*: *one of the first fraternal benefit societies in the United States, was organized in 1890 by Joseph Cullen Root. Among its social and fraternal benefits, W.O.W. provided life insurance. Membership was originally restricted to white males between the ages of 15 and 52. By 1977 these restrictions had been relaxed)*

Davis Bend, Mississippi

Prior to 1865, when Davis Bend was simply referred to as the "Joseph Davis plantation Davis Bend, Mississippi was an all-black town near Vicksburg, sometimes referred to as Davis Bend colony. It was a 4,000-acre cooperative community made up of former enslaved African Americans seeking equality, justice, and race pride in a society they called their own. In 1865, this community was one of the first black towns to develop after the Civil War. The architect of Davis Bend was African American Benjamin Montgomery. Prior to 1865, when Davis Bend was simply referred to as the "Joseph Davis plantation," an enslaved Montgomery functioned as its overseer and owned the plantation store. After the war, Davis sold the land that his plantations rested on to Montgomery for $300,000 in gold at a 6 percent interest rate. The largest plantation at Davis Bend was Hurricane. In 1872, Benjamin Montgomery's son, Isaiah, ran Hurricane as its property manager, informal counsel, and diplomat to white neighbors, agents, and suppliers from Vicksburg, Cincinnati (Ohio), New Orleans (Louisiana), and St. Louis (Missouri).

Made in the USA
Lexington, KY
06 September 2017